X-RAY ARCHITECTURE

To Katy and Andrea

Beatriz Colomina

X-RAY ARCHITECTURE

Lars Müller Publishers

1

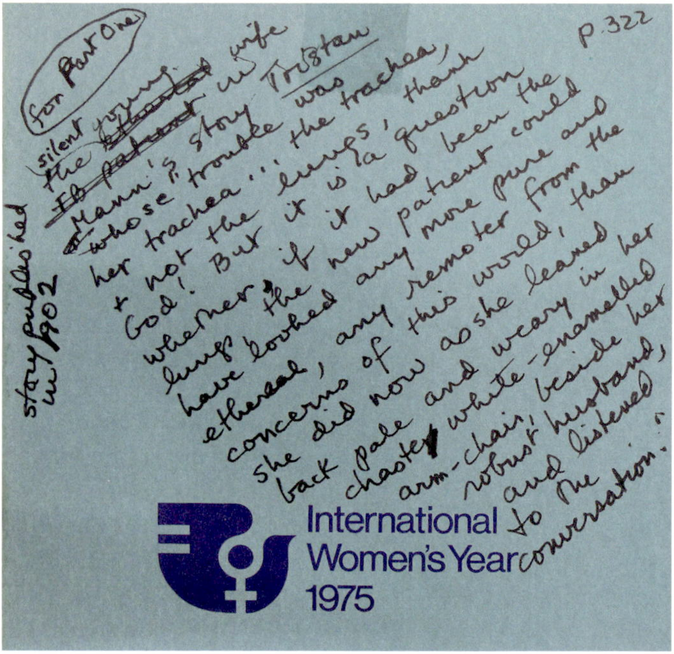

P.322

(for Part One)

story published in 1902

the silent young ~~[illegible]~~ wife in ~~[illegible]~~ Mann's story Tristan whose trouble was the trachea, ... the trachea, her trachea ... not the lungs, thank God! But it is a question whether, if it had been the lungs the new patient could have looked any more pure and ethereal, any remoter from the concerns of this world, than she did now as she leaned back pale and weary in her chaste white-enamelled arm-chair, beside her robust husband, and listened to the conversation."

International Women's Year 1975

Introduction

The bond between architecture and illness is probably my longest preoccupation. It goes back at least to the year I arrived in New York, at the end of 1980, after studying architecture in Barcelona. By some impossibly good luck, I landed as a visiting fellow at the New York Institute for the Humanities, then run by Richard Sennett, and with some extraordinary figures as senior fellows—Carl Schorske, Wolfgang Schivelbusch, and Susan Sontag, among others. I was deeply attracted to the kind of interdisciplinary work they were doing. In particular, Sontag's *Illness as Metaphor,* which had recently been published, had an enormous influence on me. I started seeing modern architecture in terms of all the pathologies related to it, real or imagined—agoraphobia, claustrophobia, nervous disorders, and, above all, tuberculosis and the obsession with hygiene, with germs, with fresh air.... I thought this would be a great topic for my dissertation and actually wrote about one hundred pages on it in some kind of feverish state induced by my intoxication with New York.

But there was not yet a climate for that kind of interdisciplinary research in architecture—not in Barcelona, and not at Columbia University, either, where I was a visiting scholar the following year. So I ended up working on two canonical figures, Adolf Loos and Le Corbusier, and the relationships between modern architecture and the emerging media of its time—photography, illustrated magazines, film, and so on. It turned out that the field of architecture was not ready for that, either. Talking about media in architecture was anathema in the early 1980s, as if it were an attack on

2

1 Susan Sontag, handwritten notes on tuberculosis patient in Thomas Mann's *Tristan*, ca. 1975
2 Susan Sontag (1933–2004), November 3, 1972

3

4

the object, or revealing a dirty secret, or even as if the media were a kind of illness.

Returning to the project on tuberculosis and modern architecture is for me like the return of the repressed. Except that it has always been there in some kind of latent form, like a virus that surfaces every now and then in essays and conference papers, but never completely takes over.[1] So this is the project that I decided to work on during a sabbatical year at the American Academy in Berlin and the Getty Research Institute in Los Angeles. I was planning to do something else. But on one of my first days at the academy in Wannsee, I discovered that there had been several tuberculosis sanatoriums in the area. The air there was famously cleaner, and people from elsewhere in Berlin came to Wannsee for the cure. **FIG. 3**

So I decided, or perhaps it was decided for me, to change my topic and take up again this question that had been with me for such a long time. Indeed, that fall, I immediately imagined myself as a patient in a sanatorium taking the cure, along with all the wonderful, witty fellows and partners with their various ailments—a feeling that made perfect sense of the academy's retired location, the lake, the fresh air, the terraces, the forest, the light, the extraordinary and abundant food, the great care of the team of professionals in the house, and the beautiful pavilion in the garden by the lake that Regine Leibinger and Frank Barkow had recently completed as a kind of sun pavilion for the cure, **FIG. 4** where I wrote these lines.

Likewise, arriving at the Getty in the spring of that academic year, to a very white building on top of a hill, I thought

3 Open-air terrace for the cure, Heckeshorn pulmonary clinic, Berlin-Wannsee, in the 1950s
4 Barkow Leibinger architects, pavilion at the American Academy in Berlin-Wannsee, 2014

about it as almost like a Magic Mountain, with terraces outside every room where patients in the Getty Research Institute could take the sunlight-and-air cure and where I walked past a photograph of Sontag, who had been a fellow there, on the way to my office every day and I waved to her as if to remind myself how it all started.

That year, the theme at the Getty Research Institute was the canon of art history. There is today an ever more nuanced understanding of the canon in architecture, yet the central mythology of modern architecture remains remarkably intact after almost one hundred years—perhaps because it was never true. Concealed within the standard narratives about modern architecture are other stories that have been forgotten or repressed, stories that energized and rationalized the work of the avant-garde, but were pushed to the background in favor of a simplistic rhetoric of technical and visual efficiency.

Reyner Banham, probably the first historian to challenge the mythology of modern architecture as functionalist, contrasted the way his teacher Nikolaus Pevsner could never escape the short list of canonical figures that he himself had canonized with Henry-Russell Hitchcock's "extra-canonical" vision, which picks up peripheral and unexpected figures and ideas.[2] In these terms, I think of my research as "intra-canonical"—attentive to the unexpected within the canon itself. And in this case, the unexpected is disease.

So what is this surprisingly resilient canonical view?

Modern architecture, launched in the 1920s by an international group of avant-garde architects, has usually been understood in terms of functional efficiency, new materials (glass, iron, reinforced concrete), new technologies of construction, and the machine aesthetic. In contrast, the hypothesis of this book is that modern architecture was shaped by the dominant medical obsession of its time—tuberculosis—and the technology that became associated with it—X-rays. That technology produced a new and widespread change in the conception of space and the relation of inside to outside. This change can be understood as a specific historical event, a twentieth-century twist in the ancient, intimate relationship between architecture and medicine that is ongoing today. Just as medical technologies and the treatment of illness played a major role in determining the characteristics of modern architecture, new medical technologies are today creating new forms of architecture as the relationship between inside and outside passes through another transformation. Yet we are still living in the architecture shaped by a specific disease, tuberculosis, and its primary diagnostic tool, the X-ray. Modern architecture remains the default everyday environment, the norm produced by vast industrial systems, rather than the transgressive work of an avant-garde inspired by a specific disease.

It is as if the widespread success of modern architecture depended on its association with health, its internationalism the consequence of the global spread of the disease it was meant to resist. A map showing the distribution of modern architecture would echo a map of the distribution of the illness. Tuberculosis is fundamentally urban, as was modern architecture. One in seven people on the planet died from it in the nineteenth century, but in the city of Paris alone, it was close to one in three.

Modernity was driven by illness. The engine of modern architecture was not a heroic, shiny, functional machine working its way across the globe, but a languid, fragile body suspended outside daily life in a protective cocoon of new technologies and geometries. It is the difficulty of each breath and therefore the treasure of each breath: the melancholy of modernity.

Modern architecture is inseparable from an intimate, even romantic, relationship between a new kind of medical image and a new kind of space—each intriguing and inspiring the other. The point here is not to pin this relationship down and ossify it, but to release it, to reactive it, to stimulate reflection by offering a kind of portrait at the intersection of biology, psychology, biography, sexuality, and technology—to invite the reader to look again, to see modern architecture through different eyes. What does it mean when everyone—the client, the architect, the theorist, the critic, the worker—is a patient?

1 Some of the texts I published on this theme include: "Krankheit als Metapher in der modernen Architektur," *Daidalos* 64 (1997); "The Medical Body in Modern Architecture," in *Anybody*, ed. Cynthia Davidson (Cambridge, MA: MIT Press, 1997); "Skinless Architecture," in *The State of Architecture at the Beginning of the 21st Century*, ed. Bernard Tschumi and Irene Cheng (New York: Columbia University Press, 2003); "X-Ray Architecture: Illness as Metaphor," *Positions* 0 (Fall 2008); "Unclear Visions; Architectures of Surveillance," in *Engineered Transparency: The Technical, Visual, and Spatial Effects of Glass*, ed. Michael Bell and Jeannie Kim (New York: Princeton Architectural Press, 2009); "Röntgen-Architektur," in *Elektromagnetismus in Architektur, Design und Kunst*, ed. Stephan Trüby (Munich: Wilhelm Fink, 2009); "Illness as Metaphor in Modern Architecture," in *Caring Culture: Art, Architecture and the Politics of Public Health*, ed. Andrea Phillips and Markus Miessen (Berlin: Sternberg Press, 2011); "X-Ray Architecture: The Tuberculosis Effect," *Well, Well, Well, Harvard Design Magazine* no. 40 (Spring–Summer 2015); X-Screens: Röntgen Architecture," *e-flux journal* no. 66, October 2015.

2 Reyner Banham, "Actual Monuments," (1988) in *A Critic Writes: Selected Essays by Reyner Banham*, ed. Mary Banham, Paul Barker, Sutherland Lyall, and Cedric Price (Berkeley: University of California Press, 1999), p. 283.

CHAPTER 1

Health and Architecture: From Vitruvius to Sick Building Syndrome

Architecture and medicine have always been tightly interlinked. Just as classical theories of the Greek polis followed theories of the four humors, contemporary ideas of health organize design theories today. Architectural discourse weaves itself through theories of body and brain, constructing the architect as a kind of doctor and the client as patient.

Vitruvius in the first century BC launched Western architectural theory by insisting that all architects needed to study medicine: "Healthfulness being their chief object."[1] He devoted a large part of the first book of his *Ten Books on Architecture* to the question of health, giving detailed instructions on how to determine the healthiness of a proposed site for a city by returning to the ancient method of sacrificing an animal that lives there and inspecting its liver to make sure it is "sound and firm." Likewise, for the healthy site of each building, he discusses the theory of the four humors and emphasizes the direction of the winds and the sun. Too much of one humor enfeebles and "impairs the fluids of the human body." In reverse, those who are unwell can be cured more quickly through design, rebuilding the system of those "exhausted by disease," including "consumption" (tuberculosis). Vitruvius discusses the internal workings of the body just as much as he discusses the internal working of buildings. Theories of medicine are used as a kind of foundation for architectural theory. Architecture itself thus becomes a branch of medicine. Symptomatically, Vitruvius didn't simply import the theory of the four humors, which was treated skeptically by many

1

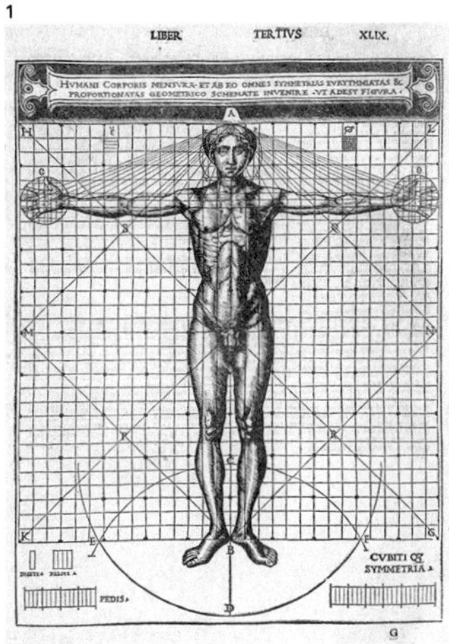

1 Measure of the human body, Cesare Cesariano's translation of Vitruvius's *De Architectura*, 1521

2

3

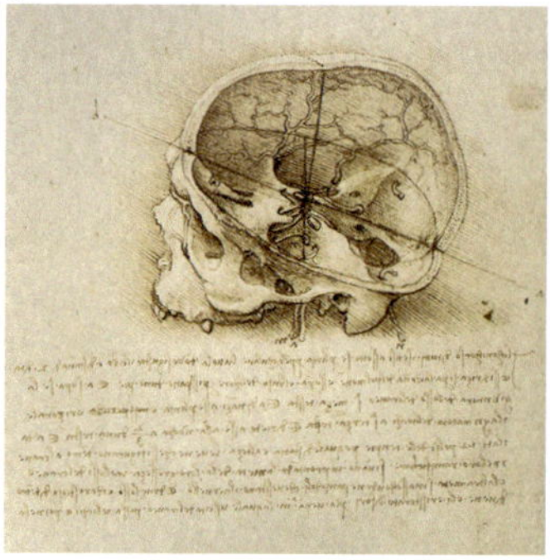

4

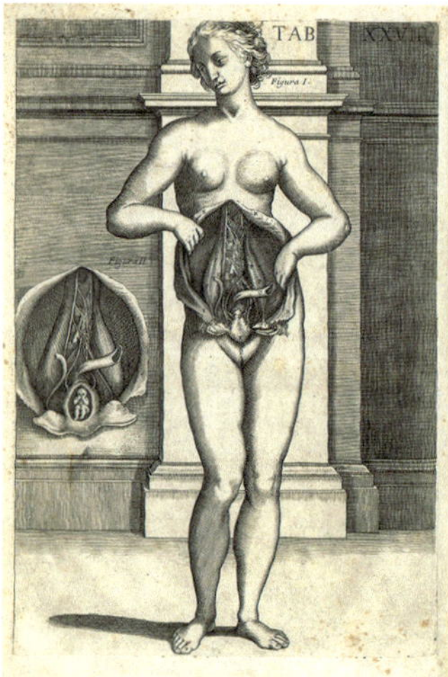

5

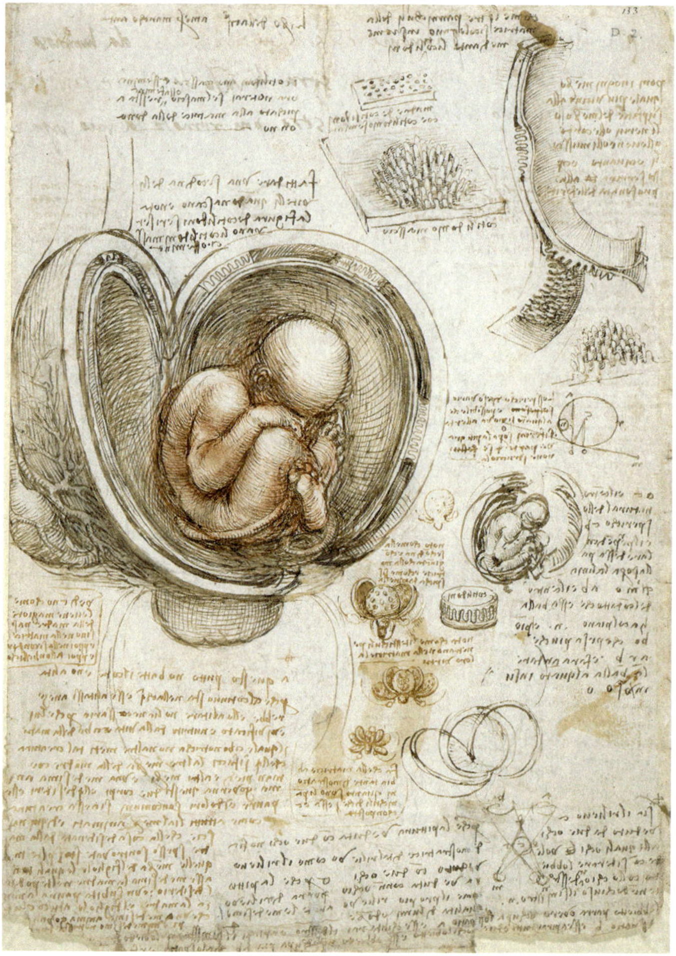

2 John Banister delivering an anatomical lecture at the Barber-Surgeons' Hall, ca. 1580

3 Leonardo da Vinci, *View of a Skull*, ca. 1489

4 Pietro Berrettini da Cortona, *Tabulae anatomicae*, Plate XXVII, engraving by Luca Ciamberlano, Rome 1741, original drawing ca. 1618

5 Leonardo da Vinci, *Embryo in the Womb*, ca. 1510

6

7

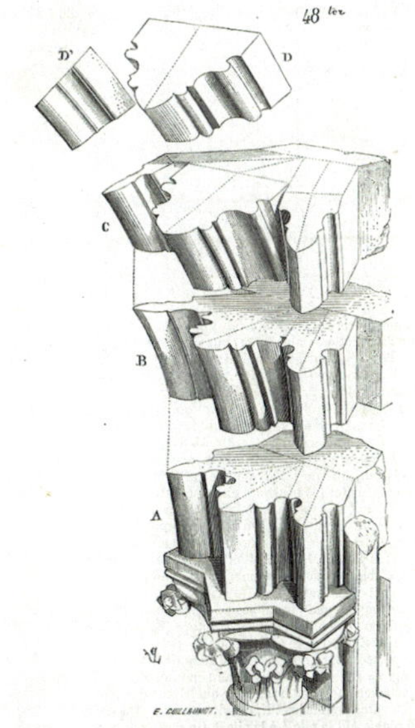

8

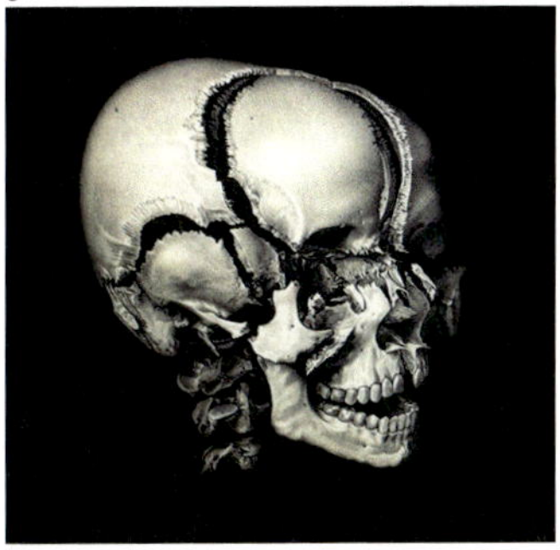

physicians, but elaborated on it, adjusting it to develop his own architecturally based theory of health or health-based theory of architecture.[2]

By the Renaissance, however, the central reference for architecture was no longer the whole body, its health determined by the four humors, but a dissected, fragmented, analyzed body. Just as Renaissance schools of medicine used casts of body parts, design schools such as the very first one, the Accademia delle Arti del Disegno in Florence, founded in 1563 by Giorgio Vasari, used cast fragments of historical buildings for teaching, and anatomical dissection at the Santa Maria Nuova hospital was a central part of the training to which all students of Vasari's academy were required to attend and draw for days on end, even as the body putrefied and some students fell ill.[3] As doctors investigated the mysterious interior of the body by cutting into and dissecting it, architects tried to understand the interior of buildings by slicing section cuts through them. In the sketchbooks of Leonardo da Vinci, cutaway views of architectural interiors appear beside anatomical drawings. He even understood the interiors of the brain and the womb in architectural terms, as enclosures that must be cut through to reveal their secrets. **FIGS. 3, 5** Likewise, in the mid-nineteenth century, Viollet-le-Duc illustrated his *Dictionnaire raisonné de l'architecture française du XIe au XVIe siècle* (1854–1868) with perspectival sectional cutaway drawings showing medieval buildings as if dissected. **FIG. 7** Influenced by George Cuvier's *Leçons d'anatomie comparée* (1800–1805) **FIG. 6** and Jean-Marc Bourgery's *Traité complet de l'anatomie de*

6 Lessons of anatomy of the baron Georges Cuvier (1769–1832), in the Jardin des Plantes of Paris, ca. 1800
7 Eugène Viollet-le-Duc, *Tas-de-charge* drawing, in his *Dictionnaire raisonné de l'architecture française du XIe au XVIe siècle*, 1854–1868
8 Jean-Baptiste Marc Bourgery, exploded view of the skull, in *Traité complet de l'anatomie de l'homme comprenant la médecine opératoire*, Paris, 1831

9 B. Čermák, the Viewing Glass Tower of the Chamber of Commerce Pavilion, Exhibition of Contemporary Culture in Czechoslovakia, Brno, 1928
10 A chest X-ray in progress at Professor Maxime Menard's radiology department at the Cochin hospital, Paris, 1914
11 Robert Koch, "Die Aetiologie der Tuberculose" (The etiology of tuberculosis), published in the *Berliner Klinische Wochenschrift* on April 10, 1882. First publication of the discovery of the tuberculosis bacillus

9

10

l'homme, comprenant la médecine opératoire (1830–1849), **FIG. 8** he treated medieval architecture as a body to be analyzed—an "animate being" requiring "dissection" to allow separate study of its parts. His new mode of drawing revealed the functional role of each dissected fragment. His own interventions into medieval buildings were understood as surgical procedures, with modern iron technology used as a prosthesis.[4]

EXERCISING ARCHITECTURE

As medical representations changed, so did architectural representations. In the twentieth century, the widespread use of X-rays made a new way of thinking about architecture possible. Modern buildings even started to look like medical images, with transparent glass walls revealing the inner secrets of the structures. **FIG. 9** Indeed, the architecture of the early twentieth century cannot be fully understood without grasping its relationship with disease and especially with tuberculosis, a disease for which X-rays were by chance particularly well adapted as a means of diagnosis and monitoring of treatment. **FIG. 10**

The symptoms, if not the principles, of modern architecture seem to have been taken straight out of a medical text on the disease. A year before the German microbiologist Robert Koch discovered the tubercle bacillus in 1882, **FIG. 11** a standard medical book gave the cause of the disease as, among other things, lack of exercise, sedentary indoor life, defective ventilation, deficiency of light, and depressing emotions.[5] It took a long time for these notions to lose

11

Die Berliner Klinische Wochenschrift erscheint jeden Montag in der Stärke von wenigstens 1½ Bogen gr. 4. Preis vierteljährlich 6 Mark. Bestellungen nehmen alle Buchhandlungen und Post-Anstalten an.

Einsendungen wolle man portofrei an die Redaction (W. Königgrätzerstrasse 125.) oder an die Verlagsbuchhandlung von August Hirschwald in Berlin (N.W. Unter den Linden 68.) adressiren.

BERLINER KLINISCHE WOCHENSCHRIFT.

Organ für practische Aerzte.

Mit Berücksichtigung der preussischen Medicinalverwaltung und Medicinalgesetzgebung

nach amtlichen Mittheilungen.

Redacteur: Professor Dr. C. A. Ewald. Verlag von August Hirschwald in Berlin.

Montag, den 10. April 1882. № 15. Neunzehnter Jahrgang.

I. Die Aetiologie der Tuberculose.

(Nach einem in der physiologischen Gesellschaft zu Berlin am 24. März cr. gehaltenen Vortrage.)

Von

Dr. **Robert Koch,**

Regierungsrath im Kaiserl. Gesundheitsamt.

Die von Villemin gemachte Entdeckung, dass die Tuberculose auf Thiere übertragbar ist, hat bekanntlich vielfache Bestätigung, aber auch anscheinend wohlbegründeten Widerspruch gefunden, so dass es bis vor wenigen Jahren unentschieden bleiben musste, ob die Tuberculose eine Infectionskrankheit sei oder nicht. Seitdem haben aber die zuerst von Cohnheim und Salomonsen, später von Baumgarten ausgeführten Impfungen in die vordere Augenkammer, ferner die Inhalationsversuche von Tappeiner und Anderen die Uebertragbarkeit der Tuberculose gegen jeden Zweifel sicher gestellt und es muss ihr in Zukunft ein Platz unter den Infectionskrankheiten angewiesen werden.

Wenn die Zahl der Opfer, welche eine Krankheit fordert, als Massstab für ihre Bedeutung zu gelten hat, dann müssen alle Krankheiten, namentlich aber die gefürchtetsten Infectionskrankheiten, Pest, Cholera u. s. w. weit hinter der Tuberculose zurückstehen. Die Statistik lehrt, dass $^1/_7$ aller Menschen an Tuberculose stirbt und dass, wenn nur die mittleren productiven Altersklassen in Betracht kommen, die Tuberculose ein Drittel derselben und oft mehr dahinrafft. Die öffentliche Gesundheitspflege hat also Grund genug, ihre Aufmerksamkeit einer so mörderischen Krankheit zu widmen, ganz abgesehen davon, dass noch andere Verhältnisse, von denen nur die Beziehungen der Tuberculose zur Perlsucht erwähnt werden sollen, das Interesse der Gesundheitspflege in Anspruch nehmen.

Da es nun zu den Aufgaben des Gesundheitsamtes gehört, die Infectionskrankheiten vom Standpunkte der Gesundheitspflege aus, also in erster Linie in Bezug auf ihre Aetiologie, zum Gegenstand von Ermittelungsarbeiten zu machen, so erschien es als eine dringende Pflicht, vor Allem über die Tuberculose eingehende Untersuchungen anzustellen.

Das Wesen der Tuberculose zu ergründen, ist schon wiederholt versucht, aber bis jetzt ohne Erfolg. Die zum Nachweis der pathogenen Microorganismen so vielfach bewährten Färbungsmethoden haben dieser Krankheit gegenüber im Stich gelassen und die zum Zwecke der Isolirung und Züchtung des Tuberkel-Virus angestellten Versuche konnten bis jetzt nicht als gelungen angesehen werden, so dass Cohnheim in der soeben erschienenen neuesten Auflage seiner Vorlesungen über allgemeine Pathologie „den directen Nachweis des tuberculösen Virus als ein bis heute noch ungelöstes Problem“ bezeichnen musste.

Bei meinen Untersuchungen über die Tuberculose habe ich mich anfangs auch der bekannten Methoden bedient, ohne damit eine Aufklärung über das Wesen der Krankheit zu erlangen. Aber durch einige gelegentliche Beobachtungen wurde ich dann veranlasst, diese Methoden zu verlassen und andere Wege einzuschlagen, die schliesslich auch zu positiven Resultaten führten.

Das Ziel der Untersuchung musste zunächst auf den Nachweis von irgend welchen, dem Körper fremdartigen, parasitischen Gebilden gerichtet sein, die möglicherweise als Krankheitsursache gedeutet werden konnten. Dieser Nachweis gelang auch in der That durch ein bestimmtes Färbungsverfahren, mit Hülfe dessen in allen tuberculös veränderten Organen characteristische, bis dahin nicht bekannte Bacterien zu finden waren. Es würde zu weit führen, den Weg, auf welchem ich zu diesem neuen Verfahren gelangte, zu schildern und ich will deswegen sofort zur Beschreibung desselben übergehen.

Die Untersuchungsobjecte werden in der bekannten, für Untersuchungen auf pathogene Bacterien üblichen Weise, vorbereitet und entweder auf dem Deckglas ausgebreitet, getrocknet und erhitzt, oder nach Erhärtung in Alkohol in Schnitte zerlegt. Die Deckgläschen oder Schnitte gelangen in eine Farblösung von folgender Zusammensetzung. 200 Ccm. destillirten Wassers werden mit 1 Ccm. einer concentrirten alcoholischen Methylenblau-Lösung vermischt, umgeschüttelt und erhalten dann unter wiederholtem Schütteln noch einen Zusatz von 0,2 Ccm. einer 10 % Kalilauge. Diese Mischung darf selbst nach tagelangem Stehen keinen Niederschlag geben. Die zu färbenden Objecte bleiben in derselben 20 bis 24 Stunden. Durch Erwärmen der Farblösung auf 40° C. im Wasserbade kann diese Zeit auf $^1/_2$ bis 1 Stunde abgekürzt werden. Die Deckgläschen werden hierauf mit einer concentrirten wässrigen Lösung von Vesuvin, welche vor jedesmaligem Gebrauche zu filtriren ist, übergossen und nach ein bis zwei Minuten mit destillirtem Wasser abgespült. Wenn die Deckgläschen aus dem Methylenblau kommen, sieht die ihnen anhaftende Schicht dunkelblau aus und ist stark

12

13

12 Willi Baumeister, poster of the Werkbund exhibition *Die Wohnung*, 1927
13 Woman exercising on the terrace of Richard Döcker's house in the Weissenhof Siedlung, *Die Wohnung* exhibition, Stuttgart, 1927
14 CIAM Algiers team, presentation panel on tuberculosis in Bidonville Mahieddinne, for the 9th CIAM congress in Aix-en-Provence, 1953

credibility. Tuberculosis was thought to be a "wet" disease produced by damp cities. In an uncanny echo of Vitruvius, the TB patient was thought to need a new environment to dry out the inside of their bodies. Modern architects offered health by providing exactly such a change of environment. Nineteenth-century architecture was demonized as unhealthy, and sun, light, ventilation, exercise, roof terraces, hygiene, and whiteness were offered as means to prevent, if not cure, tuberculosis. **FIGS. 12–14** The publicity campaign of modern architecture was organized around contemporary beliefs about tuberculosis and fears of the disease.

In engaging TB, architects were not just tuning in to one illness among others. The TB scare was key in the emerging bond between the body, the military, industry, and politics. As Susan Sontag argued, few diseases have been so "spectacularly, and similarly, encumbered by the trappings of metaphor" as tuberculosis and cancer.[6] In *The Human Motor,* Anson Rabinbach goes as far as locating TB as part of a complete reconceptualization of the human body.[7] He argues that the obsession with fatigue that took over between 1895 and World War I marked rising anxiety about the industrial age. Diseases such as TB were blamed on fatigue, and exercise programs offered to combat them. There was a widespread call for organized sports. Gymnastic exercises, which had been limited to the military throughout the nineteenth century, were now advocated for schools. Furthermore, the military itself was reorganized on the basis of the new "sciences of work." Medicine and biology became the basis of political theory. Through this "biologiza-

14

tion of politics," the sciences of the body were firmly established as the basis of "social hygiene." By 1910, they were split into physiology and psychology, but successfully recombined as "psychotechnics" during the war. On the basis of this military success, an amalgamation of European scientific research and US Taylorism became standard equipment of modern industrial management. The dream of a body without fatigue finally reached its sinister peak in the dictatorial regimes of the 1930s.

We can see this trajectory in architecture. Architects repeatedly used disease imagery to express concern for social order. Architecture's traditional role of imposing order takes on different meanings with different diseases. The reconfiguration of the medical body by new sciences leads to a reconfiguration of architecture. Take Le Corbusier, the opening pages of *Vers une architecture* (1923) give his "diagnosis" of the state of architecture, condemning the traditional house for producing the debilitating effect of tuberculosis ("consumption"). He goes on to promote the healthy engineer over the unhealthy architect:

> We have become sedentary beings, that is our lot. The house eats away at us in our immobility, like consumption. We will soon need too many sanatoria.... Engineers are healthy and virile, active and useful, moral and joyful. Architects are disenchanted and idle, boastful or morose. That is because they will soon have nothing to do. *We have no more money* to pile up historical keepsakes. We need to cleanse ourselves....

15 Le Corbusier explaining the *Plan Voisin* using a map of the city of Paris. Film still from *L'Architecture d'aujourd'hui*, 1929
16 Film stills from *L'Architecture d'aujourd'hui*, 1929, by Pierre Chenal and Le Corbusier

15

> The diagnosis is clear. Engineers make architecture.... People still believe, here and there, in architects, just as people blindly believe in doctors.[8]

Throughout the book, health is a battle cry. The final chapter opposes the healthy modern workplace to the unhealthy private house: "The machine that we live in is an old coach full of tuberculosis."[9] Like so many architects, Le Corbusier expanded the medical argument from the house to the city. In *Urbanisme* (1925) he opposes the fatiguing city and looks for a "cure," concluding that "surgery" is required to remove the "cancer" of degenerate street layouts and "rotten old houses full of tuberculosis."[10]

In his film *L'Architecture d'aujourd'hui* (1929), made in collaboration with the young filmmaker Pierre Chenal, Le Corbusier argues that disease breeds in cities because, in the twentieth century, people still live as if in the Middle Ages. His solution: cut through the fabric of the old city and exercise on the roof garden. **FIG. 15** The film's tour through his villas of the 1920s emphasizes once again the value of sunbathing and exercise. It culminates in close-ups, shot on the diagonal from below, of a man and two women excitedly working out in a kind of sexualized intensity on the roof garden of Villa Church in exercise clothing and (for the women) high heels. **FIG. 16** The house is first and foremost a machine for health, a form of therapy.

In *La ville radieuse* of 1935, **FIG. 17** Le Corbusier insists on detaching the house, with the help of pilotis (thin columns), from the "wet, humid ground, where disease breeds" and on

16

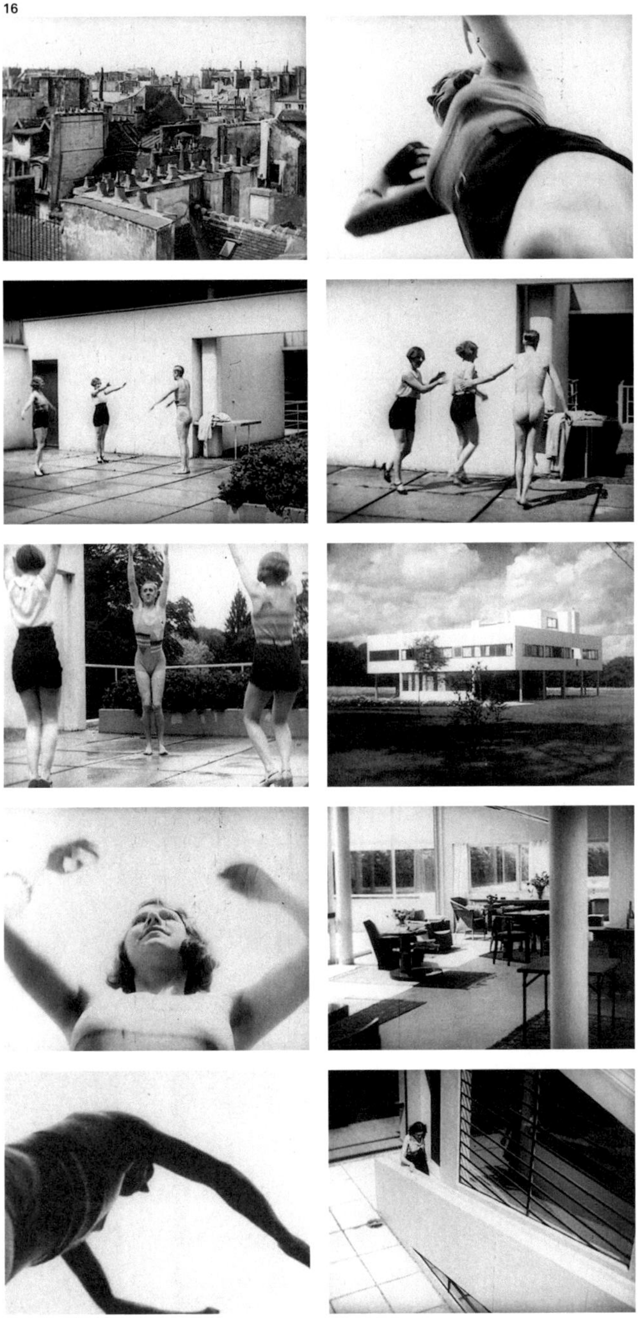

17 Terrace of the villa Stein at Garches. Film still from *L'Architecture d'aujourd'hui*, 1929, by Pierre Chenal and Le Corbusier
18 Le Corbusier, *The Radiant City*, first English edition, 1967, cover
19–21 Illustrations from Le Corbusier's *The Radiant City*, 1967

17

using the roof as a garden for sunbathing and exercise.[11] FIG. 17 Nobody seems to have known anything about skin cancer yet. To reinforce the point, Le Corbusier uses pictures taken from medical texts as architectural illustrations, showing the lungs and their inner workings, FIG. 20 while giving architectural illustrations medical labels, as when a photograph of an old part of the city becomes "Historic Paris, tubercular Paris."[12] FIG. 19 In this book, Le Corbusier develops a concept of "exact air" whereby the outdoor air is continually circulated and cleaned, made "dust free, disinfected … and ready to be consumed by the lung."[13] FIG. 21 One by one, Le Corbusier thus presents the characteristic features of modern architecture—pilotis, roof garden, glass walls, and clean air—as medical devices, and the overall effect is that of a sanatorium devoted to both preventive and reactive cure. There is no line between domestic architecture and medicine.

Le Corbusier had long been obsessed with his own health. Moving in 1917 to Paris from his small hometown, La Chaux-de-Fonds in Switzerland, he complained about feeling exhausted all the time until he met Dr. Pierre Winter, who introduced him to exercise as a way of combating fatigue and stress. They played basketball together twice a week, and Winter subsequently turned Le Corbusier into a boxer, FIG. 23 runner, and eventually a swimmer. Winter would become a contributor to Le Corbusier and Amédée Ozenfant's journal *L'Esprit nouveau,* which regularly covered sporting events and informed its readers of new athletic records. In an article in *L'Esprit nouveau* entitled "Sports," Winter writes:

18

19

History. Historic Paris, tubercular Paris.

20

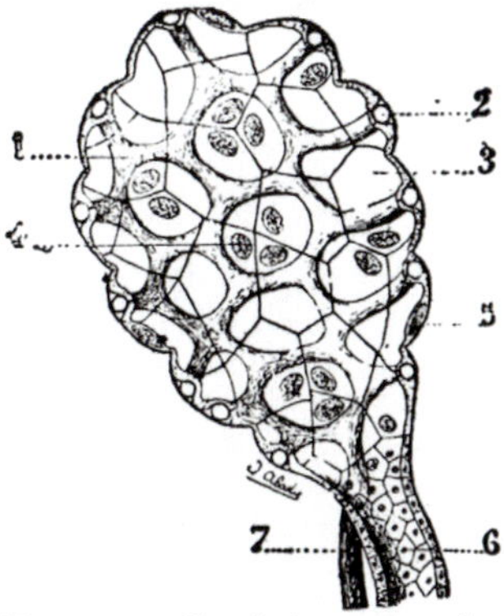

Fig. 253. — Circulation à la surface d'un lobule pulmonaire.

1 et 2. réseau capillaire; 3. paroi de l'alvéole; 4 et 5. noyaux des cellules épithéliales. 6. bronchiole. 7. vaisseau sanguin afférent.

Fig. 253. Circulation at the surface of a pulmonary lobule.

1 and 2, capillary network. 3, Alveole wall. 4 and 5, nuclei of epithelial cells. 6, Bronchial tube 7, Afferent blood vessel.

21

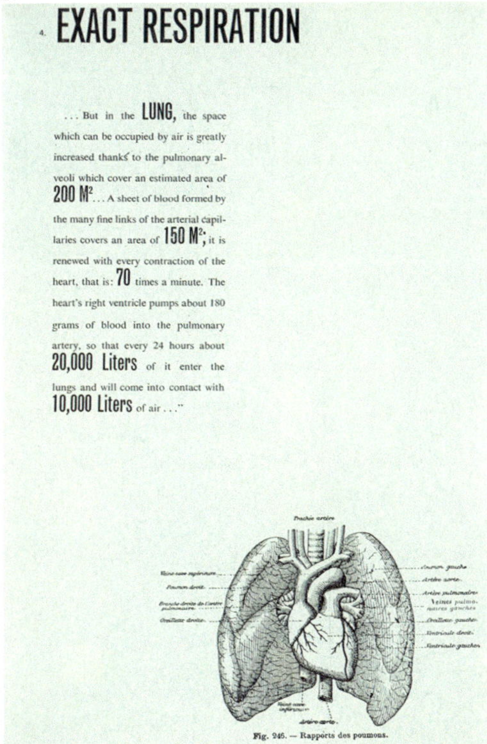

4. EXACT RESPIRATION

. . . But in the **LUNG,** the space which can be occupied by air is greatly increased thanks to the pulmonary alveoli which cover an estimated area of **200 M²** . . . A sheet of blood formed by the many fine links of the arterial capillaries covers an area of **150 M²**; it is renewed with every contraction of the heart, that is: **70** times a minute. The heart's right ventricle pumps about 180 grams of blood into the pulmonary artery, so that every 24 hours about **20,000 Liters** of it enter the lungs and will come into contact with **10,000 Liters** of air . . ."

Fig. 246. — Rapports des poumons.

22

23

22 Children dancing in the Dalcroze method school of Albert Jeanneret, *L'Esprit nouveau* 2, 1920
23 Le Corbusier and Pierre Jeanneret boxing on the beach at Piquew, 1933
24 *L'Esprit nouveau* 15, February 1922, cover
25 Pierre Winter, "Le corps nouveau," *L'Esprit nouveau* 15, February 1922

> Let us put our personal life and our social life in order. If everybody methodically studies his daily timetable with a view to taylorizing his acts and gestures ... if we all banished idle habits and lackadaisical work, wasted effort ... if sleep were better regulated ... when all those extra minutes were added up, one might find time for sport, for tending to the body.... [T]o regulate one's life is to control it and is a great source of deep joy.... Sport introduces an element of ORDER in life.[14]

FIGS. 24, 25

Winter was an enthusiast of the authoritarian wing of the syndicalist movement in France and a follower of Georges Valois (the self-proclaimed French Mussolini), who founded the short-lived fascist party Le Faisceau in 1925. In 1928, Winter joined the fascist revolutionary party of Philippe Lamour, made of old members of Faisceau. In a 1926 article for Valois's journal *Le nouveau siècle* on Le Corbusier's plan for a new kind of city, Winter writes: "Only a strong program of urbanism—the program of a Fascist government—is capable of adapting the modern city to the needs of all."[15]

This intimate bond between architecture, urbanism, disease, war, industry, and politics is explicit throughout the work of Le Corbusier and many of his colleagues in the interwar period. In a lengthy statement prepared to introduce Le Corbusier's lecture in L'Académie de la Coupole, Paris, in 1936, Winter describes "Le Corbusier ... the architect, the painter, the poet, as inseparable from the less known Le Corbusier that I have the particular mission to

24

25

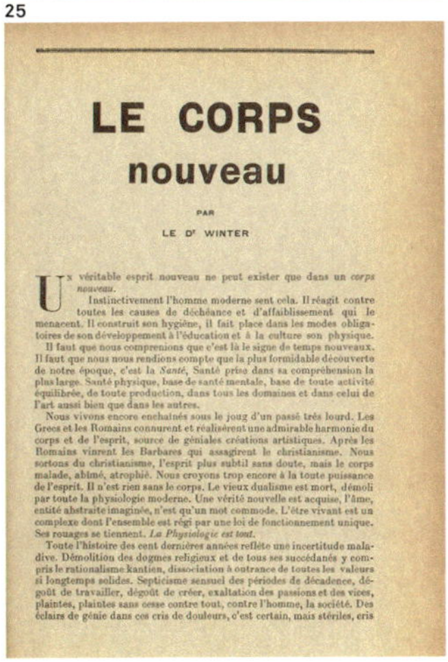

LE CORPS nouveau

PAR

LE Dr WINTER

Un véritable esprit nouveau ne peut exister que dans un *corps nouveau*.

Instinctivement l'homme moderne sent cela. Il réagit contre toutes les causes de déchéance et d'affaiblissement qui le menacent. Il construit son hygiène, il fait place dans les modes obligatoires de son développement à l'éducation et à la culture son physique.

Il faut que nous comprenions que c'est là le signe de temps nouveaux. Il faut que nous nous rendions compte que la plus formidable découverte de notre époque, c'est la *Santé*, Santé prise dans sa compréhension la plus large. Santé physique, base de santé mentale, base de toute activité équilibrée, de toute production, dans tous les domaines et dans celui de l'art aussi bien que dans les autres.

Nous vivons encore enchainés sous le joug d'un passé très lourd. Les Grecs et les Romains connurent et réalisèrent une admirable harmonie du corps et de l'esprit, source de géniales créations artistiques. Après les Romains vinrent les Barbares qui assagirent le christianisme. Nous sortons du christianisme, l'esprit plus subtil sans doute, mais le corps malade, abimé, atrophié. Nous croyons trop encore à la toute puissance de l'esprit. Il n'est rien sans le corps. Le vieux dualisme est mort, démoli par toute la physiologie moderne. Une vérité nouvelle est acquise, l'âme, entité abstraite imaginée, n'est qu'un mot commode. L'être vivant est un complexe dont l'ensemble est régi par une loi de fonctionnement unique. Ses rouages se tiennent. *La Physiologie est tout.*

Toute l'histoire des cent dernières années reflète une incertitude maladive. Démolition des dogmes religieux et de tous ses succédanés y compris le rationalisme kantien, dissociation à outrance de toutes les valeurs si longtemps solides. Septicisme sensuel des périodes de décadence, dégoût de travailler, dégoût de créer, exaltation des passions et des vices, plaintes, plaintes sans cesse contre tout, contre l'homme, la société. Des éclairs de génie dans ces cris de douleurs, c'est certain, mais stériles, cris introduce you to—under the labels, too pompous for their modesty … Biologist (with a big B), sociologist (with a big S), and I would add athlete, who could have perhaps become a champion"[16] and goes on to describe how he had encountered Le Corbusier in the early twenties in bad shape: "he disregarded his body … worked day and night … 7 days a week … didn't care about his sleep … had forgotten his breathing … his muscles. He was surprised that did not go well and he complained and invoked bizarre gods, those that doctors have invented to deceive their ill."[17]

Winter, who in 1925 became chief surgeon in the Faculty of Medicine in Paris, was militantly in favor of homeopathy and actively searching for alternative forms of medicine, including the curative capabilities of exercise and diet. The polemical pages of *L'Esprit nouveau* offered a number of theories of health: from Dr. Winter's hygiene and exercise through Dr. Allendy's homeopathy to Jaques-Dalcroze's rhythmic gymnastics. **FIG. 22** Each produced a unique image of the healthy body.

The modern body housed by modern architecture thus was not a single body, but a multiplicity of bodies. The body was no longer a stable point of reference around which an architecture could be built. It was a construction site. Architects such as Le Corbusier and his colleagues in the architectural avant-garde actively redesigned the body with their architecture, rather than housing it or symbolizing it. A new spirit (*l'esprit nouveau*) requires a new body, as Winter writes in his article "Le corps nouveau":

> A truly new spirit can exist only in a new body. Instinctively, modern man knows that.... We have to realize that the most formidable discovery of our time is *Health*, understood in this more comprehensive sense. Physical health: the basis of mental health, the basis of every balanced activity, of all production, in all domains, and in that of art as much as in all the others.... The body will emerge naked in the sun, washed, muscled, supple.[18]

Modern architecture likewise presented itself as lean and fit, all the excess weight of neoclassical tradition stripped off to reveal a muscular and agile body in a white sports outfit. The modern house was understood not just as a kind of medical equipment, a mechanism for caring for the body, but as a piece of exercise equipment designed to enhance it, to produce a strong and healthy body. Think of all the body-building houses in modern architecture: Marcel Breuer's bedroom for Erwin Piscator in Berlin (1927) **FIG. 26**, with its gymnastic equipment, and his apartment with Gustav Hassenpflug for Hilde Levi in Berlin (1930) **FIG. 27**; Walter Gropius's gyms in his communal apartments for the Werkbund exhibition in Paris (1930) **FIG. 28** and for the German Building Exhibition in Berlin (1931) **FIG. 29**; Richard Döcker's rooftop gym at the Weissenhofsiedlung in Stuttgart (1927); Theo Effenberger's roof terrace gym at the Werkbund building exhibition in Breslau (1929) **FIG. 31**; the sports room and solarium on the top of Johannes Brinkman and Leendert Cornelis van der Vlugt's van der Leeuw house in Rotterdam (1928–1930). **FIG. 30** Then there are Le Corbusier's Immeuble Villas

26 Marcel Breuer, bedroom for Piscator, Berlin, 1927
27 Marcel Breuer, apartment for Hilde Levi in Berlin, 1930
28 Walter Gropius, communal gym for apartment house, Werkbund exhibition, Paris, 1930
29 Walter Gropius, communal gym for apartment house, German Building Exhibition, Berlin, 1931
30 Leendert Cornelis van der Vlugt and Johannes Brinkmann, gym in C. H. van der Leeuw House, Rotterdam, 1928–1929
31 Theo Effenberger, house in the Werkbund housing exhibition, Breslau, 1929

26

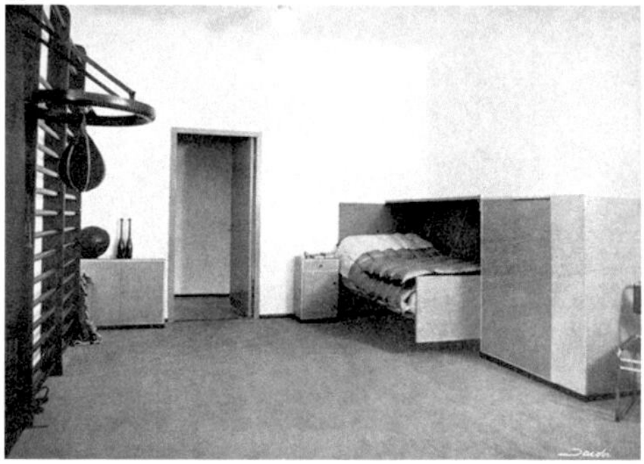

27

28

29

30

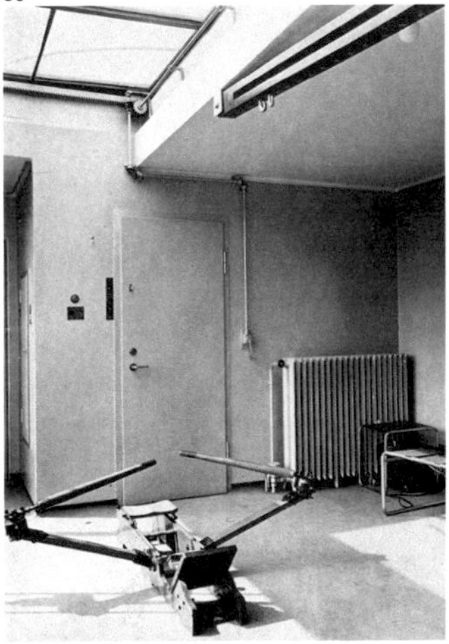

31

32

LE POINT DE VUE DU BIOLOGISTE

par le Docteur PIERRE WINTER

De quel biologiste ?

De celui qui centre volontairement ses recherches sur les problèmes humains et désire, avant tout, mettre « au service de l'homme » leurs résultats.

Peu importent à ce biologiste les savantes et minutieuses analyses des faits de la vie, si elles n'aboutissent pas à la connaissance de lois dont on puisse déduire des applications pratiques — applications pratiques qui, pour lui, ne doivent pas concerner exclusivement le corps physique de l'homme, mais

— 29 —

33

34

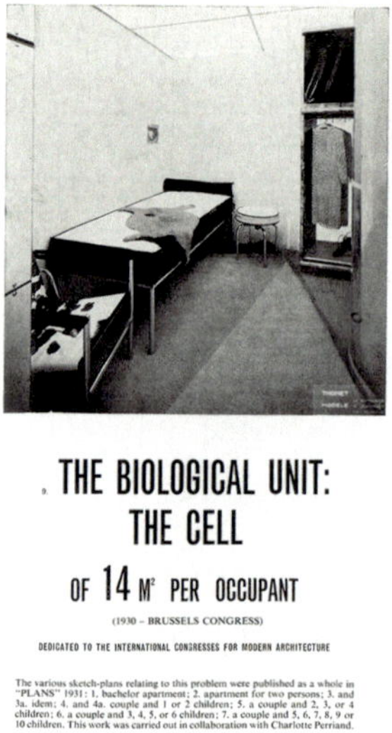
THE BIOLOGICAL UNIT: THE CELL OF 14 M² PER OCCUPANT

(1930 – BRUSSELS CONGRESS)

DEDICATED TO THE INTERNATIONAL CONGRESSES FOR MODERN ARCHITECTURE

The various sketch-plans relating to this problem were published as a whole in "PLANS" 1931: 1. bachelor apartment; 2. apartment for two persons; 3. and 3a. idem; 4. and 4a. couple and 1 or 2 children; 5. a couple and 2, 3, or 4 children; 6. a couple and 3, 4, 5, or 6 children; 7. a couple and 5, 6, 7, 8, 9 or 10 children. This work was carried out in collaboration with Charlotte Perriand.

(1922), where each apartment was to have its own sports room. "On the roof of the building there is a 1000-meter track on which to run in the fresh air, and there are also the gymnasiums, where the gym instructors would direct parents as well as children; there are solariums too (which have proved so successful in the United States in combating tuberculosis)."[19] **FIG. 33** The athletic figure is one of the paradigmatic clients of modern architecture and tuberculosis lurks as the ever-present threat.

But the body was not seen as simply physical. *L'Esprit nouveau* was also obsessed with the relationship between psyche and body. It published articles by Dr. Allendy and his colleague Dr. Laforgue on the relationship between Freudian psychoanalysis and French psychiatry, with titles such as "The Conscious and the Unconscious," "Neuroses," "Dreams," and "The Oedipus Complex." While Le Corbusier was sometimes dismissive of psychoanalysis, he repeatedly spoke of the intimate relationship between mind and body, portraying mental stability as the product of a healthy physical environment. In *Urbanisme,* he argues that the degeneration of the city leads to "physical and nervous sickness," and in *La ville radieuse,* he proposes that the new living cell be a machine for the "recuperation of physical and nervous energy ... the upkeep of the human machine: cleaning, draining the toxic substances, recuperating nervous energy, maintenance or increase of physical energy."[20] **FIG. 34** Once again, the architect was a doctor, practicing a form of preventive medicine that nurtures and rebuilds the body and psyche.

32 Le Corbusier portrayed as a biologist. Pierre Winter, "The Point of View of a Biologist," 1933
33 Le Corbusier, *Architecture et urbanisme,* suspended garden, Immeuble Wanner, Geneva, 1928–1929
34 The Biological Unit, Illustration from Le Corbusier's *The Radiant City*

MODERN NERVES

The history of modern design uncannily parallels that of modern anesthetics. Every element of modern architecture addressed both physiological and mental sickness. Le Corbusier saw the smooth white surfaces he was strongly advocating with his architecture not just as hygienic, a way to prevent the spread of germs, but as an anesthetic to calm "the nerves shattered in the aftermath of war," at the same time that actual anesthetics (cocaine) were being "peddled" in the street of Paris, as he noted.[21] Cocaine was one of the first substances used as anesthetic for surgery by Karl Koller (on the recommendation of Freud) in 1884. **FIG. 36**

Anesthesia is the removal of feeling, the temporal suppression of the central nervous system in order to achieve lack of sensation, and by minimizing friction, the smooth surfaces of modern architecture anesthetize bodily sensation. Smooth white planes restore the "calm" that preceded the brutality of the arrival of the mass-produced ornaments of modern industry. Le Corbusier repeatedly uses the word "calm" as an ideal, as if the purpose of design was stress reduction. For him, even the touch of the modern object becomes a reassuring visual effect: "Our hand reaches out to it [the modern object] and our sense of touch *looks* in its own way as our fingers close around it."[22]

The shock of war, the shock of the machine age, the shock of the metropolis have in common anesthesia, the temporary removal of feeling, whether physical or psychological. In "Experience and Poverty" (1933) Walter Benjamin wrote about people returning from World War I "poorer in

35

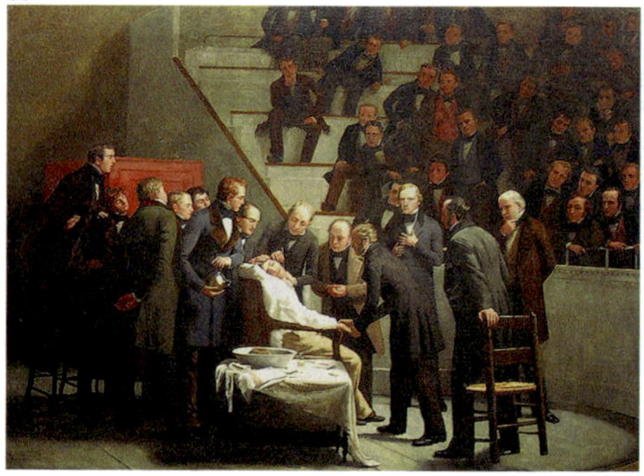

36

37

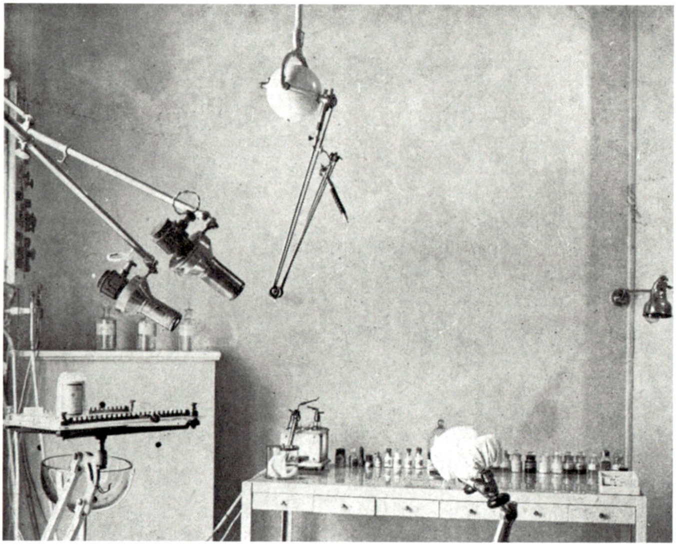

experience," unable to communicate, silent, in shock after feeling the full force of modern technology: "A generation that had gone to school in horse-drawn streetcars now stood in the open air, amid a landscape in which nothing was the same except the clouds, and, at its center, in a force field of destructive torrents and explosions, the tiny, fragile human body."[23] Until the nineteenth century, *aesthetics*, from the Greek, had nothing to do with the intellect or the ideal and everything to do with sensation, with perception by bodily feeling.[24] But now, feeling was no longer possible. Humans were anesthetized by the shock, yet sought further anesthetics. This poverty of experience finds its parallel in

35 Robert C. Hinckley, first operation under ether, 1846, painted 1882–1893
36 Opium Poppy, in Otto Wilhelm Thomé, *Flora von Deutschland, Österreich und der Schweiz,* 1885
37 The equipment of a dentist, published by Le Corbusier and Ozenfant in their article "Formation de l'Optique Moderne" in *L'Esprit nouveau* 21, 1924

modern architecture in glass-and-steel buildings on whose smooth surfaces the inhabitant cannot leave any traces, any memory. In his writings on Baudelaire, Benjamin speaks of the smile of passersby in the metropolis ("keep smiling") that protect them from an unprecedented number of close encounters with strangers by developing mimetic tactics. The smile "functions as mimetic shock absorber."[25] Modern design is likewise a shock absorber, its frozen smile barely hiding the terror it tries to cover over.

Benjamin's understanding of modern experience is neurological, as Susan Buck-Morss has written.[26] "The shock experience which the passer-by has in the crowd corresponds to what the worker 'experiences' at his machine."[27] War, machine, and metropolis are all shock environments, conditions of danger where one has to be able to react quickly to protect oneself from sudden, unforeseeable threats. Nerves are on the periphery.

The elimination of ornament is not simply an aesthetic choice, but a neurological or even narcotic one. Adolf Loos argued that we moderns no longer have the nerves necessary to eat, dress, and decorate as in previous centuries. In "Ornament and Crime," he speaks of his "horror" in front of the decorated animals in culinary displays, particularly if he thinks he has to eat "one of these stuffed animal corpses. I only eat roast beef!" He feels the same nausea in the face of any excessive ornament, whether on food or architecture: "We lack the steady nerves to drink from an elephant's ivory tusk on which an Amazon battle scene has been engraved.... Our temples are no longer painted blue, red, green, and white,

38

39

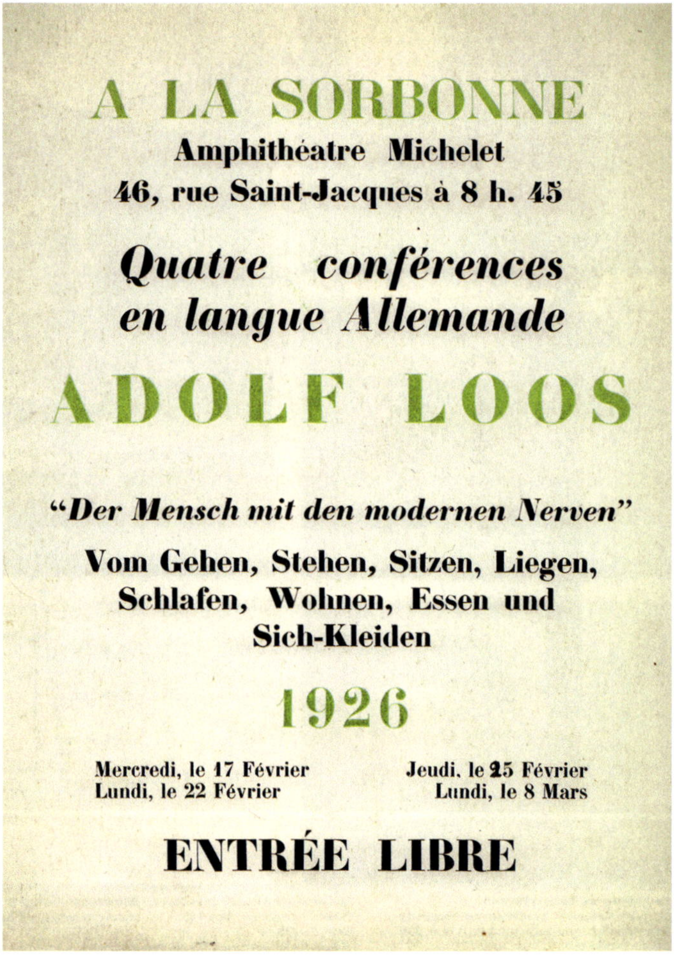
A LA SORBONNE
Amphithéatre Michelet
46, rue Saint-Jacques à 8 h. 45
Quatre conférences
en langue Allemande
ADOLF LOOS
"Der Mensch mit den modernen Nerven"
Vom Gehen, Stehen, Sitzen, Liegen,
Schlafen, Wohnen, Essen und
Sich-Kleiden
1926
Mercredi, le 17 Février
Lundi, le 22 Février
Jeudi, le 25 Février
Lundi, le 8 Mars
ENTRÉE LIBRE

38 Adolf Loos after a stomach operation, Sanatorium der Kaufmannschaft, 1918
39 "The Man with the Modern Nerves," poster for a series of lectures by Adolf Loos in La Sorbonne, Paris, 1926
40 Hydrotherapy at the sanatorium "Lebendige Kraft," full body wrap by Dr. Maximilian Bircher-Brenner, Zurich, 1910

40

like the Parthenon, no, we have learned to appreciate the beauty of naked stone."[28] Modern man has a whole new set of nerves with completely different sensitivities.

In "Karl Kraus," Walter Benjamin quotes Robert Scheu, brother of Gustav Scheu (for whom Adolf Loos built a controversial house in Vienna in 1912): "Kraus discovered a great subject that had never before set in motion the pen of a journalist: the rights of the nerves.... He became the advocate of the nerves ... but the subject grew under his hands, to become the problem of private life."[29] Private life, the interior, becomes newly fragile, like that of the nervous individual analyzed by psychoanalysis or the vulnerable body of the tuberculosis patient penetrated by X-rays. Everybody becomes like a child or a patient needing to be wrapped in soft lining. **FIG. 40** It is as if the new nerves are so new that the modern individual has only just been born and needs a protective incubator to survive, to gain the necessary strength. Loos's architecture is such an incubator.

Loos was himself fragile. He suffered from numerous nervous and physical ailments throughout his life. He contracted syphilis as a young man, and it left him sterile. He had stomach cancer and underwent a number of major surgeries. **FIG. 38** All his life he suffered from poor hearing, and he eventually became completely deaf. At the end of his life, he checked himself into the sanatorium run by his friend, the neurologist Dr. Norbert Schwarzmann, in Kalksburg, where he died in 1933. A year earlier, Buckminster Fuller had included "nerve shock proofing" in his list of basic requirements for all houses.[30] Frederick Kiesler and Richard

41 Frederick Kiesler, *Contemporary Art Applied to the Store and Its Display,* 1930, cover

41

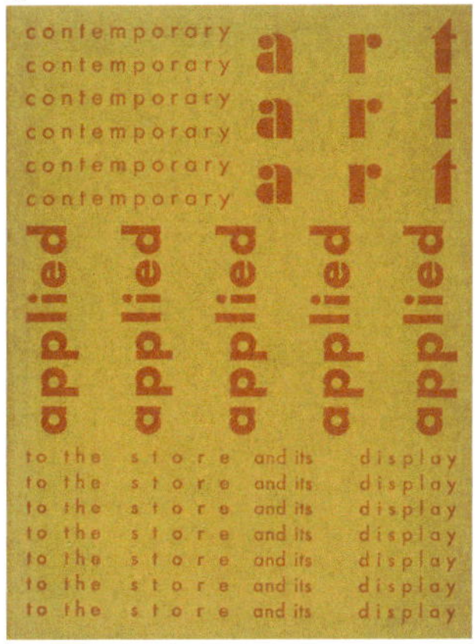

Neutra would develop entire theories of design based on the nerves. It is as if nerves themselves were the true clients of modern architecture.

Modern architecture was not just a form of medical equipment or an exercise machine. It also was a cocoon for sheltering the fragile psyche traumatized by exposure to war, loss of stable borders, and the new rhythms and speeds of modern industrialized technology. Every room became a recovery room, every building a trauma center. Architecture became a psychological craft.

"PSYCHO-FUNCTION," OR ARCHITECTURE AS EATING DISORDER

Take, for example, the extraordinary concept of "psycho-function" that Friedrich Kiesler introduced in his 1930 book *Contemporary Art Applied to the Store and Its Display:* FIG. 41 "The 'psycho-functional' influence is exhibited not only in lines, planes and form, but also in materials and colors. Glass has a different psychological effect from leather, wood from metal. The same applies, of course, to color schemes. Function and efficiency alone cannot create art works. 'Psycho-function' is that 'surplus' above efficiency which may turn a functional solution into art."[31] Kiesler continues the argument in the later essay "Pseudo-Functionalism in Modern Architecture": "We must strive from the outset *to satisfy the psyche of the dweller.*"[32] The house, he says, is a human body, "a living organism with the reactivity of a full-blooded creature," with organs (the stairs are the feet, the ventilation system is the nose, and so on), a nervous system, and a digestive system that can "suffer from constipation."[33] More than that, he insists, the house, like man, lives "in emotions and dreams through the medium of his physique." The psyche cannot be separated from the body. Indeed, the house is the product of "the erotic and creative instinct," and our experience of it is erotic.[34]

In the press release for the 1969 exhibition of *Galaxies* at the Howard Wise Gallery in New York, Kiesler claims to have "discovered architecture" when, at the age of three, he crept under the "voluminous peasant skirts of his Ukrainian nanny and struck a match." Architecture for him is always erotic. Of his Endless House, **FIGS. 42, 43** he writes: "There is no beginning and no end to it, like the human body.... The 'Endless' is rather sensuous, more like the female body in contrast to sharp-angled male architecture."[35] The building is meant to produce a kind of high—in 1961, he likened the experience of the Endless House to that of smoking marijuana. In the course of an interview, he was asked: "What do you think would happen if architects generally became interested in what you have done and in your approach? Isn't it a terribly dangerous, undisciplined sort of architecture for most people?" To which he responded: "I can assure you, it will be like giving them marijuana, architecturally speaking."[36] For him, the occupant of modern architecture yearns to be spaced out.

In 1947 Kiesler generated the first version of his Endless House. The house was not just one project among others. It was his whole life—his philosophy and even his body. He built it, literally, from the inside and saw himself

42, 43 Frederick Kiesler, Endless House, interior models, 1960

42

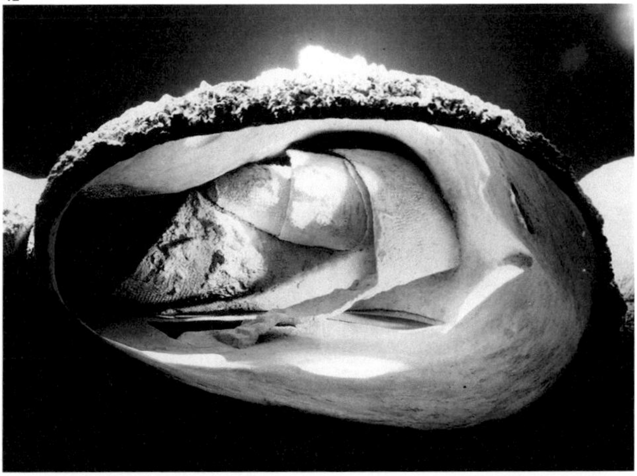

43

being swallowed by it. The house was like a stomach, full of folds, absorbing juices and nutrients. The occupant thus becomes a kind of food. In an extraordinary confusion of his own body with architecture, he described modern architecture as architecture on a diet in the aftermath of World War I:

> We had nothing to eat. I recall very well my own situation: after the war I lived on the dole for many years; I got about seven Kronen a week, which would be the equivalent of seven dollars per week now. But one could live on that monastically; I had rice, chiefly, and mushrooms. I remember only too well the mushrooms which I dried and reheated again just as I did with tea-leaves. As in our living habits, we started to clean off everything that was surplus in design—ornamentation, certain luxurious materials, moldings, this and that. Everything became, over the years, simpler, cleaner, whiter, and ... you know, what we call functionalism was on its natural way.
>
> So functionalism was really a reaction to the overstuffing of the Victorian age. Architecture had to be put on a diet. And the rectangular style did it. Now the period of diet is over and we can eat normally again. However that does not mean that we should overeat, stuff ourselves with whipped cream, ice cream—or with architecture either.[37]

Modern architecture is an eating disorder. The result was what Kiesler called "the rectangular style," the skin-and-

44 Frederick Kiesler, Endless Theater, floor plan, Vienna, 1924–1925
45 Frederick Kiesler, Space Stage, International Exhibition of New Theater Techniques, Vienna, 1924
46 Frederick Kiesler, Endless Theater, longitudinal section, Vienna, 1924–1925

44
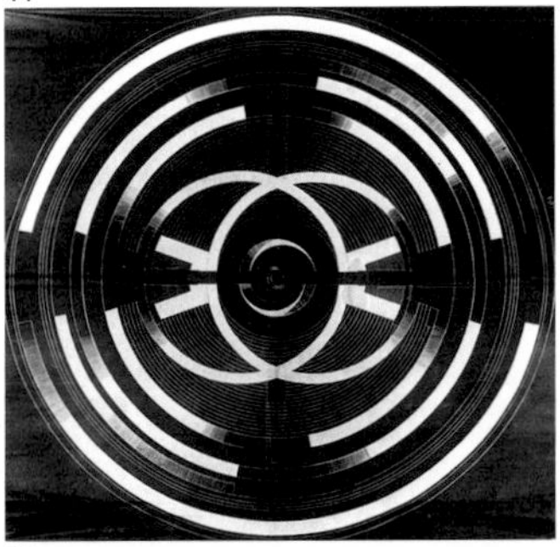

46
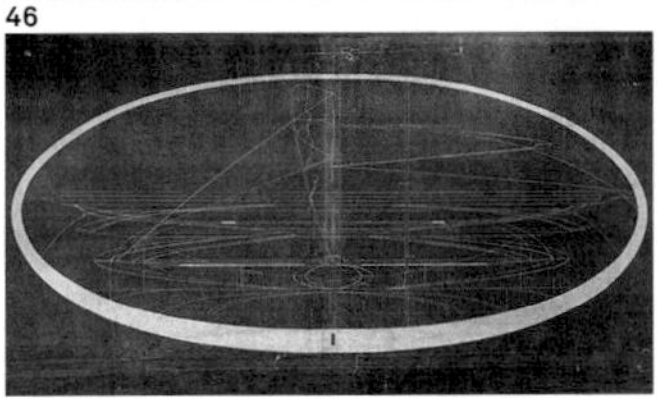

45

bones architecture of the modern period. For him, a well-balanced diet meant his Endless House: the elimination of any constipating residue. Everything in the Endless House is skin. The skin is the structure, as in an egg. Kiesler claimed to have worked on this idea for a long time. In fact, he insisted that he worked on just one idea throughout his life. He traced it back to his Space Theater of 1923, **FIGS. 44–46** his "first Endless." When he came to the United States in 1926, he said, he carried the Endless with him, but no one understood it. The organizers of the International Style exhibition of 1932 at MoMA reviewed his work when they were preparing the exhibition. This is how Kiesler recalls their meeting:

47

48

> Philip Johnson came with Henry-Russell Hitchcock to see plans of my work. Among our friends of the De Stijl group it was known that I have deviated from the "quadrat," but van Doesburg stood by enthusiastically, as did Mondrian. The others were doubtful; Mies was neutral and reserved. I was terribly poor.... Here were the plans for a building that looked like an egg, not like the customary box. It wasn't square, it wasn't in steel, it wasn't in glass, it wasn't in aluminum, it was absolutely outside the mode of the International Style.[38]

Kiesler was starving. Apparently he survived thanks to a coffee shop owner on Sixth Avenue who fed him and his wife Stefi Frischer every day. When he was finally thrown out of his apartment because he could not pay the rent, he was let in every day by the doorman while the new tenants were out so he could use the drafting table, which had been confiscated by the landlord, to work on his project for the shop windows of Saks Fifth Avenue. *Inside the Endless House* describes his inability to afford even basic expenses in terms of the same emaciated body that he identifies with modern architecture: "All in all, I'm down at the bottom and have practically nothing left: these expenses are the bone structure, and there is no hope for either skin or flesh with which to cover the skeleton."[39]

Just as Le Corbusier's idea about health and architecture started with his obsessions about his own body, Kiesler's physical condition organized his theories and designs. He could not separate himself from his architec-

47 Frederick Kiesler with his model of the Endless House, New York, 1959–1960
48 Frederick Kiesler inside the Bucephalus, Amagansett, Long Island, 1964–1965
49, 50 Two studies of human perception/ Vision Machine (Shortest–Longest), New York, ca. 1937–1941
51 Portrait of Frederick Kiesler, 1965
52 Frederick Kiesler, *Inside the Endless House*, 1966, cover

49

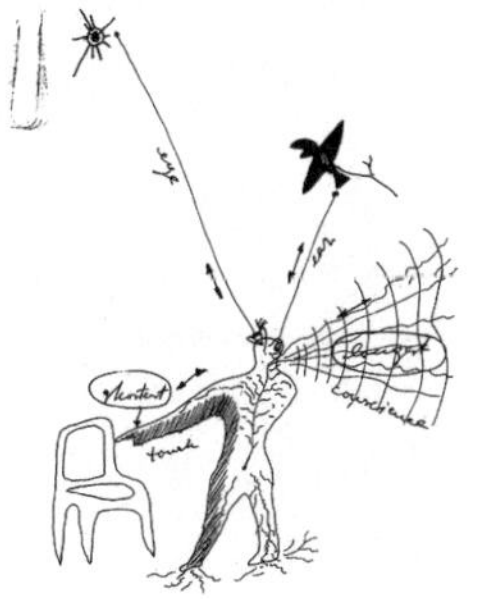

50

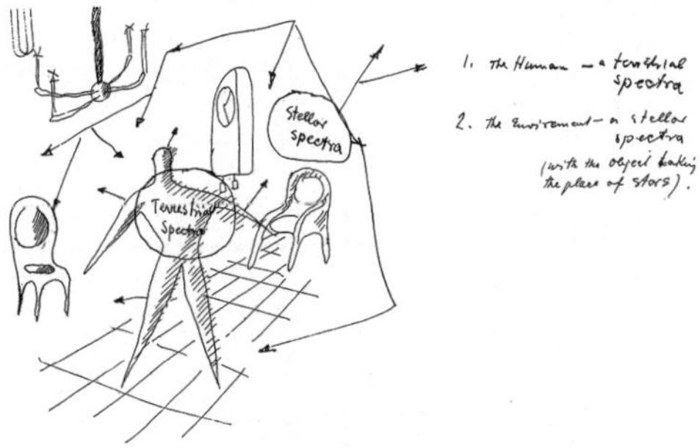

ture. Not by chance, he always photographed his own body inside the body of the building. **FIGS. 47, 48** With his fragile frame inside the egg, it is as if the house became his surrogate body. He replaced the heroic, athletic, muscular body of modern architecture with a frail body in need of protection by architecture. Architecture here becomes an infinite, uterine cave, nurturing a kind of translucent body so that the brain can thrive and feel. The body for Kiesler quivers, sheltered in a kind of spiral, not in order to be disconnected from the world, but on the contrary, in order to connect itself to the world.

The polemical sensuality of Kiesler's designs extends the nerves from the psyche through the tactile to the cosmic. A series of sketches make this point. In one, the interaction of the nervous system with a chair becomes part of a multisensual engagement with the world. In another, the chair becomes part of an interior, and the human is described as "a terrestrial spectra," the environment as a "stellar spectra (with the objects taking the place of stars)." **FIGS. 49, 50** Space for Kiesler is always outer space. Everything in his architecture floats. The floors go up and down, the structure hangs, and even the furniture, the cabinets, the tables, the lighting fixtures are suspended in a Surrealist project that begins with the thought of the body as a kind of house and of the house as a body. It is not by chance that his memoirs are entitled *Inside the Endless House.* **FIG. 52** Psyche, sexuality, the body, and architecture are inseparable.

Indeed, in *Inside the Endless House* Kiesler refers to "the house of the human body." The book is a kind of diary

51

52

(covering the years 1956 to 1964) that revolves around the condition of the architect's body. It is filled with references to his medical problems, from rheumatism to asthma, allergies, colds, and fevers. Much of it involves eating, or the desire to eat. Detailed descriptions of numerous meals are preceded by comments such as "a hunger rose from my stomach incessantly" or "My solar plexus signaled hunger. And starved I was." Even a client's final agreement to commission Kiesler is interrupted by the stomach: "I was desperately hungry.... I ate a naked piece of meat."[40] The modern subject is like the first humans surviving in their caves after the occasional hunt.

Le Corbusier's fatigue and Kiesler's malnourishment completely organized their thinking about architecture. Their rhetoric of the healthy and health-inducing building is underpinned by the actual experience of sick bodies. The wasting away of the body became the countermodel for a healthy architecture. But their therapeutic proposals are very different, as is clear in a section of *Inside the Endless House* entitled "The Correalism of the Plastic Arts": "nobody has ever defined the meaning of the roots of function; it has not been recognized that any function is subject to evolution just as man is. Function is now frozen in hygiene, light and air-conditioning."[41] Kiesler dismisses the aesthetic of sun, air, and hygiene as a "magic fake of pseudo-functionalism" that is "vomiting its indigestion."[42] Modern architecture is not as healthy as it looks. *Inside the Endless House* suggests that healthy architecture has to avoid threats like the "cancerous growth of ducts"[43] imposed on all building types by engineers and the filling of basements with the "excrement from the digestion of our house-life."[44] A whole different attitude toward the body of the building is required.

For Kiesler, the healthy body is first and foremost the sensual body. Indeed, sensual pleasure is the organizing principle of his work. At one point, he describes the model of the Endless House as "rolled up like a sex kitten." The architect's primary role is to satisfy appetites, whether sexual or gastric: "If art could be accepted like sex and sex like eating, men and women would not feel like perverts, shamelessly obscene in the presence of modern art or architecture."[45] For Kiesler, the International Style is filled with disorders and repressions. Unblocking architecture in the name of pleasure does not mean abandoning the medical body. On the contrary. Kiesler's twisted forms are meant to be healthier than Le Corbusier's "machine à habiter." Dissidents such as Kiesler expose that modern architecture is an always failed attempt to repress its own sensuality and like every person is full of secrets, obsessions, and forbidden pleasures hidden behind its attempts to project the image of a new normality.

NUDITY, FREE LOVE, AND THE HEALTH HOUSE

R. M. Schindler and Richard Neutra are well known in the history of modern architecture for their respective "health houses" for Doctor Phillip Lovell in California: Schindler's Lovell Beach House in Newport Beach (1922–1926) **FIG. 54** and Neutra's Lovell House in Los Angeles (1927–1929), also known as the Health House. **FIG. 63** Less well known is that the

53 Rudolph Schindler bathing at Illilouette Falls, Yosemite, 1921
54 R. M. Schindler, Beach House for Dr. Phillip Lovell, Newport Beach, 1925–1926
55 Pauline Schindler and Leah Lovell, "school in the garden," ca. 1925
56 Adolf Koch's socialist body culture school, Lake Motzen, near Berlin, ca. 1930

53

54

55

56

57

58

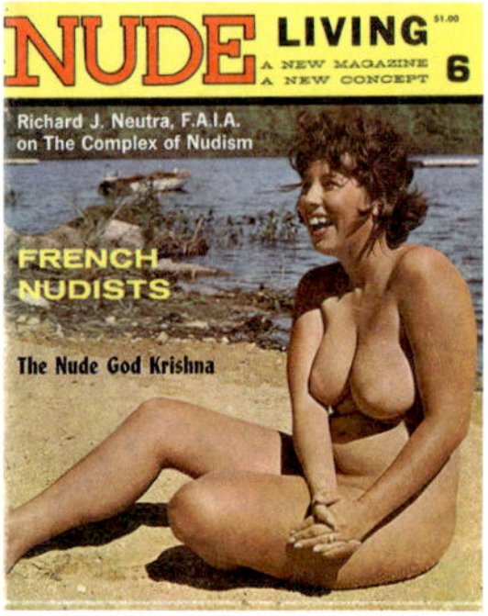

59

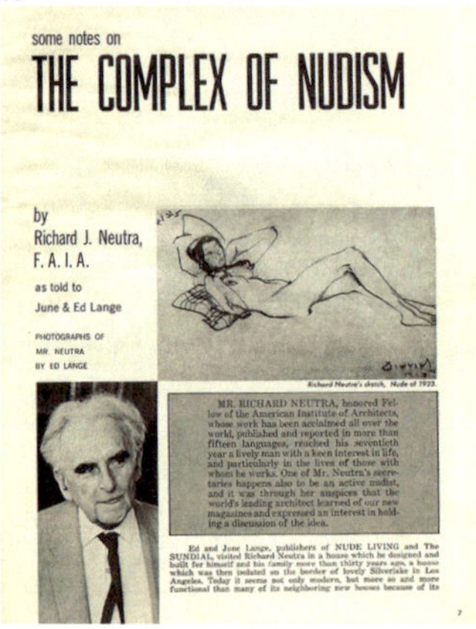

some notes on

THE COMPLEX OF NUDISM

by
Richard J. Neutra,
F. A. I. A.
as told to
June & Ed Lange

PHOTOGRAPHS OF
MR. NEUTRA
BY ED LANGE

Richard Neutra's sketch, Nude of 1923.

MR. RICHARD NEUTRA, honored Fellow of the American Institute of Architects, whose work has been acclaimed all over the world, published and reported in more than fifteen languages, reached his seventieth year a lively man with a keen interest in life, and particularly in the lives of those with whom he works. One of Mr. Neutra's secretaries happens also to be an active nudist, and it was through her auspices that the world's leading architect learned of our new magazines and expressed an interest in holding a discussion of the idea.

Ed and June Lange, publishers of NUDE LIVING and The SUNDIAL, visited Richard Neutra in a house which he designed and built for himself and his family more than thirty years ago, a house which was then isolated on the border of lovely Silverlake in Los Angeles. Today it seems not only modern, but more so and more functional than many of its neighboring new houses because of its

7

57 Image in *Nude Living*, April 1962
58 Cover of *Nude Living*, April 1962
59 Article by Richard Neutra in *Nude Living*, April 1962
60 Richard Neutra, Lovell Health House, under construction
61 Back cover of Richard Neutra, *Survival Through Design*, 1954, with the Health House under construction superimposed on an image of the nervous system of the body

impulse behind both houses came not so much from straight modern architecture theories as from theories about sex, health, psychoanalysis, and nudism. **FIGS. 53, 55** Modern architecture was here inseparable from a new lifestyle, which included a vegetarian diet, exercise, sunbathing in the nude, sleeping in the open air, and dressing in simple robes made from natural fibers. Many of these ideas came from the late nineteenth-century *Lebensreform* movement in Germany, **FIG. 56** which advocated a back-to-nature lifestyle of fresh air, gardening, health food, alternative medicine, nudism, sexual liberation, and the avoidance of alcohol, tobacco, and vaccines. These ideas had arrived in California, where many proponents of the movement had emigrated. Neutra even contributed to the magazine *Nude Living* on the recommendation of his secretary, Audre Hardy, who was featured naked in its pages.[46] **FIGS. 57–59**

Dr. Lovell was a naturopath and drugless practitioner who thought all diseases have a dietary origin. He never studied medicine, but his theories of diet, exercise, sun therapy, and open-air sleeping were very influential in Southern California. He wrote a column for the *Los Angeles Times* entitled "Care of the Body." The publisher of the newspaper, Harry Chandler, was one of his patients. The Lovell Houses of Schindler and Neutra were organized around his full regime of sun, air, exercise, fasting, and diet strategies. The Health House of Neutra, in particular, became a public demonstration of Lovell's theories, with en-suite sleeping porches outside every room, "nude sunbathing opportunities" throughout the house, and "hydrotherapy equipment"

60

61

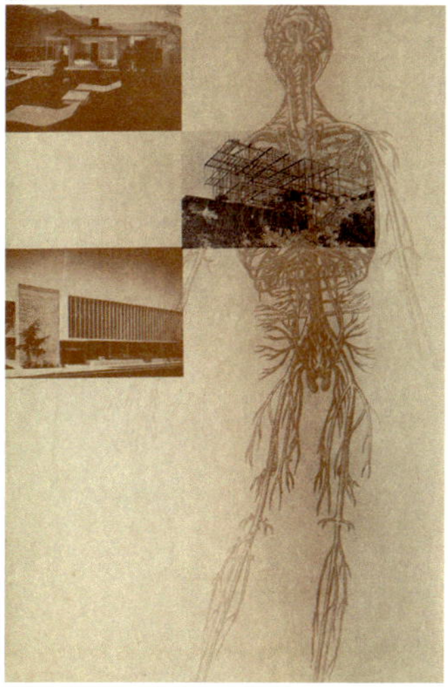

and "marathon showers" in the master bathroom, which was also equipped with a "built-in enema fixture with various douches and nozzles devices, thermostatically controlled."[47] Lovell opened the house to the public for two weekends, announcing it in his *Los Angeles Times* column, which included photographs, a description of the house, and a map showing how to get there. **FIG. 62** Around fifteen thousand people showed up, and Neutra himself gave the tours. **FIG. 63** Two photographs of the "House of Health" appear in this column alongside ads for treating "sagging flabby chins," "pelvic troubles: men and women," "severe cases of chronic constipation," "Prostate troubles," and "eczema,"[48] a testament to the increasing preoccupation of Americans with the physical appearance and performance of their bodies.

Lovell saw in modern architecture a model for health, a mechanism for reconstructing the human: "When we learn to build our bodies with the same careful precision and the same scientific accuracy with which the modern builder constructs his houses" we finally will become healthy.[49] Neutra, on the other hand, saw architecture as a "branch of preventive medicine." Influenced by Lovell's theories of drugless health, he was proud of resisting what he called the "drugs of ornamentation" in the design of the house, avoiding the "corpulent excesses of ornament and curvature."[50] Neutra had his own theories about the relationship between health and architecture and wrote extensively about it. In *Survival through Design* (1954), **FIG. 61** for example, he argues that the very survival of the human species depends on having designers focus on "physiological space." Design, for

CARE OF THE BODY

By Philip M. Lovell, *N. D.*

Author of "Diet for Health" and "The Health of the Child"

The Home Built for Health

For years I have periodically written articles telling you how to build your home so that you can derive from it the maximum degree of health and beauty service. I have written on miscellaneous problems such as lighting, heating, hydrotherapy equipment, labor-saving devices, sleeping porches, material for construction and other health features. Always at the end of each article was the thought, "If I ever build a home myself—"

At last the day has arrived. We have built such a home—a home premised on the fundamental health principles and construction ideas which I have presented in my writings in the past.

Front View of Dr. Lovell Home of Health.

I know that there are many who are interested, and with this in mind we are opening it for public inspection before furnishing and occupying it.

Hence, consider this an invitation for all Care of the Body readers to visit this newly constructed home built for health. It is located at 4616 Dundee Drive, Los Angeles, in the Los Feliz hills adjacent

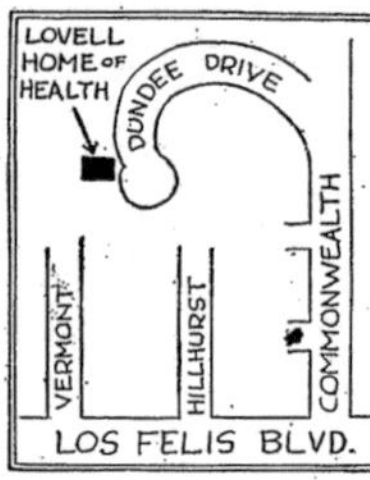

to Griffith Park. The accompanying sketch will show the way of getting there.

The house will be open for public inspection today, Sunday, the 15th inst., and Saturday and Sunday, the 21st and 22nd inst., respectively, from 8 a.m. to 5 p.m.

Mr. Richard T. Neutra, architect who designed and supervised the construction, will lecture at 3 p.m. on each of these days on building the home for health and will conduct the audience from room to room and place to place, describing in detail the purposes of each innovation.

The house is located at the end of a blind street with a wide turning radius. In order to avoid confusion it is requested that everyone visiting the house by automobile go to the end of the road, turn around at the turning basin and park on the right curb with your car facing downhill. I shall also ask that you please drive slowly and carefuly on Dundee Drive, as there will probably be many people coming and going and there are several blind turns.

For those who cannot inspect this home, a brief description will not be amiss.

The main construction is steel, built on a deep, reinforced concrete foundation. The walls, floors, ceilings and roof are all steel-girded, being covered with fireproof expanded steel and plaster.

The window sashes are steel and there is a greater profusion of them than in any home I have ever seen.

There are plenty of opportunities throughout the house for nude sun baths privately taken for each member.

Many of the windows are of the latest invention of glass, admitting ultra-violet light.

The bathrooms are completely equipped with hydrotherapy equipment, including such things as sitz baths, multiple marathon showers and the latest type of sanitary fixtures.

Sanitation and hygiene are the keynote.

The ventilation, sunshine and light ideas are exceedingly modern.

The bedrooms are built "en suite"; that is, every inside bedroom has its accompanying sleeping porch so that sleeping can be done outdoors.

The lighting is indirect—mostly recessed inside the ceiling—and shows behind ribbed glass.

The kitchen would be interesting to every practical housewife, for it incorporates not only the principles of hygiene and sanitation, but also most of the labor-saving devices so dear to the average woman. There is, for instance, an electric dishwasher, a vegetable-washer, a water filter, a grinder for grains or coffees, if one wishes, heaps of closet space, a gas incinerator and similar conveniences.

From the photographs of the exterior of the residence you can see the quantity of glass which makes the house really an outdoors home whenever so desired.

This home, in a sense, is being built mainly for the little ones. It is really a social school in which they will learn their life habits. Their customs will be molded and shaped therein.

With this in view, it has many of the features which schools should have, but most of them do not. There are, for instance, ample playground facilities with playground equipment to be added. There is a wading pond, where they can sail their boats and grow their fish.

Photograph by Willard D. Morgan, architect, Richard D. Neutra

Side view of home and garage.

An out-of-doors, yet inclosed area, is a schoolroom proper with provision for their carpenter work, clay modeling and other hand tools.

There are facilities for swimming, basketball, handball and, in fact, any other provision which can be developed in a reasonably small area of ground.

Yet most of these are available to the average small home—the cottage of modest means.

The entire home should be considered from a social sense rather than from a restricted private family residence—a place where friends and kin can gather —where children of the neighborhood will prolong their stay voluntarily.

The pictures will show some of it. The best can be seen on the residence.

These are some of the primary objectives in opening this home for public inspection. The thought and care that

63

Neutra, operates at the intersection of biology and psychology as a therapeutic defense against the "disastrous effects" of all the accumulated conditions of modern life.

Neutra thought his buildings could improve not just the health, but also the sex lives of their inhabitants. The desire for self-improvement in every aspect of one's life resonated with Californians who had become increasingly concerned with their bodies' appearance and performance.[51] Exercise, bodybuilding, dieting, therapy, surgery, and cosmetics became a major part of a continuous self-construction. Already by midcentury, the preoccupation had extended to mental health. As tuberculosis became controlled with antibiotics, particularly streptomycin (the first antibiotic cure for tuberculosis, discovered in 1943), Neutra switched his idea of the architect as a doctor to the idea of the architect as a kind of psychoanalyst. The function of the house was to provide not just physical health, but also psychological well-being. Many clients of Neutra talked to him about their "nervous" problems, their marital problems, their fertility problems. In fact, his theory of architecture was ultimately a theory about the nerves, the intersection of body and brain.

A symptomatic figure was Wilhelm Reich, a protégé of Freud who deviated from his theories, was expelled from psychoanalytic circles, and settled in America in 1939. He was the inventor of the "orgone energy accumulator," popularized as an "orgasm machine" in films such as Woody Allen's *Sleeper* (1973) and Roger Vadim's *Barbarella* (1968). Several clients of Neutra were followers of Reich, especially Josephine and Robert Chuey, who commissioned a house by

62 Philip M. Lovell, "Care of the Body," *Los Angeles Times*, December 15, 1929
63 Richard Neutra pointing to the Lovell House, Los Angeles, 1927–1929

64

65

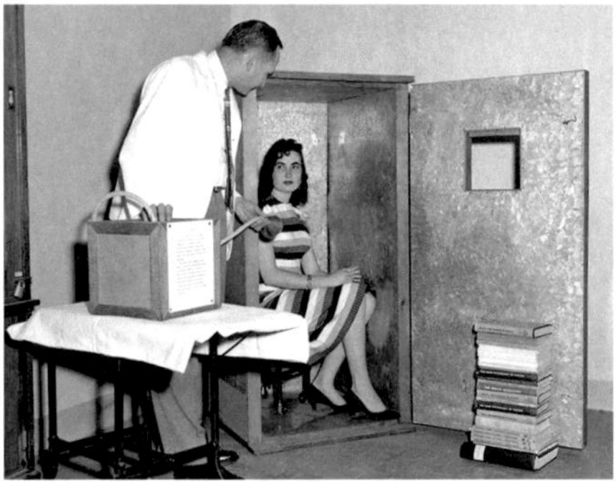

him that became a salon for orgone users and early experiments with LSD.[52] **FIG. 64**

Reich thought the libido is affected by physical space and—unlike Freud, who saw sexual dysfunction as a symptom of neurosis—Reich thought it is the cause of the neurosis and sought to alleviate it with "orgone," a previously unaccounted-for form of energy. His "orgone energy accumulator" **FIG. 65** was a primitive box the size of a telephone booth, composed of up to twenty layers of organic and nonorganic materials, that was supposed to accumulate the energy and transmit it to the body inside it. Reich wrote about the need for regular, daily sessions in the machine and claimed it could cure anything from headaches to chronic fatigue, arthritis, heart disease, cancer, brain tumors, and impotence. The orgone accumulator became best known as a machine to increase sexual performance, or what Reich called "orgastic potency," a complete release of energy that could be measured as an electrical discharge. Several clients of Neutra had accumulators in their houses. More important, Neutra thought of the house itself as a kind of orgone accumulator, a machine not just for health, but also for desire—or rather, desire as health.

64 Richard Neutra, Chuey House, Los Angeles, 1956
65 Wilhelm Reich, Orgone Energy Accumulator
66 Charles and Ray Eames, wartime splint made of molded plywood, 1943
67 Charles and Ray Eames, mass production of plywood leg splints, 1943

SHOCK ABSORBER

The bond between design, medicine, war, and psychology keeps running through architectural discourse into the second half of the century. Charles and Ray Eames's famous designs of the 1940s and 1950s, for example, are usually understood as reacting against the cold materials and

66

67

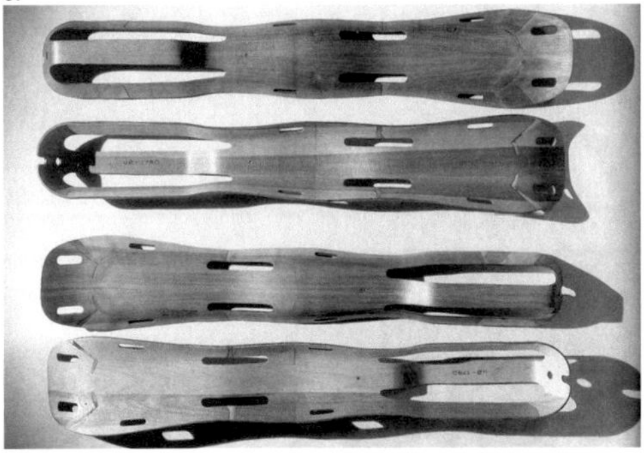

austere forms of 1920s and 1930s furniture design, which looked like doctor's equipment, and as expressing a new concern for the body, for natural materials, and for organic forms. But there is nothing "natural" about them. In fact, the Eameses' plywood furniture and toys are the result of medical and military research.

During World War II, Charles and Ray Eames had formed a company with John Entenza to mass-produce plywood war products with military funding. In 1941 and 1942, they developed a molded plywood splint for the US Navy to replace a metal leg splint that did not sufficiently secure the leg and even led to gangrene and death. By the war's end, more than one hundred and fifty thousand Eames splints had been shipped to the navy. FIGS. 66, 67 The splint performed very well in the field and was praised for its lifesaving features. In addition, the company designed and developed a plywood body litter and an arm splint, molded plywood aircraft parts, and more. By 1945, the Eameses were producing molded plywood chairs with the technology they had developed for the military. A photograph of the plywood lounge chair of 1946 shows Charles Eames reclining on it, the position of his leg sticking straight out indicating that he had not forgotten where the idea came from. In addition, the Eameses produced molded plywood children's furniture, molded plywood animals, lightweight plywood cabinets, and even plywood Christmas decorations made out of leftover splints. Military and medical equipment had become the basis of domestic equipment.

For the Eameses, as for Le Corbusier, the designer is a surgeon. In the course of an interview, Charles Eames said:

"The preoccupation with self-expression is no more appropriate to the world of art than it is to the world of surgery. That does not mean I would reduce self-expression to zero; I am sure that really great surgeons operate on the edge of intuition. But the rigorous constraints in surgery—those are important in any art."[53] Yet the Eameses' orthopedic body is not Le Corbusier's tuberculoid body or Kiesler's emaciated body. At any one time there was more than one such theory at the intersection of medicine and architecture. Architectural discourse is shaped by a continuous debate and tension between alternative medical scenarios.

After World War II, Charles and Ray Eames defined the house itself as a "shock absorber." "The house must make no insistent demands for itself, but rather aid as a background for life in work ... [and] acts as re-orientor and 'shock absorber.'"[54] But what is this shock? The shock in the postwar years was the shock of nuclear annihilation. **FIGS. 68, 69** Domestic life could no longer be taken for granted. It became an art form carefully constructed and marketed by a whole new industry: a form of art therapy for a traumatized nation, a reassuring image of the "good life" to be bought like any other product. The interior becomes a showroom full of objects. **FIG. 70** Shock is presumably absorbed through the consumption of design. "Good design" offers a "good life," a galaxy of happy, self-contained objects for people who do not feel safely contained and cannot be sure of life itself.

The Eameses perfected the "keep smiling" strategy that Benjamin had observed after World War I. Perhaps no other designers can be seen smiling so often and so polemically. **FIG. 71** While the ever-scowling Adolf Loos had insisted in "Ornament and Crime" that the craftsman is "so healthy he cannot invent ornament," the ever-beaming Eameses, the poster children of good design, encouraged the postwar consumer to keep clinging to smooth design as if to a psychological life raft. The real function of good design remained anesthetic, a symptom of a trauma that cannot be expressed, a smooth line of defense.

If architectural discourse has from its beginning associated building and body, the body that it describes is the medical body, reconstructed by each new theory of health. Throughout the twentieth century, designers positioned architecture against medical and psychological trauma. Each new instrument of medical diagnosis implied new positions for design and new systems of architectural representation. The occupant is a patient, with modernity itself being both a disease and a possible cure.

68

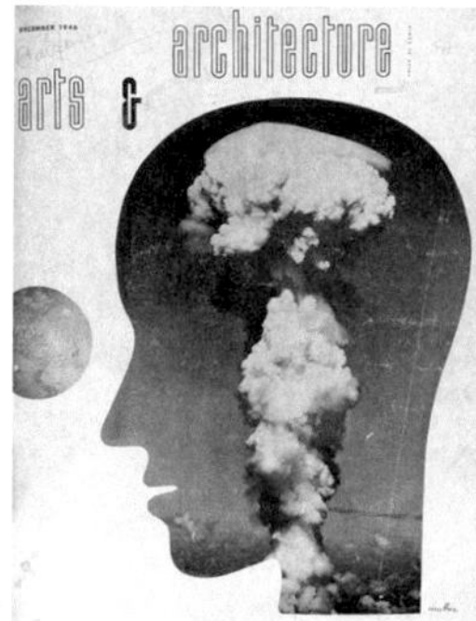

69

68 Cover of *Arts & Architecture*, December 1946
69 "Containment at Home: A Cold War Family Poses in their Fallout Shelter," *Life* magazine, August 1, 1961
70 Charles and Ray Eames in the living room of the Eames House, 1958
71 Charles and Ray Eames at Christmas 1944, with plywood sculpture by Ray

70

71

1 Vitruvius Pollio, *The Ten Books on Architecture,* trans. Morris Hicky Morgan (Cambridge, MA: Harvard University Press, 1914), p. 20.
2 Vitruvius argued that objects can be a combination of the four elements in different proportions, rather than just of two, as in the original medical theory. "Commentary: Book 2," in *Vitruvius: Ten Books on Architecture,* trans. Ingrid D. Rowland, (Cambridge: Cambridge University Press, 1999), p. 178.
3 Karen-Edis Barzman, *The Florentine Academy and the Early Modern State: The Discipline of Disegno* (Cambridge: Cambridge University Press, 2000), pp. 163–64. The requirement of attending the annual dissection was added to the founding statutes in 1563.
4 Martin Bressani, "Prosthetic Fantasies of the First Machine Age: Viollet-le Duc's Iron Architecture," *AA Files* 68 (2014), pp. 43–49.
5 Austin Flint and William H. Welch, *The Principles and Practice of Medicine,* 5th ed. (Philadelphia: Henry C. Lea's Son & Co., 1881), p. 206. See also Susan Sontag, *Illness as Metaphor* (New York: Farrar, Straus and Giroux, 1977), p. 54.
6 Sontag, *Illness as Metaphor,* p. 5.
7 Anson Rabinbach, *The Human Motor: Energy, Fatigue, and the Origins of Modernity* (New York: Basic Books, 1990).
8 Le Corbusier, *Toward an Architecture,* trans. John Goodman (Los Angeles: Getty Research Institute, 2007), pp. 94–95; originally published in 1923 as *Vers une architecture.*
9 Ibid., p. 297.
10 Le Corbusier, *The City of To-morrow and Its Planning,* trans. Frederick Etchells (New York: Dover Editions, 1987), pp. 256–57; originally published in 1925 as *Urbanisme.*
11 Le Corbusier, *The Radiant City,* trans. Pamela Knight, Eleanor Levieux, and Derek Coltman (New York: Orion Press, 1967), pp. 55–56; originally published in 1933 as *La ville radieuse.*
12 Ibid., p. 100. Le Corbusier had already symptomatically ended his book *Urbanisme* (1925) with an appendix featuring highly detailed sectional medical images of lungs. Le Corbusier, *Urbanisme* (Paris: Crès 1925), unpaginated appendix.
13 Ibid., p. 48.
14 Dr. Winter, "Sports," *L'Esprit nouveau,* no. 16 (May 1922), p. 1952.
15 Pierre Winter, "La ville moderne," *Le nouveau siècle,* May 16, 1926, quoted in Robert Fishman, *Urban Utopias in the Twentieth Century* (New York: Basic Books, 1982), p. 224.
16 "Le Corbusier … l'architecte, le peintre, le poète se confondent et ne sont pas séparables des le Corbusier moins connus que j'ai la particulière mission de vous présenter,—sous les étiquettes trop pompeuses pour sa modestie … Biologiste (avec un grand B) du Sociologue (avec un grand S) et j'ajouterai de l'athlète, qui aurait peut-être pu arriver champion." Dr. Pierre Winter, "Le Corbusier, Biologiste, Sociologue," in Le Corbusier and Pierre Jeanneret, *Œuvre complète, 1934–1938,* (1936; Zurich: Girsberger, 1964), pp. 13–15.
17 Ibid., p. 14.
18 Dr. Winter, "Le corps nouveau," *L'Esprit nouveau,* no. 15 (February 1922), p. 1755.
19 Le Corbusier, *Urbanisme* (Paris: Crès, 1925), p. 207. In English, Le Corbusier, *The City of To-morrow and Its Planning,* p. 216, translation slightly modified.
20 Le Corbusier, *The City of To-morrow and Its Planning,* p. 84; Le Corbusier, *The Radiant City,* p. 36.
21 Le Corbusier, *The Decorative Art of Today,* trans. James I. Dunnett (Cambridge, MA: MIT Press, 1987), p. 96; originally published in 1925 as *L'Art décoratif d'aujourd'hui.* See also Nina Rosenblatt, "Empathy and Anaesthesia: On the Origins of a French Machine Aesthetic," *Grey Room,* no. 2 (Winter 2001), pp. 78–97. The first public demonstration of an operation under anesthesia (with ether) took place at Massachusetts General Hospital in 1846.
22 Le Corbusier, *The Decorative Art of Today,* p. 112.
23 Walter Benjamin, "Experience and Poverty," trans. Rodney Livingstone, in *Walter Benjamin: Selected Writings, Volume 2: 1927–1934,* ed. Michael W. Jennings, Howard Eiland, and Gary Smith (Cambridge, MA: Belknap Press of Harvard University Press, 1999), p. 732.
24 Susan Buck-Morss, "Aesthetics and Anaesthetics: Walter Benjamin's Artwork Essay Reconsidered," *October* 62 (Fall 1992), pp. 3–42.
25 Walter Benjamin, *Charles Baudelaire,* trans. Harry Zohn (London: Verso, 1983), p. 133.
26 Susan Buck-Morss, "Aesthetics and Anaesthetics: Walter Benjamin's Artwork Essay Reconsidered," *October* 62 (Fall 1992), pp. 3–42.
27 Walter Benjamin, "On Some Motifs on Baudelaire," trans. Harry Zohn, in *Illuminations,* ed. Hannah Arendt (New York: Harcourt, Brace & World, 1968), p. 155.
28 Adolf Loos, "Architecture," in *The Architecture of Adolf Loos: An Arts Council Exhibition,* ed. Yehuda Safran and Wilfried Wang (London: Arts Council of Great Britain, 1985), p. 107.
29 Walter Benjamin, "Karl Kraus," trans. Edmund Jephcott, in *Walter Benjamin:*

Selected Writings, Volume 2: 1927–1934, p. 438. Benjamin often confuses Loos with the architecture of glass. Nothing could be further from Loos. But where he is surgical is with the dismantling of the private from within and the resolute defense against the intrusive gaze of public authority.
30 Buckminster Fuller, "Universal Conditions of the Industrially Reproducible Shelter," *T-Square* 2, no. 2 (February 1932), p. 37.
31 Frederick Kiesler, *Contemporary Art Applied to the Store and Its Display* (New York: Brentano's, 1930), p. 87.
32 Frederick Kiesler, "Pseudo-Functionalism in Modern Architecture," *Partisan Review* 16 (July 1949), p. 735. Emphasis in the original.
33 "A house must be practical. To be practical means to serve. To be serviceable in every respect. In any direction. If any directions are closed, the house suffers from constipation." Ibid., p. 739.
34 Ibid. pp. 733–42.
35 Frederick Kiesler, *Inside the Endless House: Art, People, and Architecture—A Journal* (New York: Simon and Schuster, 1966), p. 566.
36 "Kiesler: Pursuit of an Idea," interview by Thomas H. Creigton, *Progressive Architecture* (July 1961), p. 115.
37 Ibid., p. 106.
38 Ibid., pp. 113–14. Twenty years later, Johnson supported Kiesler's work. In 1950, he acquired, for the Museum of Modern Art the model of the Endless House that had been exhibited in the Kootz Gallery. He also facilitated Kiesler's subsequent exhibitions of the Endless House in the Museum of Modern Art: *Two Houses, New Ways of Building* (1952), with Buckminster Fuller; and *Visionary Architecture* (1960), with Bruno Taut, Frank Lloyd Wright, Buckminster Fuller, and Le Corbusier.
39 Frederick Kiesler, *Inside the Endless House: Art, People, and Architecture—A Journal*, p. 229.
40 Ibid., p. 203.
41 Ibid., p. 154.
42 Ibid., p. 155.
43 Ibid., p. 338.
44 Ibid., p. 272.
45 Ibid., p. 236.
46 Richard Neutra, "Some Notes on The Complex of Nudism," *Nude Living* 1, no. 6 (April 1962), pp. 7–10, and "Audre: Able and Agile," ibid., pp. 11–13. I am grateful to Thomas Hines for pointing this out to me and lending me his own copy of the magazine.
47 Willard Morgan, "Plumbing and Heating for a Modern Health Home," *Domestic Engineering* (April 5, 1930), p. 52.
48 Philip Lovell, "Care of the Body," *Los Angeles Times Sunday Magazine,* December 15, 1929, p. 26.
49 Philip Lovell and Leah Lovell, *Diet for Health by Natural Methods: Together with Health Menus and Recipes; Complete Instructions for the Cure of the Sick Without the Use of Drugs* (Los Angeles: Times-Mirror Press, 1927), p. 16, quoted in Victoria Jane Solan, "Built for Health" (PhD diss., Yale University, 2004), p. 140.
50 Richard Neutra, quoted in "Steel Construction with Plaster," *California Plasterer,* 1929, clipping in Neutra archives, UCLA. See Solan, "Built for Health," pp. 145–46.
51 Sara Schrank, "Naked Houses: The Architecture of Nudism and the Rethinking of the American Suburb," *Journal of Urban History* 38, no. 4 (2012), p. 638.
52 Sylvia Lavin, *Form Follows Libido: Architecture and Richard Neutra in a Psychoanalytic Culture* (Cambridge, MA: MIT Press, 2004), p. 76.
53 Charles Eames, interview with Digby Diehl, "Charles Eames: Q&A," *Los Angeles Times WEST Magazine,* October 8, 1972, p. 14, reprinted in Digby Diehl, *Supertalk* (New York: Doubleday, 1974). The original transcript is in the Eames archives, Library of Congress.
54 "Case Study Houses 8 and 9 by Charles Eames and Eero Saarinen, Architects," *Arts & Architecture* (December 1945), p. 44.

CHAPTER 2

Tuberculosis

One could write an entire encyclopedia just about the impact of tuberculosis on early twentieth-century architecture, beginning with the active collaborations between architects and doctors in the design of tuberculosis sanatoriums such as Alvar and Aino Aalto's Paimio (1929–1933) in Finland,[1] **FIG. 1** considered by Sigfried Giedion one of "three institutional buildings inseparably linked to the rise of contemporary architecture"—the other two being the Bauhaus at Dessau by Walter Gropius (1926) and the unrealized project for the League of Nations Palace at Geneva by Le Corbusier (1927). Giedion claimed that in all three projects, "the various parts are fully integrated—like the organs of a body."[2] The most

1

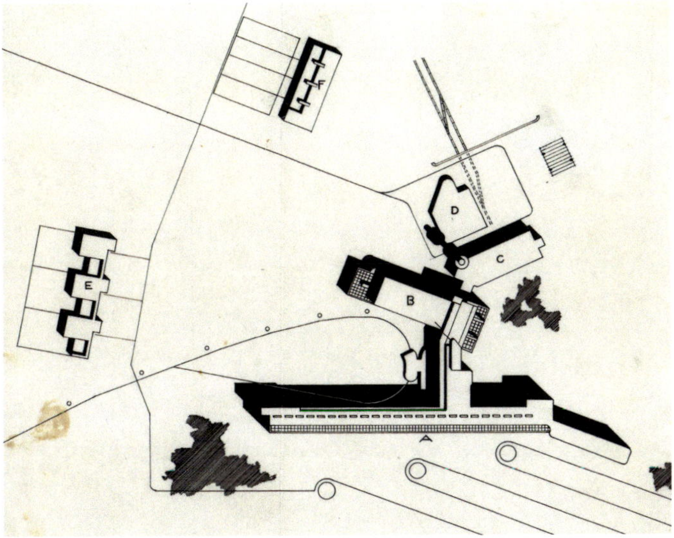

1 Alvar Aalto, Paimio Sanatorium, site plan

Alvar and Aino Aalto, Paimio Sanatorium, 1929–1933
2 Exterior view with sundeck balconies, ca. 1934
3, 4 Patient room
5 Alvar Aalto, drawing of curved floor under window, 1929
6 Alvar Aalto, drawing of noiseless sink, 1932

2

3

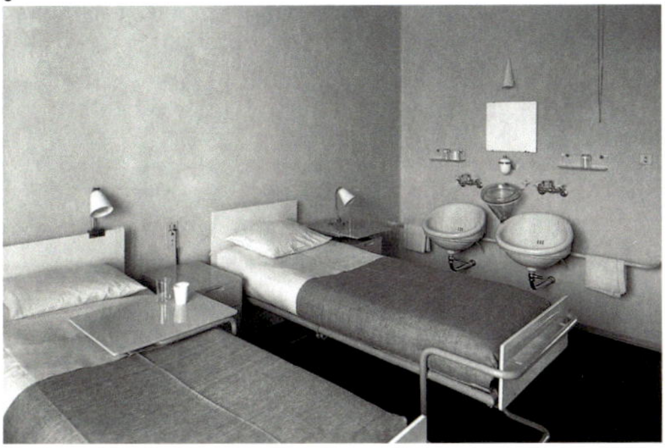

4

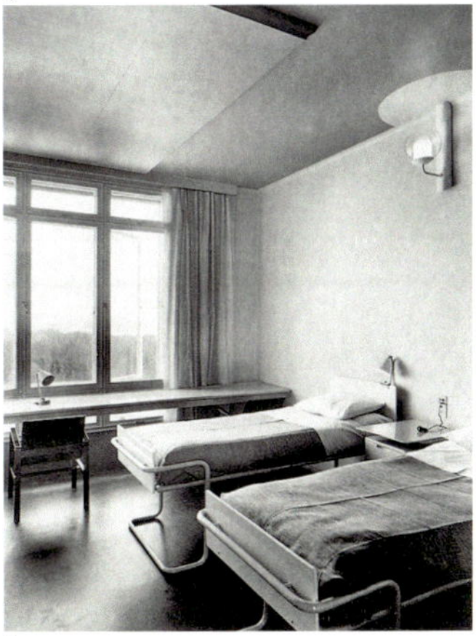

modern of buildings are themselves healthy bodies, in an update of the Vitruvian idea, with the twist that one of the three buildings is devoted to sick bodies.

With its dramatic terraces in the sky, the Paimio Sanatorium even bears an uncanny resemblance, in canonical photographs, to ribs in an X-ray, FIG. 2 the primary diagnostic tool for TB. Its clean-lined bedrooms, void of ornament, were designed to minimize surfaces where dust could accumulate. FIGS. 3, 4 Even the intersection of floor and wall beneath the window curved to stop dust buildup. FIG. 5 The rooms were equipped with furniture and sanitary fittings designed by the architects, including chairs whose back was angled to facilitate breathing and expectoration, FIG. 16 sinks designed to reduce splashing, FIG. 6 and spittoons to minimize sound. Door handles were carefully designed not to catch the sleeves of the doctors' white coats. FIG. 12 But the building's main equipment was the top-floor terrace, FIGS. 8, 9 seven stories above the forested landscape, where patients were wheeled out for regular doses of fresh air and sun in the lounge chairs specially designed by Aino Aalto. FIG. 10 Eventually, the terrace had to be closed off, because the nurses couldn't keep desperate patients from throwing themselves from it every time they turned their backs on them.[3] The discovery and success of streptomycin in 1943 revealed that there was little scientific basis for the air-and-sun therapy of the sanatorium.[4] Sometimes the therapy even precipitated the end—at Paimio, quite literally.

Tuberculosis helped make modern architecture modern. It is not that modern architects made modern sanatoriums.

5

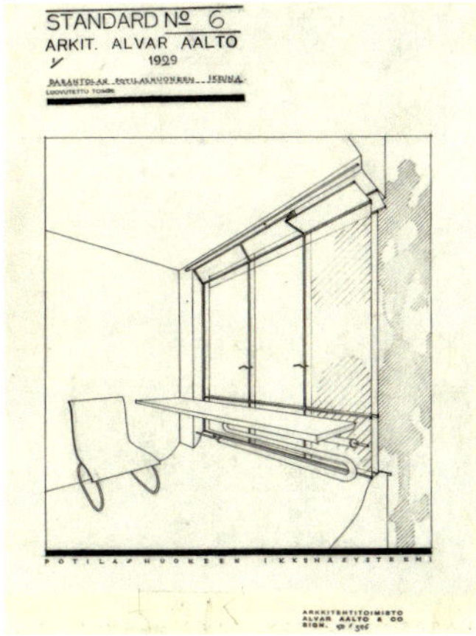

6

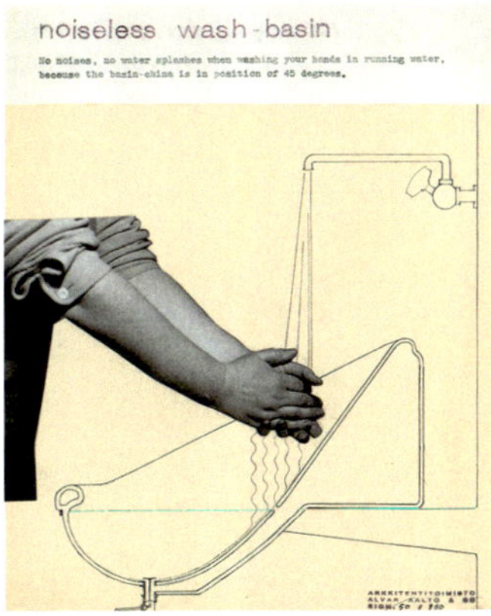

7 Alvar Aalto, Kinkomaa tuberculosis sanatorium project (not realized), perspective drawing, 1927

Alvar and Aino Aalto, Paimio Sanatorium, 1929–1933

8 Upper sun terrace with patients taking the fresh-air cure, 1933

9 Upper sun terrace with patients

10 Drawing of chaise longue designed by Aino Aalto for Paimio Sanatorium, 1932

7

8

9

10

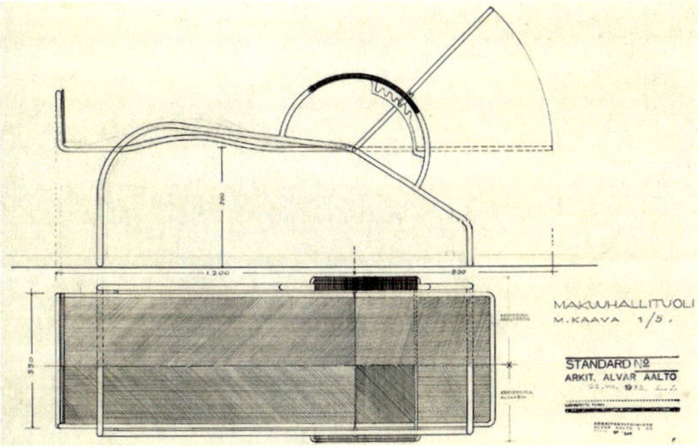

Rather, sanatoriums modernized architects. Aalto was a neoclassical architect before his "conversion to functionalism" in the 1927 competition entry for a tuberculosis sanatorium at Kinkomaa, Finland—an unrealized project of horizontal lines and wide terraces for the cure that anticipates Paimio.[5] **FIG. 7**

For Aalto, the sanatorium was not architecture in the service of medicine, but integral to medicine as such—an apparatus devised as a means of treatment:

> The main purpose of the building is to function as a medical instrument.... The room design is determined by the depleted strength of the patient, reclining in his bed. The colour of the ceiling is chosen for quietness, the light sources are outside of the patient's field of vision, the heating is oriented towards the patient's feet, and the water runs soundlessly from the taps to make sure that no patient disturbs his neighbour.[6] **FIG. 11**

Aalto himself had been sick at the time of the competition for the building and claimed that having to lie in bed for an extended period of time had been crucial to his understanding of the problem. Architecture always had been conceived for the vertical person, but here was a client permanently in the horizontal.

The whole design of the room and the building had to change accordingly. Light fixtures could not remain in the ceiling, irritating the eyes of the occupant lying in bed, for

11 Drawing by Alvar Aalto of an ordinary room for a "vertical person" and a room in Paimio for a "horizontal person" to illustrate his 1940 article "The Humanizing of Architecture," November 1940

11

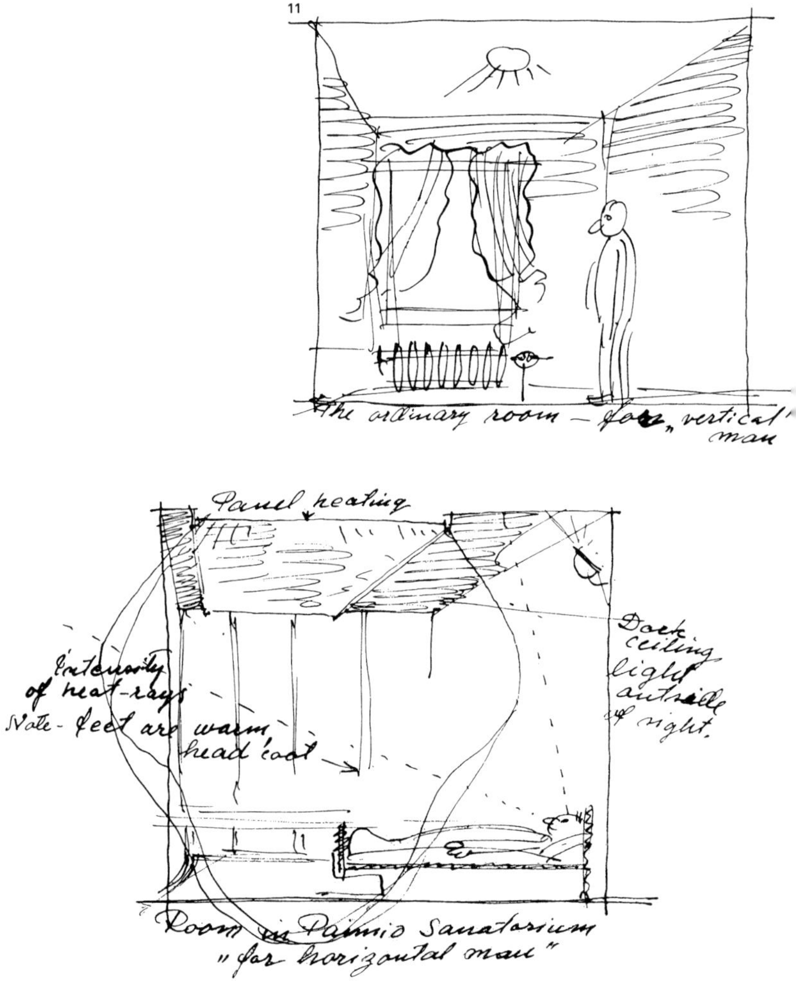

whom the ceiling had all of a sudden acquired maximum importance—a new kind of facade, one could say. The view through the window to the forest outside also had to be calculated from the point of view of the bed. In the terrace, the low parapet and thin rail above allowed the eye of the horizontal person to travel far above the forest. Even when in movement, the patient often remained horizontal in a sanatorium. Elevators encased in transparent glass, placed at the end of the corridor to avoid disturbing patients in the rooms, allowed the traveling patient, in a bed on wheels, a horizontal cross-section view of the architecture and the landscape beyond. The unconstrained horizontal view was itself a medical instrument, calming the eye and brain.

The colors of the room and the building had to be thought in these terms too—soothing, "quiet, dark hues" of blue for the ceiling, the walls in lighter shades. Bright canary yellow in the reception booth by the entrance and in the linoleum of the lobby, staircase, and corridors evoked "sunny optimism even in cold, cloudy days." **FIG. 13** Just as heating by radiant ceiling panels was directed at the patients' feet, and not their heads, windows were of special construction so the cold outside air would enter diagonally through the window boxes in which the intake openings were "as far as possible away from the patient."[7] "Mechanical ventilation does not enter the picture because natural ventilation with fresh, ozone-rich air is of the utmost importance in the healing process," Aalto wrote.[8] Psychological factors were also to be carefully considered:

12

13

Alvar Aalto, Paimio Sanatorium, 1929–1933
12 Patient room door handle designed not to catch doctor's lab coat sleeves
13 Main staircase
14 Diagram of the sun rays and heating rays in a patient's room
15 Diagram showing the heat environment in a patient's room

14

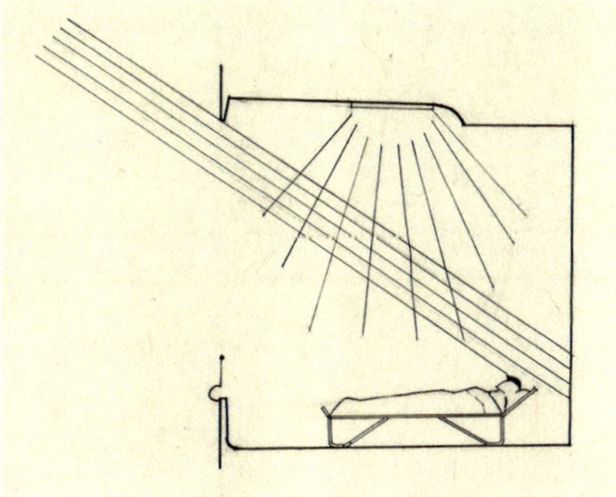

15

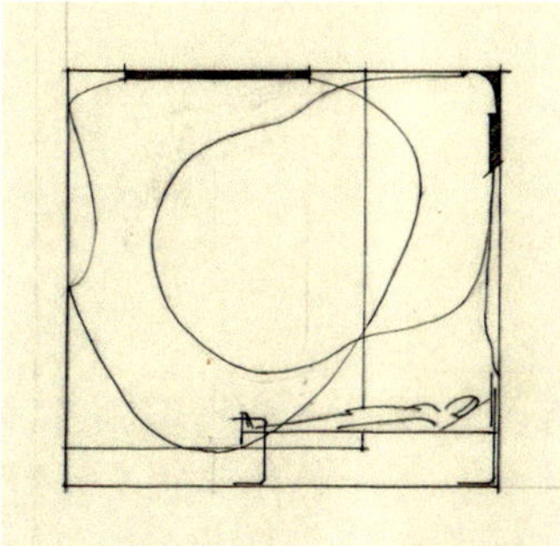

> An extended period of confinement can be extremely depressing for a bed-ridden patient. Furthermore, conventional hospital rooms are never designed for constant bed-ridden patients. The contrasts in color and mass between vertical walls and horizontal ceilings resulting from both natural and artificial light are not particularly well-suited for patients who are especially sensitive because of their illness.... A tuberculosis sanatorium is, to all intents and purposes, a house with open windows.[9] **FIGS. 14, 15**

Architecture was not only part of the treatment, it had to address the patient's way of life. Living in a sanatorium for long periods makes it home. The hospital had to be thought as a new kind of house. And in reverse, the generic house needed to be a sanatorium. Aalto later wrote:

> I was able to discover that special physical and psychological reactions by patients provide good pointers of ordinary housing. If we proceed from technical functionalism, we shall discover that a great many things in our present architecture are unfunctional from the point of view of psychology, or a combination of psychology and physiology. To examine how human beings react to forms and constructions, it is useful to use for experimentation especially sensitive persons, such as patients in a sanatorium.[10]

16

17

The bodily and psychological sensitivity of the sick person was used to recalibrate architecture. Even the specialized furniture became ordinary everyday pieces. If the cantilevered birch-wood Paimio chair, for example, was designed to open the chest of the patient, allowing him or her to breathe easier, soon enough, that chair became everybody's chair. Likewise with the rest of the furniture specially designed for Paimio: "The sanatorium needed furniture which should be light, flexible, easy to clean and so on. After extensive experimentation in wood, the flexible system was discovered ... to produce furniture which was more suitable for the long and painful life in a sanatorium."[11] A workshop was set up with a local company to carry out the first experiments, and in 1935, barely two years after completing Paimio, Alvar and Aino Aalto founded the Finnish furniture company Artek, **FIG. 17** with "the ambition to support and nourish human beings' physical and psychological wellbeing."[12] It is not by chance that the official time line of the company starts with Paimio Sanatorium, since it is there where the first experiments in modern furniture by the Aaltos took place. The Aalto that became known as one of the so-called masters of modern architecture did so by engaging with disease. Aalto designs, after Paimio, had the aura of health.

The reference point was the seriously ill. Aalto claimed that the architect had to design for the person in the "weakest position." The tuberculosis patient becomes the model for modern architecture. In other words, sickness was no longer seen as the exception, but as the norm—and varying degrees of sickness were seen to define the human condi-

16 Paimio Sanatorium lounge recreation room with Paimio chairs, 1933
17 The Artek store in Helsinki, 1939
18 Engraving after a drawing by Robert Koch of fresh bacilli from the lungs of a tuberculosis patient, as seen under the microsope
19 Engraving after a drawing by Robort Koch of tuberculosis bacilli, after two weeks growth under a culture, as seen under the microscope

tion. The modern subject has multiple ailments, physical and psychological, and architecture is a protective cocoon not just against the weather and other outside threats, but in modernity, more notably against internal threats: psychological and bodily ailments.

Symptomatically, Aalto compared his experiments in Paimio and their application to everyday use to the "exaggerated" forms of analysis that scientists use "in order to obtain clear more visible results," such as "stained bacteria" for microscope examination.[13] He saw design as a form of medical research, with the sanatorium acting as a kind of research lab for modern architecture—a way of testing architecture, looking more closely, in a rigorous examination, and experimenting—looking at what has been hidden, exposing the invisible forces.

THE INVISIBLE CLIENT

Sigmund Freud, the X-ray, bacteriology, and the germ theory of disease all emerged in the same short period of time, and they are all about looking inside, acknowledging the invisible: the unconscious, the skeleton, the microelement of bacteria and the bacillus of TB. Architecture, likewise, turns itself inside out: the threat is no longer outside, but inside, in the "invisible." The micro scale of bacteria becomes the base for furniture, rooms, houses, and cities: the micro and the macro; the bacterium and the city. Cities were suddenly thought to be teeming with unseen occupants that in a sense became the new clients of modern architecture and urbanism. **FIGS. 18, 19**

18

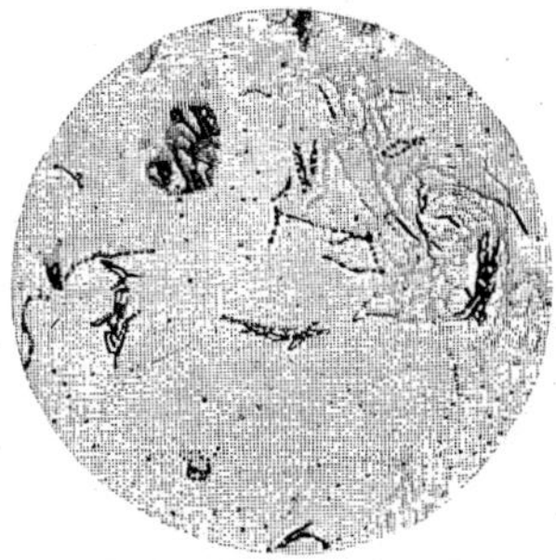

FRESH BACILLI FROM THE LUNGS OF A CONSUMPTIVE PATIENT, AS SEEN UNDER THE MICROSCOPE.

19

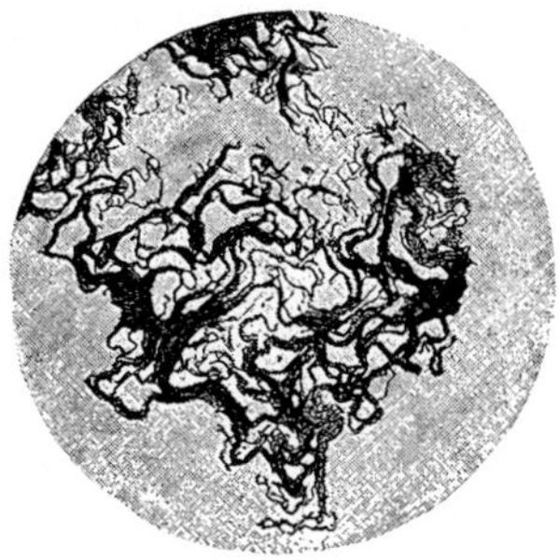

BACILLI AFTER TWO WEEKS' GROWTH, UNDER THE MICROSCOPE.

20

21

22

20 Josef Hoffmann, Purkersdorf sanatorium, original design, west facade, 1903
21 Otto Pfleghard and Max Haefeli, with engineer Robert Maillart, Queen Alexandra Sanatorium, Davos, 1907
22 Otto Wagner, project for Palmschoss heliotherapy center, Brixen, Italy, 1914
23 Bernard Bijvoet and Jan Duiker, Zonnestraal sanatorium, Hilversum, 1927, postcard
24 Richard Döcker, Waiblingen sanatorium, 1926–1928

23

24

The architect-doctor became a bacteriologist, generating design principles out of the laboratory scrutiny of microbes. Architecture itself became bacterial. As Le Corbusier put it:

> We need a diagnosis and a line of conduct. In 1922 I tried to delve into an analysis, I did some laboratory work. Isolating my microbe. I watched it develop. The biology of my microbe appeared in indisputable clarity. Certitudes acquired; diagnosis. Then, by an effort of synthesis, I drew up the fundamental principles of modern city planning.[14]

Microbes were both the literal and metaphorical basis of a new architecture and urbanism. Modern architecture paradoxically had to represent this new invisible order with bright, transparent images, seen as clean, clear, and healthy in a kind of visual hygiene. The whiteness of modern architecture is unambiguously that of the hospital, surfaces that, as it were, demonstrate their cleanliness.

The history of modern architecture is full of sanatoriums: Josef Hoffmann's Purkersdorf outside Vienna (1903) FIG. 20; Otto Wagner's Steinhof, Vienna (1907) and project for Palmschoss heliotherapy center in the mountains near Brixen in Italy (1914) FIG. 22; the Queen Alexandra Sanatorium in Davos (1907) FIG. 21, by the architects Otto Pfleghard and Max Haefeli and engineer Robert Maillart; Jan Duiker and Bernard Bijvoet's Zonnestraal in Hilversum (1925–1928) FIG. 23; Richard Döcker's sanatorium in Waiblingen (1926–1928) FIG. 24; Werner Hebebrand and Willi Kleinertz's Sonnen-

25 Pablo Zabalo, Sanatorio de Leza, Alava, Spain, 1934, postcard
26 William Ganster and William Pereira, Lake County Tuberculosis Sanatorium, Waukegan, Illinois, 1939
27 Werner Hebebrand and Wilhelm Kleinertz, Sonnenblick Sanatorium, Marburg, 1929–1931
28 Cover of the *Revista Nacional de Arquitectura* 126, June 1952, with an image of Lake County Tuberculosis Sanatorium superimposed on an X-ray of lungs

25

blick sanatorium in Marburg (1929–1931) FIG. 27; Jaromír Krejcar's Machnáč sanatorium in Trenčianske Teplice (1929–1932) FIG. 29; Josep Lluís Sert's Dispensario Antituberculoso in Barcelona (1934) and hillside sanatorium project for Barcelona (1936); Pablo Zabalo's Sanatorio de Leza, Alava (1934) FIG. 25; William Ganster and William Pereira's Lake County Tuberculosis Sanatorium in Waukegan, Illinois (1939) FIGS. 26, 28; so on and on. Many modern architects did a sanatorium at some point, and often it defined them. The sanatorium was the testing ground of new materials and techniques of construction and often involved experimental collaborations between architects, engineers, and doctors.

The sanatorium buildings were typically disconnected from cities, floating like ships on mountainsides, in forests, by lakes, or at the coast, with their row upon row of sun terraces treated like little beaches—sometimes linked to artificial beaches on the inside of the building or to real beaches on the outside. FIGS. 30, 31 This sense of floating outside its normal urban habitat and angling itself to the sun to heal fragile bodies challenged the definition of architecture. It is as if architecture itself took the cure.

In fact, the sanatorium modernized architecture. It is not a traditional building with balconies added to it to catch the sun, but a set of deep sun terraces understood as the crucial medical instrument to be propped up and serviced by a transformed building. The whole building ultimately adjusted itself into a solar device, sometimes stacking itself at a steep angle, as with Marcel Breuer and Gustav Hassenpflug's 1930 project for a 1100-bed

26

27

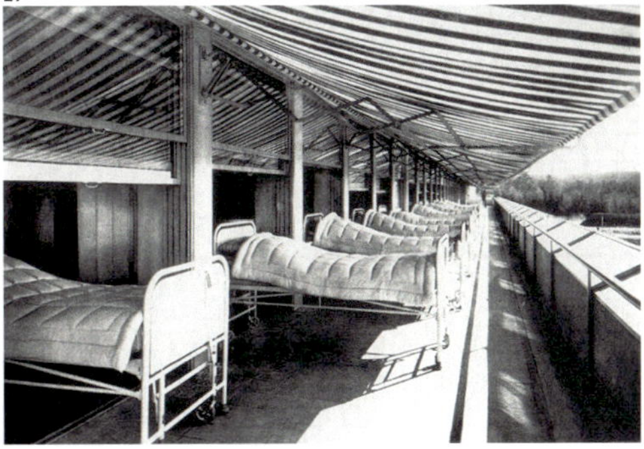

28

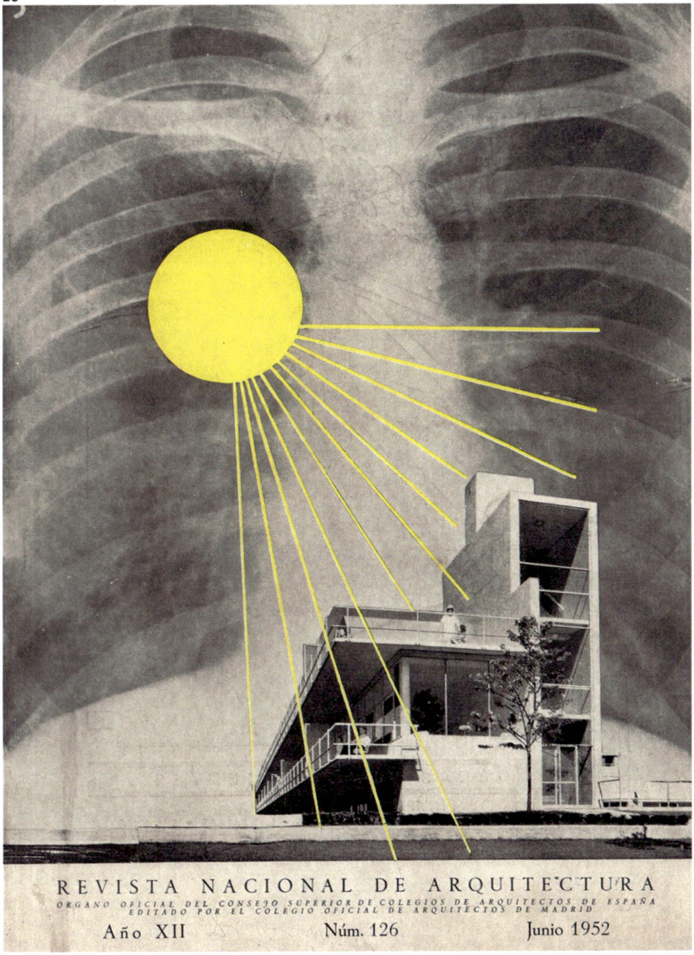
REVISTA NACIONAL DE ARQUITECTURA
ORGANO OFICIAL DEL CONSEJO SUPERIOR DE COLEGIOS DE ARQUITECTOS DE ESPAÑA
EDITADO POR EL COLEGIO OFICIAL DE ARQUITECTOS DE MADRID
Año XII
Núm. 126
Junio 1952

29

30

La plage artificielle constitue un progrès important dans l'hygiène sociale moderne ; elle permet d'arriver à la certitude d'une prophylaxie efficace antirachitique et de faire bénéficier les enfants de tous les bienfaits de l'héliothérapie sur la nutrition, le système nerveux épidermique.

31

29 Jaromir Krejcar, Machnáč, sanatorium in Trenčianske Teplice, 1929–1932
30 Artificial beach, Aix-Les-Bains
31 G. Lubarskij, Tuberculosis sanatorium near Odessa, 1930
32, 34 Jean Saidman, revolving sanatorium , Aix-les-Bains, France, 1930
33 Jean Saidman, Ranjit Institute of Poly-Radio-Therapy, revolving sanatorium Jamnagar, India, 1934
35 Inclined bed for treatment, revolving sanatorium, Aix-les-Bains

32

33

34

35

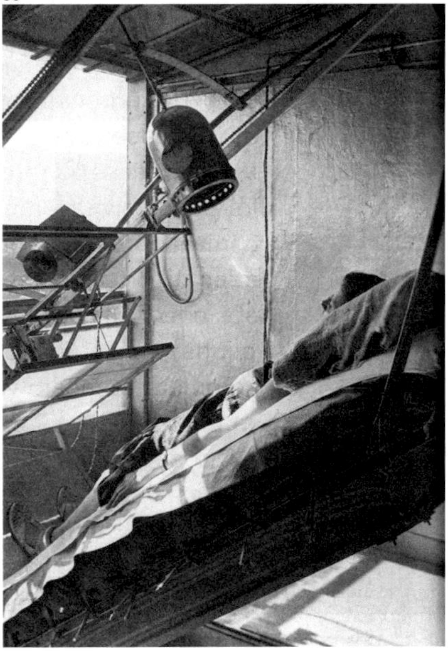

36

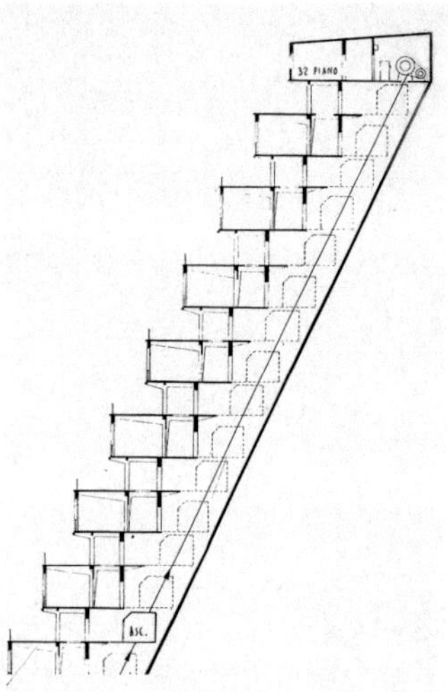

37

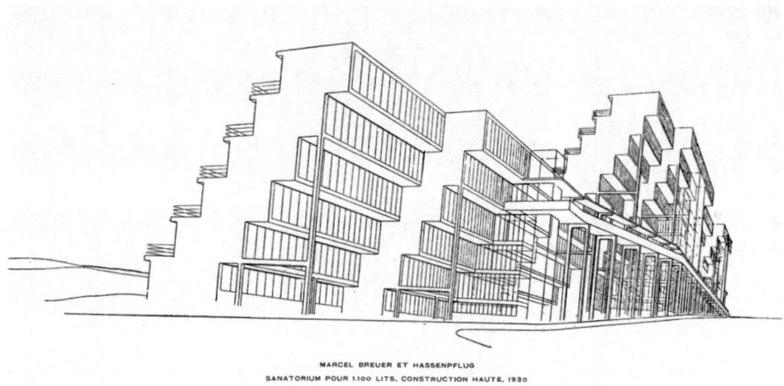

sanatorium, **FIG. 37** or at an even steeper angle with the elevator behind moving up at the same angle, as in Nicola Visontai's 1934 project for the Italian Alps. **FIG. 36** This attitude was taken to its extreme by the collaboration between the radiologist Jean Saidman and the architect André Farde to make a twenty-five-meter-long revolving solarium sixteen meters above the ground that always faced the sun for tuberculosis patients at Aix-les-Bains in 1930. **FIGS. 32, 34** It was the first of three such revolving sanatoriums that they made (the others were in Jamnagar in India **FIG. 33** and Vallauris on the Mediterranean) with sophisticated retractable glass panels and specialized focusing instruments to increase the exposure. Even the beds were suspended in metal frames that enabled them to be rotated up to a steep angle to be aligned with the instruments. **FIG. 35**

The sanatorium had from the beginning been a laboratory for incubating new attitudes toward form, spatial organization, interior design, furniture, fittings, lighting, plumbing, air, equipment, surfaces, colors, materials, and construction methods. Take Josef Hoffmann's Purkersdorf, with its purified white surfaces, radically sharp lines, cubic furniture, Hennebique construction in reinforced concrete and iron, and use of glass and electricity, all considered part of the hygienic program. Even its gridded ferroconcrete ceiling structure was exposed and painted white.[15] **FIG. 45** Not only was electricity considered more hygienic than gas as a means of illumination, ostentatiously displayed with visible cables, but it was also used for all kinds of experimental therapies, including electric massage machines,

36 Nicola Visontai, project for a sanatorium in the Italian Alps, 1934
37 Marcel Breuer and Gustav Hassenpflug, project for a 1100-bed sanatorium, 1930
38 Dr. Richard von Krafft-Ebing and his wife, Marie Luise
39 Dr. Richard von Krafft-Ebing, *Über gesunde und kranke Nerven* (On healthy and sick nerves), 1885, cover

electric baths, and chairs for strengthening the nerves. At the time that the Purkersdorf was built, critic Ludwig Hevesi described it as "the naked Hoffmann building," whose walls were lined with white porcelain tiles— "a white-painted or white-tiled 'washable world.'"[16] Hevesi was so enthusiastic as to check himself into the sanatorium to test personally some of its therapeutic devices in the "mechano-therapy room": in "this elegant white hall, full of artificial devices, with which I rapidly made closer acquaintance, [including] the electric massage machines—everything is electric."[17] FIG. 43 Electricity itself was understood as a medical instrument.

38

39

The building, commissioned by the industrialist Viktor Zuckerkandl, was constructed as an addition to an earlier sanatorium complex founded by neuropsychiatrist Dr. Richard von Krafft-Ebing FIG. 38—who died before the Purkersdorf was completed—but it was influenced by his theories. Krafft-Ebing had argued that the modern metropolis was damaging the nerves of its inhabitants and that air, light, nature, and simplicity were the most effective therapy. In 1885, he wrote *Über gesunde und kranke Nerven* (On healthy and sick nerves) FIG. 39 and a year later *Psychopathia Sexualis*. He coined the term "masochism" (after the author Leopold von Sacher-Masoch) and popularized the term "sadism." Here, once again, health was understood in psychosexual and architectural terms.

The Purkersdorf was frequented by a notable circle of patients including Gustav Mahler, Arnold Schoenberg, Hugo von Hofmannsthal, and Koloman Moser, who had designed

40

41

the furniture. **FIG. 42** Even the architect of the building, Josef Hoffmann, checked himself in now and then. He had suffered from and was treated for a "nervous disorder" prior to the commission of the Purkersdorf and was sympathetic to Krafft-Ebing's ideas. According to Eduard Sekler, that was why Hoffmann was inclined to accept the commission.[18] The Purkersdorf accepted patients with a wide range of medical conditions including "nervous" disorders, neurasthenia, eating disorders, substance abuse, and hysteria. The sanatorium had become a new kind of social space for the Viennese upper classes. Hospitals until the end of the nineteenth century were almost without exception for the poor. Members of the upper and middle class were treated at home, and hospitals were seen as abject places for the destitute.[19] But starting in the 1880s, the aristocracy and upper classes began to spend summers in sanatoriums and curative spas, largely to deal with nervous disorders and other illnesses of modernity. Bertha Zuckerkandl,[20] journalist and art critic of the *Wiener Allgemeine Zeitung,* characterized the Purkersdorf as a "cross between a modern hotel and a modern therapeutic centre."[21] And Karl Kraus described it as a "healing-swindle-institution" (*Heilschwindelanstalt*).[22] **FIGS. 40, 41**

Critics hailed the building as one of clarity and truth. The success of the institution owed enormously to the modernity of the architecture. "Modern" was becoming a new and sophisticated taste among the bourgeoisie and the intelligentsia, who were supposed to dine around a single white table at the Purkersdorf **FIG. 44** (as a kind of talking cure), sleep in spartan white rooms, **FIG. 46** and subject them-

40 Karl Kraus, *Die Fackel* 1, 1899
41 Karl Kraus, 1908
42 Koloman Moser, 1903

42

selves to regimes of treatment in white spaces. The association of cubic white forms with mental and physical health was already strong enough for architecture to act as an effective placebo.

The idea had made its way into literature. Thomas Mann's short novel *Tristan,* written in 1903, the same year as the construction of the Purkersdorf, is set in an imaginary sanatorium, the Einfried, "a long, white, rectilinear building," "warmly recommended for lung patients," but also "for patients of all sorts": "sufferers of gastric disorders ... people with defective hearts, paralytics, rheumatics, nervous sufferers of all grumblings." When one of the patients, Herr Kloterjahn's wife, asks another, "Why are you in Einfried, really?... What cure are you taking, Herr Spinell?" he answers:

> Cure? Oh, I'm having myself electrified a bit. Nothing worth mentioning. I will tell you the real reason why I am here, madame. It is a feeling for style....
> Obviously, people feel one way among furniture that is soft and comfortable and voluptuous, and quite another among the straight lines of these tables, chairs, and draperies. This brightness and hardness, this cold, austere simplicity and reserved strength, madame—it has upon me the ultimate effect of an inward purification and rebirth.[23]

"Style," is the true cure of whatever ails Herr Spinell, who wears a "white jacket" and "white hat" in this all-white building, in a "spotless white region" all covered in snow, with

Josef Hoffmann, Purkersdorf sanatorium, 1904–1905
43 Electromechanotherapy room, 1905–1906
44 Dining room, 1905–1906
45 Main hall, 1905–1906
46 Patient room, 1905

43

44

45

46

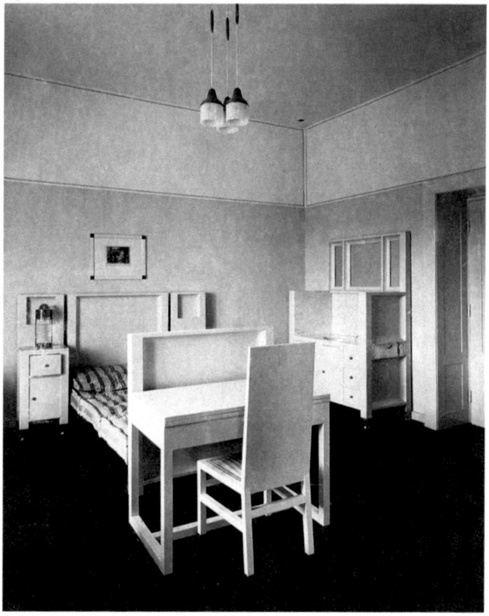

47 Camillo Sitte, manuscript page of his 1889 book *Der Städtebau nach seinen künstlerischen Grundsätzen* (City Planning according to Artistic Principles), 1899

"white-enamelled" armchairs, "white folding doors," "white-painted gallery," inhabited by the "white, slightly bloated" faces and "white hands" of the patients with their "white-veiled desire, by passion driven."[24] Whiteness is the most insistent feature of the building, the landscape, and the patients in the Einfried sanatorium.

SADO-MASOCHISM

Krafft-Ebing's ideas seem also to have influenced other architects and urban planners, such as Camillo Sitte, who criticized the design of the modern city because in his view, it was causing agoraphobia and other nervous conditions. In his 1889 book *City Planning according to Artistic Principles,* **FIG. 47** he advocated intimate urban spaces that, as in a medieval city, protect the inhabitant. Adolf Loos, also a student of masochism—there are multiple references in his writings—argues that the "man with modern nerves" can't tolerate ornament. In 1926, he gave four lectures in German at the Sorbonne, in Paris. The whole series was entitled *Der Mensch mit den modernen Nerven* (The man with modern nerves) **CHAPTER 1, FIG. 39** and dedicated to how to live one's life appropriately: how to walk, how to sit, how to lie down, how to eat, how to sleep, how to dress, and how to inhabit.[25] The subject of the nerves had preoccupied Loos all his life and permeated his writings from the turn of the century on.

For Loos, the rejection of ornament is not an aesthetic theory, but a physiological reaction, as he put it when discussing the English military uniform as a model for modern dress: "The nerves of the modern man rebel against

in Italien, nicht freistehend aufgeführt wurden. 26.
In Italien stehen mit diesem Anbauen oder Einbauen der Kirche an einer zwei oder drei Seiten auch beachtenswerthe Platzbildungen im Zusammenhang, welche nunmehr Untersuchung zu ziehen sind.

Eine ganze Musterkarte von verschiedenen Einbauungen bieten die Kirchen von Padua. Nur an einer Seite angebaut ist der S. Giustina (Fig 9) [illegible] an 2 Seiten S. Antonio, die Jesuitenkirche an 1½ Seiten; [illegible] die vorliegenden Plätze sind sehr unregelmäßig.

Fig. 9

Padua: St. Giustina

In Verona sind sämtliche Kirchen ein- oder wenigstens angebaut und nur das eine Streben deutlich erkennbar vor dem Hauptportal einen größeren Platz heraus zu bekommen. Es ist dieß so bei dem Dom (Fig. 10), bei S. Zeno Maggiore (Fig 11) bei S. Anastasia (Fig 12) und anderen. Man sieht es allen diesen Plätzen an, daß jeder seine Geschichte hat, aber wirkungsvoll sind sie alle und die Kirchen selbst kommen mit den Hauptfaçaden und Portalen zu ruhigen bedeutender Wirkung.

Fig. 10

Verona: Domplatz

Fig 11

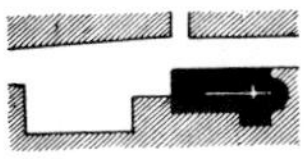

Verona: S. Zeno Maggiore

Ebenso sind auch in Piacenza alle Kirchen (selbst der Dom) eingebaut. der Domplatz liegt vor dem Hauptportal in dessen Richtung eine Straße mündet. (Fig. 13).

Fig 12

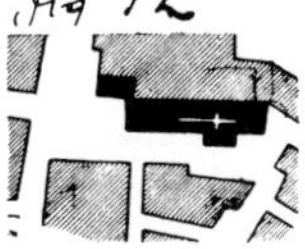

Verona: S. Anastasia

Seltener kommt die Lage des Kirchenplatzes an der Seite vor, wie in beistehender Fig. 14 welcher Fall dem Stadtplan von Palermo von S. Rita entnommen ist.

Fig: 13

Piacenza: Piazza del Duomo.

Schon diese Fälle allein und ihr Contrast zu dem ganz entgegengesetzten modernen System legen es nahe über diesen interessanten Punkt noch genauer nachzusehen. Hiezu eignet sich wohl keine Stadt besser als

a demand to go back twenty, fifty, or a hundred years."[26] He argued that human biology had evolved to give modern man a whole new set of nerves with their own needs.[27] In "Ornament and Education" (1924) he wrote: "Modern Man, the man endowed with a modern nervous system, doesn't need ornament. On the contrary, he loathes it. Every object that we call modern lacks ornament. Our dresses, our machines, our furs, and every object of everyday use don't have—since the French Revolution—any ornament."[28]

But the obsession with nerves wasn't just a Viennese hang-up. In his *Glasarchitektur* of 1914, Paul Scheerbart wrote: "Sanatoria also will want glass buildings; the influence of splendid glass architecture on the nerves is indisputable."[29] **FIGS. 48, 49** Scheerbart was obsessed with hygiene and the removal of dust, pollen, and insects, advocating the use of the recently invented vacuum cleaner at home and in the streets. He even saw building materials in these terms, enlisting doctors to further his architectural polemic against brick: "The discovery of the brick bacillus" means that "now the doctor also has a major interest in finally ousting the cult of brick."[30] The polemic against brick was now supported by medical arguments. In his telegram novella, "The Oceanic Sanatorium for Hay Fever," he imagines:

> Floating islands with breezy, colorful glass pavilions ... floating cities with grass tennis courts, sea terraces, and many other things.... Everyone in America is plagued by hay fever.... So during the flowering season, we'll have to live in the middle of the ocean.... Our

48 Paul Scheerbart, *Glasarchitektur*, Berlin, 1914, cover
49 Paul Scheerbart, 1897
50 Publicity brochure for the Waldsanatorium, Davos, Switzerland, 1911
51 Schatzalp sanatorium, Davos, ca. 1900, postcard

50

51

Oceanic Sanatorium Society for Hay Fever has found just the right thing: floating islands that will always drift hundreds of miles away from dry land and natural islands. On our islands, dirt will be nonexistent.[31]

Scheerbart saw modern technologies as both the cause and the cure of illnesses. He writes of "nerve doctors" prescribing the calming effect of colored light in sanatoriums. The idea was to counteract the "nervous effect of very bright light" that he saw as responsible in part for "the nervous ailments of our time."[32] Already in 1901, he speculated about "air-sanatoria" flying in the sky to deal with the nervous disorders produced by modern traffic.[33] But air technology, which is at the center of all Scheerbart's utopian novels, is both cure and cause. In a prewar manifesto for pacifism written in 1914, he predicted that air warfare, as the epitome of modern machinery, would produce "general insanity": "Just thinking about all these military techniques can have a deleterious effect on one's nerves." [34] For him, at least, it was prophetic. He suffered a nervous breakdown over the carnage of World War I and starved himself to death in 1915, seemingly in protest. Since he had not taken part in the war, it was as if "just thinking" had indeed provoked his death.

THE ARCHITECTURAL CURE

Davos in Switzerland was famously the epicenter of the phenomenon of the modern cure. **FIG. 50** In 1910, there were as many as twenty-six sanatoriums and forty-six hotels that catered to "consumptives." The Schatzalp, **FIG. 51** built between

52 "Liegekur" (lying cure) on the terrace of the Villa Pravenda, Davos, ca. 1900
53 Lying cure, Davos, ca. 1910, postcard
54 Katia Mann with her children (Monica, Golo, Michael, Klaus, Elizabeth, and Erika), ca. 1920

52

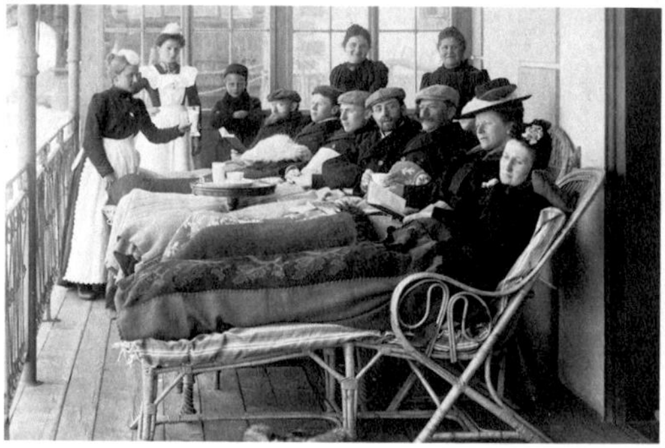

53

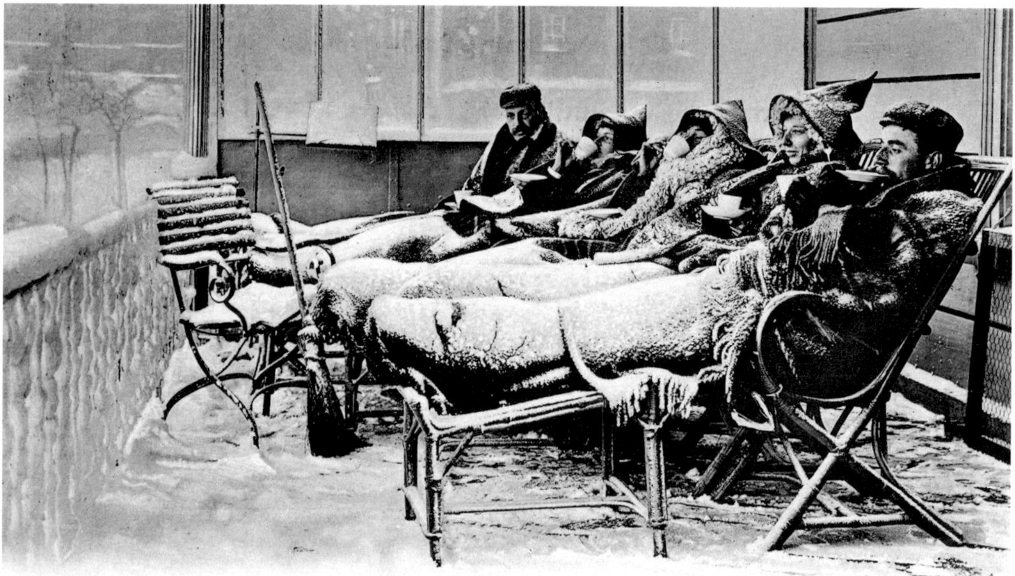

Liegekur

ARTIST. ATELIER H. GUGGENHEIM & CO., EDITEURS, ZÜRICH NO. 4658. Déposé.

54

1899 and 1900 and the only sanatorium identified by name in Thomas Mann's *The Magic Mountain,* was a collaboration between a doctor, Lucius Spengler, and two young architects from Zurich, Otto Pfleghard and Max Haefeli, with the engineer Robert Maillart, who was then working for Francois Hennebique.[35] The first building in Switzerland to be constructed of concrete and steel, it became the model for the modern sanatorium. It had steam floor heating and a flat roof with inside drainage. The most advanced medical treatment coincided with the most advanced technology in architecture.

The architecture of the Schatzalp is brutally modern in its horizontality and abstraction. With its 100-meter-long facade and endless corridors, the building is like an ocean liner. All parts are subordinated to terraces intended as therapeutic spaces, dimensioned for a patient reclining in a specially designed chaise longue, a cure to be undertaken from 7:00 a.m. to 10:00 p.m., in winter as well as in summer. A period photograph shows a group of patients lying in chairs packed closely together on the terrace, covered in a thick blanket of snow, yet seemingly happy. **FIG. 53**

Thomas Mann, always sensitive to architectural detail, describes the therapeutic chaise longue with care, evoking a philosophy of life on the edge in the horizontal. This therapy of the horizontal also was central to the Waldsanatorium, also in Davos, where Katia Mann, Thomas's wife, stayed and that inspired him to write *The Magic Mountain.* Mann's novel evokes the social life in this very modern building, where everything was wrapped in white, even the patient, who was wrapped in white to receive hydrotherapy. **FIG. 40**

Katia Mann was in fact one of the first patients in this brand-new sanatorium. She fell ill in 1912, a year after the birth of her fourth child. Her mother was convinced that Katia was suffering not from tuberculosis, but from exhaustion, having had four children and two miscarriages in less than five years, managing a large household, and even typing Mann's manuscripts.[36] Katia had been studying mathematics and experimental physics—with Wilhelm Röntgen, the discoverer of X-rays, no less—but her mother had encouraged her to abandon her studies to marry Thomas Mann at the age of twenty-one. Whatever her ailment, she stayed in and out of several sanatoriums up to 1914. Katia had no doubt that it was tuberculosis. As she wrote in her memoirs, it was "an old tubercular spot that seemed to be arrested," but she claimed she was "not seriously ill" and perhaps the "whole thing would have cleared up by itself if we hadn't been able to afford a sanatorium. It was the custom, if you had the means, to go to Davos or Arosa."[37]

Tuberculosis was often confounded with nervous disorders, and its inevitable melancholy meant the standard cure was also a psychological one. Sanatoriums offered not just an escape from the city, but an escape from normal domestic life, with the comfort of a controlled regime and a steady, yet distracting daily rhythm in the company of new friends. The hyperdesigned spaces of the clinic even represented a new form of domestic elegance. Katia Mann said the experience had strengthened her so that she could

55 Zonnestraal sanatorium, Hilversum, 1931, postcard
56 "Laat licht, lucht en zon," poster for the Zonnestraal sanatorium, ca. 1928

55

56

"stand it all."[38] And there was a lot to stand: World War II, exile to the United States, the suicide of her favorite son, Klaus, and later of her son Michael. **FIG. 54**

The modern ocean-liner environment for the rich and fabulous became democratized with sanatoriums such as Zonnestraal (1925–1928) in Hilversum, **FIG. 55** twenty miles outside Amsterdam. Zonnestraal means "sunbeam" in Dutch. It was designed by Jan Duiker and Bernard Bijvoet as a sanatorium for the General Diamond Workers' Union of the Netherlands. In this white building of reinforced concrete, the medical properties of the architecture are taken to the extreme, almost as a manifesto. **FIG. 57**

Zonnestraal was a health machine—a factory for the manufacturing of healthy bodies. Its slogan: "Laat Licht, Lucht en zon" (Allow light, air, and sun). **FIG. 56** Here, patients were wheeled out of their independent rooms and onto the terrace, which was no longer a social space, as in earlier sanatoriums. There was less interaction among patients, who seem in period photographs to keep their heads inside the room and inside their books. **FIG. 58** The real interaction was only with the sun and with machines, complex instruments such as the latest respiratory analysis devices. **FIG. 59**

The individual rooms seem to have been an advance in a working-class sanatorium, but reading Thomas Bernhard, who spent many years in and out of sanatoriums as a tuberculosis patient, which infiltrated all his writings, one becomes aware that there was nothing more terrifying to a sanatorium patient than being moved to an individual room. That could mean only one thing.[39]

57

58

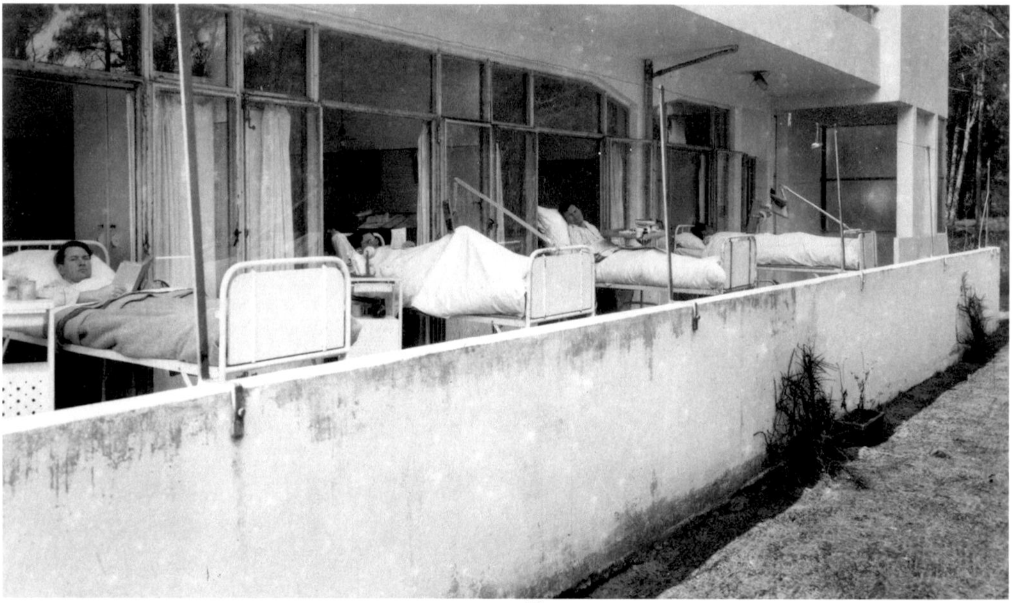

59

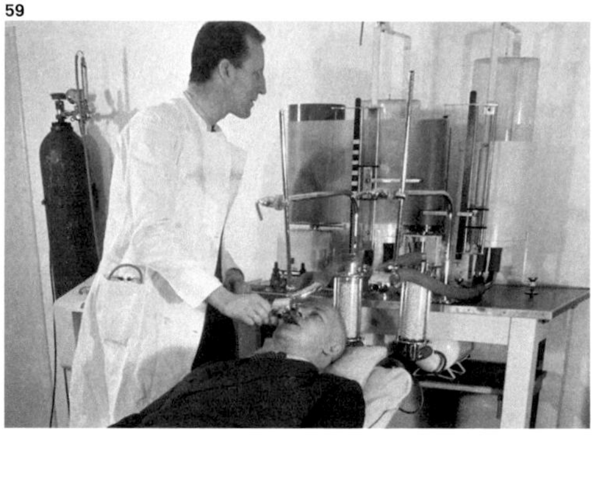

Bernard Bijvoet and Jan Duiker, Zonnestraal sanatorium, Hilversum, 1925–1928
57 Exterior view, 1928
58 Patients on the terrace, 1931
59 Treatment of Tuberculosis with respiratory analysis device, ca. 1928

Death itself was hidden. Sanatoriums in Davos and in other places did not accept very ill patients. "The sanatorium is intended for incipient and curable cases," advised the *British Journal of Diseases of the Chest* in 1908, when giving an overview of reputable sanatoriums available in Europe for prospective patients.[40] A death was a spot on their reputation. They even exaggerated their rate of cure. Subterranean tunnels carried the dead away, out of view.[41] And at the Schatzalp, 300 meters above the town of Davos, the bodies of the dead were sent down the mountain on toboggans in winter, as Thomas Mann describes in *The Magic Mountain*.

Already in *Tristan*, Mann had written: "Sometimes a death takes place among the 'severe cases....' When this happens no one knows it, not even the person sleeping next door. In the silence of the night, the waxen guest is put away and life at Einfried goes tranquilly on, with its massage, its electric treatment, douches, baths; with its exercises, its steaming and inhaling, in rooms especially equipped with all the triumphs of modern therapeutic."[42]

Paimio, which did not admit very ill patients, either, confined the most serious cases—presumably those who got worse while at the sanatorium—to the basement of the building. So much for the sun-and-air therapy. Architecture may have been seen as a medical instrument, but the patient was removed from view when the instrument didn't provide the expected results. Modern architecture represented cure but couldn't face failure. It was a bright representation of optimism inserted in place of the fear of disease.

60

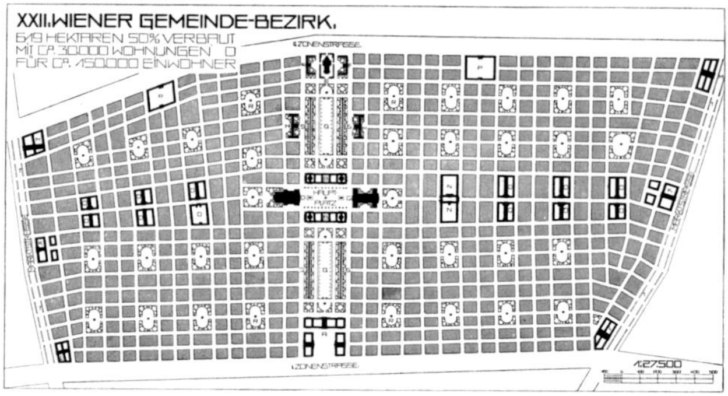

Death in modernity is hidden. Visual hygiene also means designing what you don't see or don't want to see. In Otto Wagner's plan for the *Groszstadt* (1911), **FIG. 60** high-speed trains (what was the rush?) were to remove the dead, transporting corpses in their coffins from specially designated mortuary stations to the cemeteries in the outskirts of the city: "Every large city will soon be in a position to limit the transportation of corpses to railroads, and it seems therefore proper to provide each ward with a mortuary station for this purpose."[43]

DOMESTICATING THE SANATORIUM

More significant than the architecture of the sanatorium as medical instrument is the impact of medical thought on all of modern architecture, the constant preoccupation with ventilation, sunlight, hygiene, and white walls that turned all buildings into medical equipment. As Ulrich puts it in Robert Musil's *The Man without Qualities,* a novel about 1913 Vienna, written between 1930 and 1943: "Modern man is born in hospital and dies in hospital—hence he should also live in a place like a hospital." This maxim, he adds, "had just been formulated by a leading architect, and another one, a reformer of interior decoration, demanded movable partition walls in flats."[44] **FIGS. 61, 62**

Musil was probably referring to Otto Wagner, who had already formulated the idea that modern man should live in a place like a hospital when he claimed that the hotel room should not be very different than the hospital room: clean white surfaces should replace the upholstered interiors of

60 Otto Wagner, XXIInd Viennese district, published in *Die Groszstadt*, 1911
61 Robert Musil (1880–1942)
62 Robert Musil, *Der Mann ohne Eigenschaften (The Man without Qualities)*, 1st edition, 1943, cover

61

62

the nineteenth-century hotel, where dust accumulates and illness is latent. Instead of the "princely apartments" usually requested, he proposed minimum, hygienic rooms with functional equipment that, in his view, "would give far greater comfort."[45] The medical and the domestic were interconnected. He thought "the architect has to keep fully abreast of this field [hygiene] too because these modern achievements demand truly new artistic forms."[46] New medicine called for a new architecture and a new idea of comfort. "Comfort isolates," Walter Benjamin wrote, "on the other hand, it brings those enjoying it closer to mechanization."[47] Intimacy with equipment produces detachment from the world, the very principle of the hospital room.

Wagner's lectures argued for domestic architecture to be a fusion of the machine and the hospital. As his students, recalling his teachings, put it:

> The building must function like a perfectly constructed machine; it must in its installation be on the level of the wagons-lit; and it must in matters of hygiene and cleanliness, of all objects for use, be up to clinical demands. What is needed is a synthesis of hospital, sleeping-car and machine.... It should be evident that the problem is not one of good taste or aesthetics, but entirely of technical and constructional execution.... The technical servants and helpers in our life, the lifts for food, for people, for goods, light and sound signals, cold and hot running water, central heating, internal telephones—all those mechanical and electric sys-

63 Otto Wagner, Hotel Wien on the Ringstrasse, 1910, rendering of double room
64 Wald-Oberschule in Berlin-Charlottenburg, 1904, postcard

> tems which are the nerves of the building give it a certain apparatus quality, quite apart from the kitchen in the basement which looks like a boilerhouse, from the laundry, the domestic offices and the store-rooms, all essentially in the basement.[48]

It is symptomatic that nerves are invoked once again. The nerves of the building have to be taken care of as much as the nerves of the occupant. But Wagner's nerves were not like those of Sitte or Krafft-Ebing. Wagner thought that the modern individual had become accustomed to the abstraction of long avenues and uniform facades and preferred the anonymity of the metropolis to claustrophobic, small-community life. According to him, the modern eye had lost its feelings for "small and intimate proportions, it has grown accustomed to less varied images, longer and straighter lines, larger areas and greater masses."[49] City dwellers, he believed, prefer to disappear in the crowd, to become a "number." The point of city life, for Wagner, is to make it possible to avoid social contact.[50]

> To hark back to tradition, to make "expression" or picturesqueness the controlling consideration in designing homes for the man of to-day is absurd in the light of modern experience. The number of city dwellers who to-day prefer to vanish in the mass as mere numbers on apartment doors is considerably greater than of those who care to hear the daily, "good morning, how are you" from gossipy neighbors in single houses.[51]

63

64

Both the word "hospital" and the word "hotel" derive from the Latin *hospes,* the guest or the host.[52] Wagner thought of the hotel room in much the same way he thought of the hospital room: "What is required of hotel accommodation in nearly all cases is a quiet, clean, hygienic room, where the guest is able to sleep undisturbed and attend to his physical needs."[53] The rooms for his Hotel Wien in the Ringstrasse (1910) were rendered with the sparse furniture and ascetic aesthetic of a room in Hoffmann's Purkersdorf: simple white bed, table, and chairs, without any draperies or carpets. In the foreground of one of the renderings, a woman in uniform appears to be vacuuming the floor, as if to emphasize the cleanliness, the dust-free environment. **FIG. 63**

In fact, every building, and not just hotels, became a kind of sanatorium. Take, for example, the Open Air School in Amsterdam, **FIG. 67** built in 1929, a couple of years after Zonnestraal. It was designed by the same architects, Duiker and Bijvoet, who now applied its principles of light, air, and sun to *healthy* children. They were placed inside a glass machine and even required to sit up on the roof, heads against the glass parapet, in the bright sun, with their sunglasses on. **FIG. 65** The building was conceived as a light device like those used for light therapy in the 1930s. **FIG. 66** Modern architecture went from being the cure for tuberculosis to being an apparatus for the prevention of tuberculosis.

The open-air school was an international movement, starting with the Wald-Oberschule in Berlin, Charlottenburg, which opened in 1904 for "pretubercular" children. **FIG. 64**

65, 67 Bernard Bijvoet, Jan Duiker, Open Air School for Healthy Children, Amsterdam, 1927–1930
66 French children during an indoor heliotherapy session, 1937

Eugène Beaudouin, Marcel Lods, *École de plein air* (open-air school), Mont Valérien, Suresnes (a commune outside Paris), 1931–1935
68 Cover of album of postcards of the *École de plein air*
69, 71 Postcards of children resting and bathing in the sun in Suresnes open-air school
70 Classroom with retractable walls

65

66

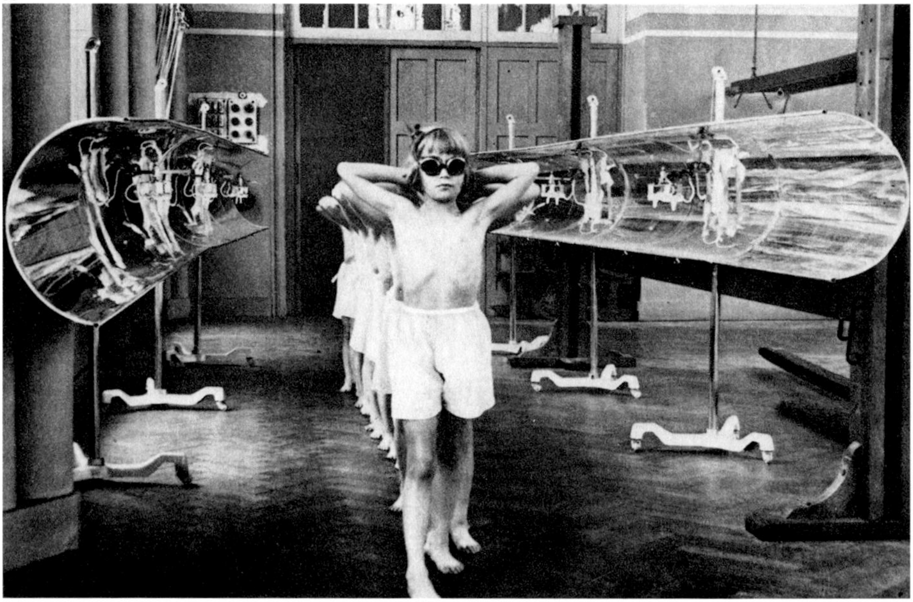

67

68

69

70

71

Richard Döcker, *Terrassentyp,* 1929
72 Otto Bartning, Children's Hospital in Lichterfelde, Berlin, terrace with patients, 1927–1928
73 Cover
74 Richard Döcker, Waiblingen sanatorium, 1926–1928, washing area in the patient rooms
75 Sections of terraced sanatoriums showing improved sun penetration

It then spread around the world with architecture ranging from lightweight structures in the forest with no walls to metal-and-concrete buildings with the bones of the structure fully exposed. The open-air school École de plein air, built by Eugène Beaudouin and Marcel Lods at Mont Valérien in Suresnes (a commune outside Paris) from 1931 to 1935, presented an uncanny resemblance between the body of the building, organized like a series of lungs, and the body of the breathing occupants. **FIGS. 69–71**

Modern architects were not the only ones advocating life in a sanatorium; their promoters, the critics, and their historians were, too. Take, for example, Sigfried Giedion's 1929 little book *Befreites Wohnen* (Liberated dwelling), **FIG. 76** subtitled *Licht, Luft, Oeffnung* (Light, air, opening), almost like the slogan of a sanatorium. Between the covers of a book about the modern house we find more than half of the illustrations dedicated to hospitals and sports: Richard Döcker's sanatorium in Waiblingen (1926–1928), **FIG. 77** Bijvoet and Duiker's Zonnestraal, sanatoriums in Davos, **FIG. 79** mountain lodges, seaside resorts, sports stadiums, images of gymnastics, sunbathing, tennis.... **FIG. 78** By the time we finally get to the houses, we may have forgotten that we were actually reading a book on the modern house. The few that Giedion included have effectively been turned into sanatoriums, with convalescents resting on long chairs on terraces (as in a picture of a Max Haefeli house in Zurich of 1928 **FIG. 81**) or gyms, as in Marcel Breuer's bedroom for Piscator in Berlin (1927–1928), **FIG. 26** André Lurcat's rooftop gym on the Guggenbühl House in Paris (1926–1927), **FIG. 80** and Richard Döcker's

72

73

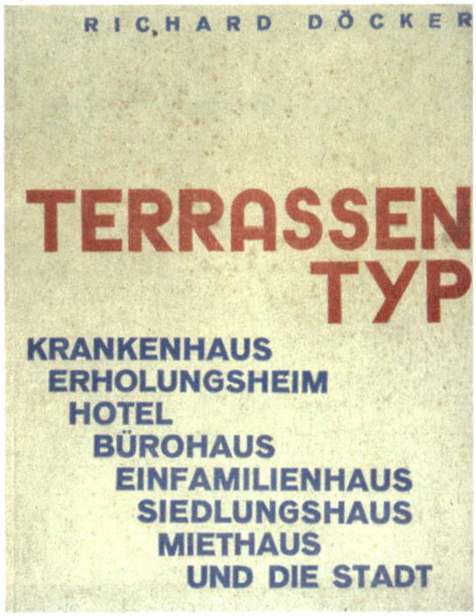

74

75

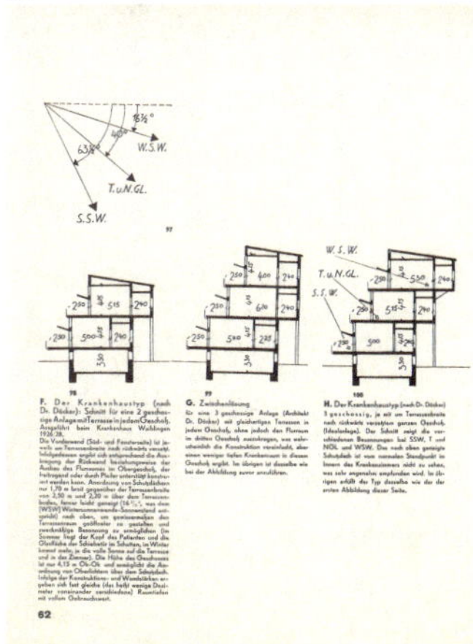

terrace with exercise equipment in his Weissenhofsiedlung house in Stuttgart (1927). **FIG. 13**

And Giedion was not the only one. Another influential book of that time, Döcker's *Terrassentyp* of 1927, **FIG. 73** follows the development of the terrace in modern architecture from the sanatorium to the home, starting with Döcker's own sanatorium in Waiblingen **FIGS. 24, 74, 77** and proceeding to Zonnestraal, Davos, and so on, delineating a seamless transition from the terraces of sanatoriums **FIG. 72** to those of modern houses. Diagrams show the penetration of sunrays in modern sanatoriums and in modern terrace houses showing how to maximize the exposure. **FIG. 75** The book concludes with a series of photographs of domestic terraces furnished with exercise equipment, as in Döcker's apartment in the Weissenhof in Stuttgart, Le Corbusier's terraces, and the terraces of Robert Mallet-Stevens's Villa Noailles (1923–1927) in Hyères.

Villa Noailles is a symptomatic case study. In one of the first articles about the house in *Art et Décoration* (July 1928) it is described as organized by a "cult of hygiene": sunlight, exercise, and fresh air take precedence over traditional forms of comfort. **FIGS. 83, 84** Bedrooms are modest in size, but each is connected to its own bathroom and its own terrace for outdoor sleeping. The master bedroom's open-air sleeping loft was designed by Pierre Chareau, with a metal bed suspended in the air, "à l'américaine," **FIG. 85** as the article in *Art et Décoration* describes it, and metal sliding doors by Jean Prouvé. The Noailles were collectors of Surrealist art, and their paintings were kept dust free with a sliding storage

Sigfried Giedion, *Befreites Wohnen* (Liberated Dwelling), 1929

76 Cover

77 Richard Döcker, Waiblingen sanatorium, 1928, with patients on the terrace

78 Woman in tennis outfit, 1920s

79 Otto Pfleghard and Max Haefeli, Queen Alexandra Sanatorium in Davos, sun terrace with patients, 1907

80 André Lurcat, gym on the terrace of the Guggenbühl House, Paris, 1926–1927

81 M. E. Haefeli, house in the Wasserwerkstrasse, with patient on the terrace, Zurich, 1928

76

77

78

Das neue praktische Tenniskostüm, dessen allgemeine
Einführung in Amerika angestrebt wird.
Spezialdienst.

79

80

81

82 Marie-Laure de Noailles, portrait by Man Ray, 1933

82

system organized like a vertical filing cabinet. A covered swimming pool had a mechanism, probably designed by Prouvé, that allowed the enormous glass walls to retreat into the ground, opening the pool to the vast outdoor exercise area. The house even had a squash court, where Charles de Noailles played with Luis Buñuel.[54] There was a personal trainer for the owners and their guests, Monsieur Taré, who features in a film by Jacques Manuel, *Biceps et bijoux* (1928), **FIG. 86** commissioned by the clients. They also commissioned Man Ray to make a film, *Les Mystères du Château du Dé* (1929), using the house as a set for endless exercise confused with Surrealist play, with the clients and their guests themselves as actors in striped exercise gear.[55] **FIGS. 87, 88**

But health, for Marie-Laure and Charles de Noailles, was more than a creative obsession. Like many of the "fragile people" who came to Hyères to "soften" their illnesses, they sought air and sun. In fact, Marie-Laure, **FIG. 82** born in Paris as the daughter of German Jewish bankers and a descendent on her mother's side from the Marquis de Sade, had for health reasons been raised in a villa in Grasse, France. Her father had died of tuberculosis when she was a baby. The radical house she commissioned from Mallet-Stevens is sited and shaped by the shadow of the disease it aims to resist.

The association of the modern house with hospital sometimes confused even professional critics and historians. Richard Neutra's Lovell Health House (1929) in Los Angeles, for example, a domestic project for a private client, was referred to as a "nursing home" by architectural historian Leonardo Benevolo.[56] The house was another doctor-architect collaboration, this time between Neutra and Dr. Philip Lovell. **FIG. 90** Design operates for Neutra at the intersection of biology and psychology as a therapeutic defense against the "disastrous effects" of all the accumulated conditions of modern life. He writes about how the "warm, moist air practically stationary, saturated with airborne bacteria, and recirculated through many lungs, had made tuberculosis endemic" and of the need for design to address both "pathology, the manifest spreading of disease," and psychological comfort, what he calls, earlier in the book, "nervous health."[57]

Neutra's sensitivity to nervous illness is autobiographical. In a letter to her mother, Dione Neutra writes that Richard suffered from "terrible depression," a recurring condition throughout his life. Ironically, it was the stresses of completing the Health House and dealing with the Lovells that seems to have caused the physical and mental exhaustion that Neutra's wife mentions in this particular letter. For Neutra, mental and physical health were always intertwined. He insisted, for example, that the success of his own tropical classroom design was not just that "airborne bacteria no longer hover in the classroom" and "expectoration dries promptly, quickly diminishing in contagiousness." It is equally in the calming and delightful sensation of cool air passing across the skin as the large fold-up doors extend the possible classroom space.[58] Neutra provides both bacteriological and nervous order, each understood as either cure or prevention of disease.

It is important to note that Neutra himself had tuberculosis and spent a year in a sanatorium in Switzerland. His

Robert Mallet-Stevens, Villa Noailles, Hyères, France, 1923–1927

83 Swimming pool

84 Terrace

85 Pierre Chareau, open-air room in the Villa Noailles, ca. 1926

86 Marie-Laure de Noailles with her gymnastic professor, St-Bernard, Hyères, 1928

87, 88 Man Ray, film stills from *Les Mystères du Château de Dé,* 1929

83

84

85

86

87

88

89

90

brother, a doctor, had tuberculosis from the age of nineteen and eventually died from the disease. Several of Neutra's clients had tuberculosis—Howard Bald, for example, who was brought to Los Angeles at the age of eight for the cure. In fact, Southern California was tuberculosis central. Many people migrated there for the cure—as did modern architecture. Even the great critic of modern architecture, Esther McCoy, originally came to California for the cure. **FIG. 89**

Modern architecture thus is occupied by and organized around two emblematic figures: the fragile tuberculosis patient seeking a cure and the athletic figure seeking prevention from the diseases of modernity. Even the body of the architect becomes part of the project. A photograph of Aino Aalto lying on the chaise longue she designed on the terrace of the sanatorium at Paimio shows the architect in the position of the patient. **FIG. 91** And a photograph of Duiker flipping into a pond portrays the architect in the active position of the healthy amateur athlete in the outdoors. **FIG. 92** Neither is exactly the typical heroic pose of the architect in front of a building.

Not only did modern architects emphasize health and exercise in opposition to the dangers of disease, sometimes presenting themselves as models, but their architecture was understood that way. The buildings became unconsciously identified with the need to produce a healthy body. For example, Mies van der Rohe's Tugendhat House (1929–1930) in Brno, which had been abandoned during the German occupation of Czechoslovakia,[59] was turned first into a physical education institute of Karla Hladká, **FIG. 96** then

89 Esther McCoy
90 Dr. Philip M. Lovell, Physical Culture Center, Los Angeles
91 Aino Aalto lying in the lounge chair she designed for the Paimio Sanatorium, ca. 1934
92 Jan Duiker diving into a pond, 1917

91

92

93

94

into a government gymnasium for children with orthopedic problems **FIG. 93** by Communist bureaucrats who presumably were unaware that the house had been photographed in its early days in exactly that spirit.[60] **FIG. 94** Early 1930s photographs of naked Tugendhat children playing in the sun on the terrace are uncannily echoed in the 1950s images of children exercising in the living room–gym and on the terrace.

The Tugendhats may have understood the house as a machine for health, too. In response to architectural critic Justus Bier, who had polemically asked the question, "Is the Tugendhat house habitable?" in the pages of the journal *Die Form,*[61] Fritz Tugendhat symptomatically invoked Davos: "After almost a year of living in the house, I can assure you without hesitation that technically it possesses everything a modern person might wish for.... On clear and frosty days, one can lowers its windows, sit in the sun, and enjoy the view of a snow-covered landscape, like Davos."[62] **FIG. 95**

In winter, the family would sit by the big glass wall in the living room, which could be lowered into the ground until it disappeared completely, taking the sun and the fresh air with the snow outside, "like Davos," a sanatorium. Photographs of the family by amateur photographer and filmmaker Fritz Tugendhat show the children playing and running around naked in the outdoor spaces of the house, evoking ideas of the *Lebensreform* movement. Grete Tugendhat, according to Irene Kalkofen, nanny of the Tugendhat children, was always afraid of the children falling ill, and whenever one of them was sick, they were isolated in Irene's

Ludwig Mies van der Rohe, Tugendhat House, ca. 1945–1950
93 Living room of the Tugendhat House transformed into rehabilitation center for children, 1966
94 Roof terrace on the upper floor with the Tugendhat children
95 View from the garden
96 Children exercising on the terrace of the physical education institute of Karla Hladká dancing school

95

96

97

98

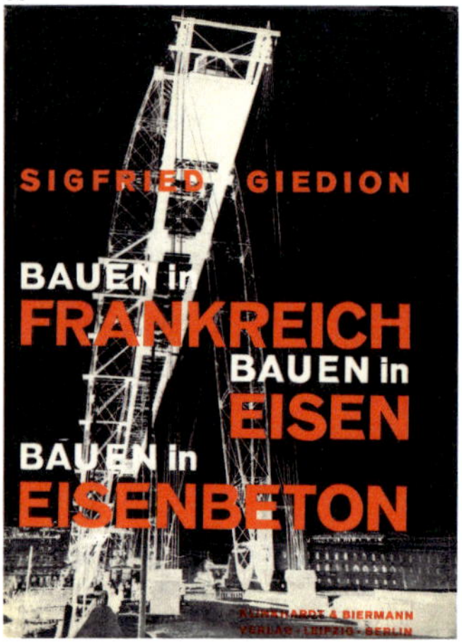

room while she slept in another child's room to avoid contagion.[63] The idea of a separate space to quarantine sick children was a standard part of a modern bourgeois house, as in Adolf Loos' Muller House in Prague.

Fritz Tugendhat himself was not in good health at the time of the commission, Mies recalls: "He was a very careful man and he was sick. He did not believe in one doctor only; he had three."[64] What Mies didn't seem to realize is that this was not that unusual. Uncertainty in the early twentieth century about the new scientific medicine made it commonplace among the bourgeoisie to consult different kinds of doctors and alternative practitioners and to follow multiple kinds of advice. In a sense, the architect was added as yet another medical consultant.

Even proposals for a modern city were imagined in health terms: from Ebenezer Howard's *Garden City* (1898) to Arturo Soria y Mata's *Ciudad Lineal* (1897), to Otto Wagner's *Die Groszstadt* (1911) to Le Corbusier's *Radiant City* (1935). Tony Garnier's influential proposal for an *Industrial City* (1904), for instance, featured the heliotherapy building **FIG. 97** of the hospital complex occupying the highest point of the plan, dominating the city from the hillside, with the sports center right in the middle of town, as if replacing the cathedral of medieval times. Health had become a new form of religion, and modern architecture built its temples.

Giedion describes Garnier's heliotherapy project in *Building in France, Building in Iron, Building in Ferroconcrete* (1928), **FIG. 98** his first book on modern architecture: "Elevators carry the convalescent in his bed to the generous terraces to

97 Tony Garnier, heliotherapy building in *Une cité industrielle*, 1904
98 László Moholy-Nagy, cover of Sigfried Giedion's *Bauen in Frankreich, Bauen in Eisen, Bauen in Eisenbeton*, 1928

which the roofs have been converted. Despite the heaviness of particular details of the design, the eye, through the interplay of the various horizontal surfaces, has an impression of the air always separating and hovering, just as our future cities will be shaped."[65] Giedion's passing comment that the therapeutic horizontality designed for the convalescents will soon shape all future cities suggests a completely new explanation for the relentless horizontal framing of modern architecture. Could it in fact be related to the horizontality of the occupant—the tuberculosis convalescent lying on the chaise and the psychoanalytic patient on the couch, the paradigmatic clients of modern architecture? As Erich Mendelsohn put it: "Modern man, amidst the flurry of his fast moving life, can find equilibrium only in the tension-free horizontal."[66] The horizontal itself becomes emblematic of health. Both the horizontal view from the inside and the view of horizontals from the outside induce health. The sanatorium aesthetic was itself medicinal—able to transform any building into a form of therapy.

1 While the sanatorium is often attributed to Alvar Aalto alone, as early as 1933 he acknowledged the collaboration with his wife, Aino Marsio-Aalto, and the participation of the Norwegian architects Erling Bjertnäs and Harald Wildhagen, as well as the Finish architects Lauri Sipilä and Lars Wiklund. Alvar Aalto, "Paimion Parantola" (Paimio Sanatorium), *Arkkitehti* 1933, pp. 79–90.

2 Sigfried Giedion, *Space, Time and Architecture: The Growth of a New Tradition* (Cambridge, MA: Harvard University Press, 1949), 8th enlarged printing, pp. 463 and 466.

3 In my first visit to Paimio in 1994, I was told by the person in charge of the building that the upper terrace of the sanatorium was off-limits and in response to my insistence claimed that it had been closed to prevent suicide. No amount of reasoning, arguments about research, or about how living in New York that offers much better opportunities for leaping from high buildings got me anywhere, but I was otherwise free to roam the building. When I reached the top of the stairs, the door of the terrace was actually open, and I took the air. I have not seen other references to suicide in Paimio, but in literature, it's a common place to commit suicide while in a sanatorium. In Thomas Mann's *Magic Mountain,* two characters commit suicide.

4 The discovery of antibiotics discredited the sanatorium movement, which was all of a sudden seen as lacking scientific proof. Indeed, there was never a scientific study of its value: "The great sanatorium movement ... was never subjected to a scientific trial of its effectiveness. But there is abundance of indirect evidence to suggest that such general measures would not cure a patient who was seriously infected. In mild and early cases, it seems likely that life could be prolonged and that the course of the disease could be slowed down, allowing the body's natural defenses a better chance of healing." Frank Ryan, *Tuberculosis: The Greatest Story Never Told* (Bromsgrove: Swift, 1992), p. 27.

5 Göran Schildt, *Alvar Aalto: The Complete Catalogue of Architecture, Design and Art,* trans. Timothy Binham (New York: Rizzoli, 1994), p. 68.

6 Alvar Aalto, in a lecture in Italy describing Paimio, 1956, quoted in Schildt, *Alvar Aalto: The Complete Catalogue,* pp. 68–69. Text in the Aalto Archives.

7 Karl Fleig and Elissa Aalto, eds., *Alvar Aalto: Das Gesamtwerk / L'œuvre complète / The Complete Work,* vol. 1, *1922–1962* (Basel: Birkhäuser, 1963), p. 39.

8 Ibid., p. 31.

9 Ibid.

10 Alvar Aalto, "The Humanizing of Architecture," *Technology Review* (November 1940). Also in *Architectural Forum* 73 (December 1940), pp. 505–506. Reprinted in Göran Schildt, *Aalto in His Own Words* (New York: Rizzoli, 1998), pp. 102–106.

11 Aalto, "The Humanizing of Architecture," p. 16.

12 "The Artek Manifesto," Artek Company, Helsinki. See also *Alvar Aalto,* vol. 1, pp. 43 and 66.

13 Aalto, "The Humanizing of Architecture," p. 15.

14 Le Corbusier, *Precisions On the Present State of Architecture and Urban Planning,* trans. Edith Schreiber Aujame (Cambridge, MA: MIT Press, 1991), p. 143. Translation of Le Corbusier, *Précisions sur un état présent d'architecture et de l'urbanisme,* (Paris: Crès et Cie, 1930).

15 About the Purkersdorf, see the detailed study of Leslie Topp, "The Purkersdorf Sanatorium and the Appearance of Science," in Topp, *Architecture and Truth in Fin-de Siècle Vienna* (Cambridge: Cambridge University Press), pp. 63–95.

16 Ludwig Hevesi, "Neubauten von Josef Hoffmann. Purkersdorf. Hohe Warte. Brüssel," in *Altkunst-Neukunst: Wien 1894–1908* (Vienna, 1909), translated and reprinted in Peter Vergo, *Art in Vienna, 1898–1918: Klimt, Kokoschka, Schiele and Their Contemporaries* (London: Phaidon, 1975), p. 135.

17 Ibid.

18 Eduard Sekler, *Josef Hoffmann: The Architectural Work* (Princeton: Princeton University Press, 1985), p. 235.

19 See Adrian Forty, "The Modern Hospital in England and France: The Social and Medical Uses of Architecture," in *Buildings and Society: Essays on the Social Development of the Built Environment,* ed. Anthony King (London: Routledge, 1980).

20 She was married to Emil Zuckerkandl, a professor of anatomy, a colleague of Krafft-Ebing, and the brother of Viktor Zuckerkandl, the industrialist who developed the Purkersdorf.

21 Quoted in Sabine Wieber, "Sculpting the Sanatorium: Nervous Bodies and Femmes Fragiles in Vienna 1900," *Women in German Yearbook* 27 (2011), p. 77.

22 Karl Krauss, *Die Fackel,* no. 167, October 26, 1904, p. 14.

23 Thomas Mann, *Tristan,* in *Stories of Three Decades,* trans. H. T. Lowe-Porter (London: Martin Secker and Warburg, 1922), p. 141.

24 Ibid., p. 154.

25 Adolf Loos, *Der Mensch mit den modernen Nerven,* February 17, 22, and

25 and March 8, according to the poster announcing the lectures.
26 Adolf Loos, "Die englische Uniform," *Neues 8 Uhr-Blatt,* May 24, 1919.
27 Adolf Loos, "Wohnen lernen!," *Neues Wiener Tagblatt,* May 15, 1921. Loos cites landscape architect Leberecht Migge on men who possess modern nerves.
28 Adolf Loos, "Ornament und Erziehung" (1924), in *Sämtliche Schriften,* ed. Frank Glück, vol. 1 (Vienna: Herold, 1962), pp. 392–93.
29 Paul Scheerbart, *Glass Architecture,* trans. James Palme (New York: Praeger, 1972), p. 62; translation of Scheerbart, *Glasarchitektur* (Berlin: Verlag der Sturm, 1914).
30 Ibid., p. 67.
31 Paul Scheerbart, "Das Ozeansanatorium für Heukranke Telegramn-Novelette," *Der Sturm* 3, no. 123–24, (August 24, 1912), trans. by Erik Born.
32 Scheerbart, *Glass Architecture,* p. 68.
33 Paul Scheerbart, "Das Luft-Sanatorium," *Gegenwart* 76 (October 1909), pp. 781–82.
34 Paul Scheerbart, "The Development of Air Militarism and the Dissolution of European Land Armies, Fortifications, and Ocean Fleets," quoted in Peter Springer, *Hand and Head: Ernst Ludwig Kirchner's Self-Portrait as Soldier* (Berkeley: University of California Press, 2002), p. 61.
35 The Schatzalp is considered Robert Maillart's first large building. It was with this building that Maillart was able to launch his independent practice.
36 Katia, née Katherina Hedwig Pringsheim, was the granddaughter of Hedwig Dohm, a famous German feminist and author, who was disappointed when Katia abandoned her studies of physics and mathematics to marry Mann. Katia Mann, *Unwritten Memories,* ed. Elisabeth Plessen and Michael Mann, trans. Hunter Hannum and Hildegarde Hannum (New York: Alfred Knopf, 1975), p. 5.
37 In fact, after six months in Davos, she spent several months the following year in Merano and Arosa. After the war, she went again for treatment to Clavadel, near Davos. Ibid., p. 68.
38 Karin Andert, *Monika Mann: Eine Biografie* (Hamburg: Mare, 1910).
39 See, for example, Thomas Bernhard, *Wittgenstein's Nephew: A Friendship,* trans. David McLintock (New York: Alfred A. Knopf, 1988) and Bernhard, *Gathering Evidence: A Memoir,* trans. David McLintock (New York: Alfred A. Knopf, 1985).
40 *British Journal of Diseases of the Chest* 2 (1908), p. 129.
41 During the recent renovation of the Schatzalp building, a secret tunnel was discovered that used to carry the dead directly from the sanatorium to the funicular station.
42 Mann, *Tristan,* p. 134.
43 Otto Wagner, "The Development of a Great City," *Architectural Record* 31, May 1912, p. 494.
44 Robert Musil, *The Man without Qualities,* trans. Eithne Wilkins and Ernst Kaiser (New York: Capricorn Books, 1965), p. 16.
45 Heinz Geretsegger and Max Peintner, *Otto Wagner 1841–1918: The Expanding City, the Beginning of Modern Architecture,* trans. Gerald Onn (London: Academy Editions, 1979), p. 140.
46 Otto Wagner, *Moderne Architektur* (Vienna: Verlag von Anton Schroll, 1896). Translated in English from the 1902 third edition as *Modern Architecture: A Guidebook for His Students to this Field of Art,* trans. Harry Francis Mallgrave (Santa Monica: Getty Center for the History of Art and the Humanities, 1988), p. 113.
47 Walter Benjamin, "On Some Motifs in Baudelaire," trans. Harry Zohn, in *Walter Benjamin: Selected Writings, Vol. 4, 1938–1940,* ed. Howard Eiland and Michael W. Jennings (Cambridge, MA: Belknap Press of Harvard University Press, 2003), p. 328.
48 Otto Wagner's students published their impression of his theories in the journal *Aus der Wagnerschule.* Extract from student Karl Maria Kerndle, quoted by Otto Antonia Graf, "Wagner and the Vienna School," in *The Anti-Rationalists,* ed. Nikolaus Pevsner and J. M. Richards (London: Architectural Press, 1973), pp. 95–96.
49 Otto Wagner, *Die Baukunst unserer Zeit: dem Baukunstjünger ein Führer auf diesem Kunstgebiete,* 4th ed. (1914; Vienna: Löcker, 1979), p. 87. Quoted in Geretsegger and Peintner, *Otto Wagner 1841–1918,* p. 43.
50 Geretsegger and Peintner, *Otto Wagner 1841–1918,* p. 37.
51 Otto Wagner, "The Development of a Great City," p. 500. Wagner had also personal reasons to prefer anonymity. He fathered two children outside his marriage and never recognized them, ultimately divorcing his wife to live with the governess of his legitimate daughter.
52 Nikolaus Pevsner, *A History of Building Types* (Princeton: Princeton University Press, 1976), p. 139.
53 Wagner, quoted in Geretsegger and Peintner, *Otto Wagner 1841–1918,* p. 140.
54 The Noailles were sponsors of many artists, including Buñuel, Salvador Dalí, and Man Ray. They produced the film

L'Age d'or (1930) by Buñuel, with script by Buñuel and Dalí. The film was banned by the police shortly after its premiere, following attacks by a right-wing group.
55 Film was not simply added to the house, but was part of its logic from the beginning. The Noailles had offered the commission first to Mies van der Rohe, who claimed to be too busy, and then to Le Corbusier, but ultimately selected Mallet-Stevens, who at that point had built only film sets.
56 Leonardo Benevolo, *History of Modern Architecture,* vol. 2 (Cambridge, MA: MIT Press, 1977), p. 640. Benevolo refers in a picture caption to Neutra's house as "Dr. Lovell's nursing home." I am grateful to Thomas Hines for pointing this out to me. About Neutra's work, see Thomas Hines, *Richard Neutra and the Search for Modern Architecture* (New York: Rizzoli, 2006) and Sylvia Lavin, *Form Follows Libido: Architecture and Richard Neutra in a Psychoanalytic Culture* (Cambridge, MA: MIT Press, 2007).
57 Richard Neutra, *Survival through Design* (New York: Oxford University Press, 1953), pp. 320 and 194.
58 Ibid., p. 322.
59 The Tugendhats went into exile in St. Gallen, Switzerland, on March 12, 1938, the day of the annexation of Austria. The house was confiscated by the Gestapo in October 1939, and the property was transferred to the Reich in 1942. Daniela Hammer-Tugendhat, Ivo Hammer, and Wolf Tegethoff, *Tugendhat House: Ludwig Mies van der Rohe* (Basel: Birkhäuser, 2015), pp. 95–98.
60 Soon after the withdrawal of Soviet troops in 1945, Karla Hladká took over the house for her private dance and rhythmic classes. In 1950, the house was registered in the Czechoslovakian Communist state under the governmental institution for physiotherapy. The house became part of a children's hospital, and the living room was turned into a gym for children with orthopedic problems. Ibid., p. 144.
61 Justus Bier, "Kann man im Haus Tugendhat wohnen?," *Die Form,* October 15, 1931, p. 392.
62 Fritz Tugendhat, *Die Form,* November 1931, pp. 437–38.
63 "Irene Kalkofen Remembers," extract from a four-hour interview with June Finfer, Chicago, 2004. *Tugendhat House,* p. 87.
64 "Interview with Mies van der Rohe," *Architectural Association* Journal, July–August 1959, quoted in Wolf Tegethoff, "The Tugendhat 'Villa': A Modern Residence in Turbulent Times," *Tugendhat House,* p. 94.
65 Sigfried Giedion, *Building in France, Building in Iron, Building in Ferro-concrete,* trans J. Duncan Berry (1928; Getty Center for the History of Art and the Humanities, 1995), p. 163.
66 Erich Mendelsohn, "Dynamics and Function" (1923), in *Programs and Manifestoes on 20th-Century Architecture,* ed. Ulrich Conrads, trans. Michael Bullock (Cambridge, MA: MIT Press, 1971), p. 72. Health was thought of in terms of equilibrium. In *Mechanization Takes Command,* Sigfried Giedion concludes his critique of mechanization by talking about the need for "equipoise," a form of equilibrium in "perfect health." He gives a detailed account of the nervous systems in the body and the importance of nervous dynamic between body and psyche. Sigfried Giedion, *Mechanization Takes Command: A Contribution to Anonymous History* (1948; New York: Norton 1969), pp. 714–23. He questions the very commitment to modern architecture that he had championed before the war. Architecture as a technical instrument was damaging the body and brain. Functionalist architecture was unhealthy in the end.

CHAPTER 3

X-Ray Intimacy

"The TB sufferer is a wanderer," Susan Sontag wrote in one her notebooks, preserved in her archives. There is a "geography of health."[1] The patient travels to find a cure. This nomadic figure is also the paradigmatic client of modern architecture, for whom entering modern buildings is like entering any other medical apparatus. Architecture here is less about shelter and more about exposure—X-ray exposure.

As X-rays became indelibly associated with tuberculosis, the tuberculosis patient became the paradigm of this new way of thinking about bodies, objects, and psychologies. In *Illness as Metaphor,* Sontag writes:

> TB makes the body transparent. The X-rays which are the standard diagnostic tool permit one, often for the first time, to see one's insides—to become transparent to oneself. While TB is understood to be, from early on, rich in visible symptoms (progressive emaciation, coughing, languidness, fever), and can be suddenly and dramatically revealed (the blood on the handkerchief), in cancer the main symptoms are thought to be, characteristically, invisible—until the last stage, when it is too late. The disease, often discovered by chance or through a routine medical checkup, can be far advanced without exhibiting any appreciable symptoms. One has an opaque body that must be taken to a specialist to find out if it contains cancer. What the patient cannot perceive, the specialist will determine by analyzing tissues taken from the body. TB patients may see their X-rays or even possess them:

> the patients at the sanatorium in *The Magic Mountain* carry theirs around in their breast pockets. Cancer patients don't look at their biopsies.[2]

Indeed, patients in the sanatorium in *The Magic Mountain* even carry the X-rays of their loved ones in their breast pockets. When Clavdia Chauchat, Hans Castor's love object, leaves the sanatorium she gives him her X-ray as a memento:

> Then he flung himself into his chair, and drew out his keepsake, his treasure, that consisted, this time, not of a few reddish-brown shavings, but a thin glass plate, which must be held toward the light to see anything on it. It was Clavdia's x-ray portrait, showing not her face, but the delicate bony structure of the upper half of her body, and the organs of the thoracic cavity, surrounded by the pale, ghostlike envelope of flesh.
>
> How often had he looked at it, how often pressed it to his lips in the time which since then had passed and brought its changes with it—such changes as, for instance, getting used to life up here without Clavdia Chauchat, getting used, that is, to her remoteness in space![3]

The X-ray is a kind of self-exposure, a new, more intimate kind of portrait of oneself or of someone close to you. To analyze the canon of modern architecture in these terms is to do a kind of X-ray of the canon, a disciplinary self-exposure, a way of getting closer to our object by allowing architecture to see itself, to see what is always there, but overlooked.

A NEW TRANSPARENCY

When Wilhelm Conrad Röntgen first published his very recent discovery of the X-ray in December of 1895 in an article translated the following month as "On a New Kind of Rays, a Preliminary Communication," **FIG. 1** he wrote about a new form of transparency in which "bodies behave to the X-rays as turbid media to light."[4] The invisible rays are described as a "medium" that penetrates objects and is revealed on screens. A technical surface acts as the most intimate witness of the otherwise hidden interior. In the early decades of the twentieth century, architects, historians, and theorists quickly absorbed the new paradigm, with its inversion of the classical relationship between inside and outside, developing an entire logic of the invisible that remains largely in place, an architecture we still live with in our countless screens monitoring endless invisible flows.

This new concept of transparency is intimately linked to the idea of a "screen." The screen that Röntgen describes was actually made of a piece of paper coated with a thin layer of barium platinum cyanide, which glows fluorescent when exposed to X-rays. He marvels at the fact that paper itself is very transparent, so the "fluorescent screen" is really just the thin layer of barium platinum cyanide. But it is not just a sheet of paper that is transparent. Even "a thousand-page book" placed behind the screen becomes transparent. "Thick blocks of wood are still transparent." It takes

1

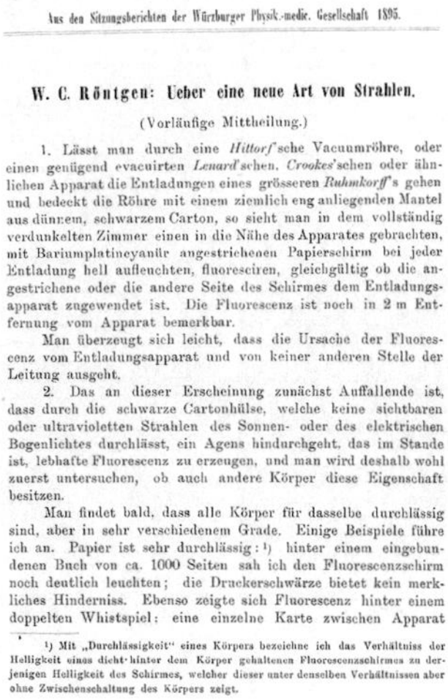

Aus den Sitzungsberichten der Würzburger Physik.-medic. Gesellschaft 1895.

W. C. Röntgen: Ueber eine neue Art von Strahlen.

(Vorläufige Mittheilung.)

1. Lässt man durch eine *Hittorf*'sche Vacuumröhre, oder einen genügend evacuirten *Lenard*'schen, *Crookes*'schen oder ähnlichen Apparat die Entladungen eines grösseren *Ruhmkorff*'s gehen und bedeckt die Röhre mit einem ziemlich eng anliegenden Mantel aus dünnem, schwarzem Carton, so sieht man in dem vollständig verdunkelten Zimmer einen in die Nähe des Apparates gebrachten, mit Bariumplatincyanür angestrichenen Papierschirm bei jeder Entladung hell aufleuchten, fluoresciren, gleichgültig ob die angestrichene oder die andere Seite des Schirmes dem Entladungsapparat zugewendet ist. Die Fluorescenz ist noch in 2 m Entfernung vom Apparat bemerkbar.

Man überzeugt sich leicht, dass die Ursache der Fluorescenz vom Entladungsapparat und von keiner anderen Stelle der Leitung ausgeht.

2. Das an dieser Erscheinung zunächst Auffallende ist, dass durch die schwarze Cartonhülse, welche keine sichtbaren oder ultravioletten Strahlen des Sonnen- oder des elektrischen Bogenlichtes durchlässt, ein Agens hindurchgeht, das im Stande ist, lebhafte Fluorescenz zu erzeugen, und man wird deshalb wohl zuerst untersuchen, ob auch andere Körper diese Eigenschaft besitzen.

Man findet bald, dass alle Körper für dasselbe durchlässig sind, aber in sehr verschiedenem Grade. Einige Beispiele führe ich an. Papier ist sehr durchlässig:[1] hinter einem eingebundenen Buch von ca. 1000 Seiten sah ich den Fluorescenzschirm noch deutlich leuchten; die Druckerschwärze bietet kein merkliches Hinderniss. Ebenso zeigte sich Fluorescenz hinter einem doppelten Whistspiel: eine einzelne Karte zwischen Apparat

[1]) Mit „Durchlässigkeit" eines Körpers bezeichne ich das Verhältniss der Helligkeit eines dicht hinter dem Körper gehaltenen Fluorescenzschirmes zu derjenigen Helligkeit des Schirmes, welcher dieser unter denselben Verhältnissen aber ohne Zwischenschaltung des Körpers zeigt.

1 Wilhelm Röntgen's first publication of the X-rays discovery, December 28, 1895

2

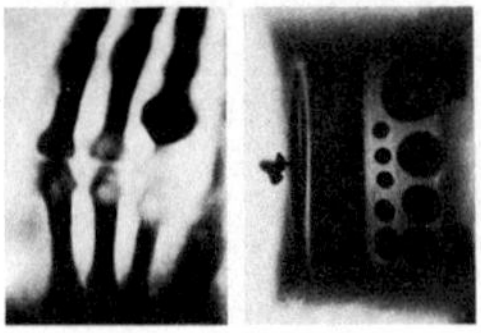

"... shadows of the bones of the hand; of a set of weights enclosed in a small box ..."

"... shadows of a compass in which the magnetic needle is entirely surrounded by metal; of a piece of metal whose inhomogeneity becomes apparent with x-rays ..."

3

many layers for tinfoil to barely cast a "shadow" on the screen, and it takes a very thick sheet of aluminum to reduce the fluorescence. **FIGS. 2, 3**

Röntgen's discovery was a radical transformation of the concepts of materiality and solidity, inverting the conventional understanding of what is visible and invisible. Röntgen's screen showed, in the words of his first report, that "all bodies possess this same transparency, but in very varying degrees."[5] Transparency, therefore, is a property of seemingly opaque bodies, including the human body. In other words, transparency is not an effect. The X-ray is not something done to an object. The object is already transparent, and the X-rays allow us to see it as such. The whole world is now understood to be transparent. More than simply affecting architecture, Röntgen's discovery was a transformation of space.

Having studied the transparency of many materials, including glass itself, which paradoxically is more opaque (because it contains lead), Röntgen looked through the human body: "If the hand be held before the fluorescent screen," he writes, "the shadow shows the bones darkly, with only faint outlines of the surrounding tissues."[6] The famous X-ray image of the hand of his wife Bertha Röntgen, with her wedding ring on the middle finger, taken only five days before he submitted the article for publication, is used as an illustration—as proof of the astonishing revelation.[7] **FIG. 4**

The story of this image, which was crucial to the popular success of the invention, is that Röntgen, afraid of revealing his stunning discovery to his colleagues, brought his

2 First X-ray images of Wilhelm Röntgen, 1895, as published in the English translation of Röntgen's article
3 Wilhelm Conrad Röntgen

wife to the laboratory the evening of December 22, 1895, after months of experimentation with inanimate objects, and exposed her hand to the X-rays for fifteen minutes, producing the first X-ray of a human body. Upon seeing the image of her hand, Bertha Röntgen famously said, "I have seen my death,"[8] anticipating a common popular reaction to such exposures—like seeing a ghost, or even seeing yourself as a ghost.

Röntgen's article stimulated an enormous double response. Scientists all around the world seized on the idea and tried to replicate the experiment. The popular press ignited a huge speculation about the possible uses and meaning of these images. Newspapers were galvanized by the idea of an invisible world. The image of Bertha's hand gave way to a whole genre of such images in both scientific and popular publications. Countless X-ray images of hands were made by Röntgen himself and others soon after the article was published. In his first public lecture about the discovery, delivered in Würzburg on January 13, 1896, Röntgen exposed the hand of Professor Albert von Kölliker, **FIG. 5** a famous anatomist and president of the Würzburg Physical and Medical Society. Summoned to Berlin by the emperor to report on the discovery, he X-rayed the hands of the Emperor Wilhelm II and the Empress Augusta Victoria. Later, he also did the hands of the Duke and Duchess of York and the Emperor and Empress of Russia, among many other notables. **FIG. 6** The hand X-ray had become a new kind of intimate portrait and the icon of a new worldview in which everything, no matter how seemingly impervious, becomes intimate.

4

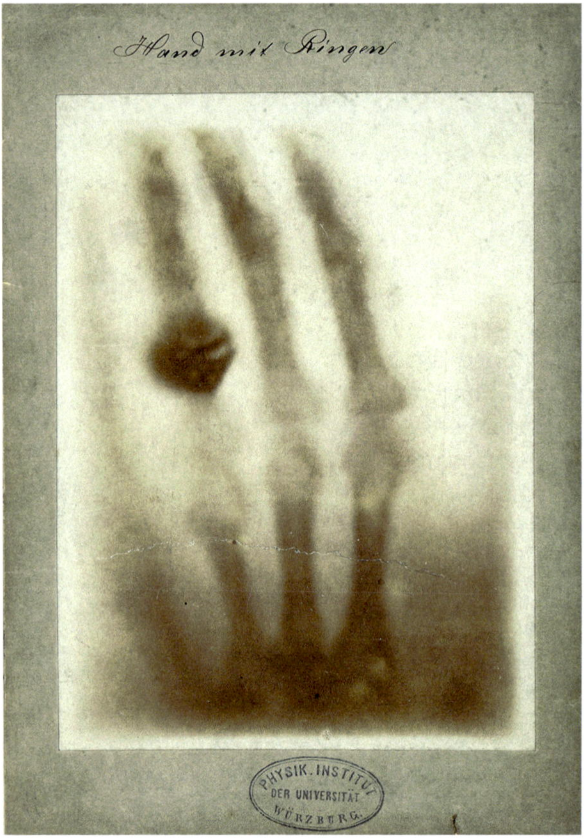

5

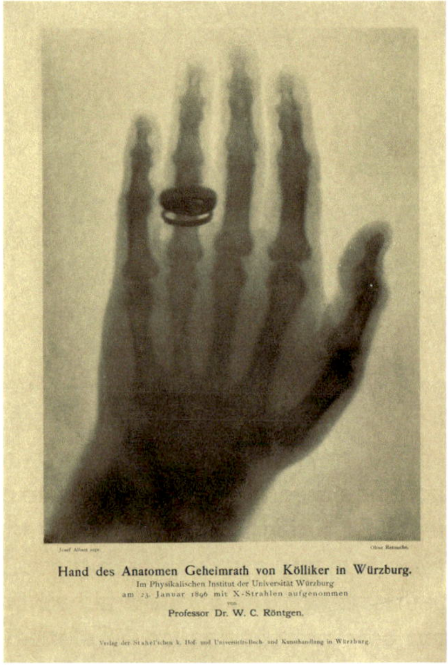

6

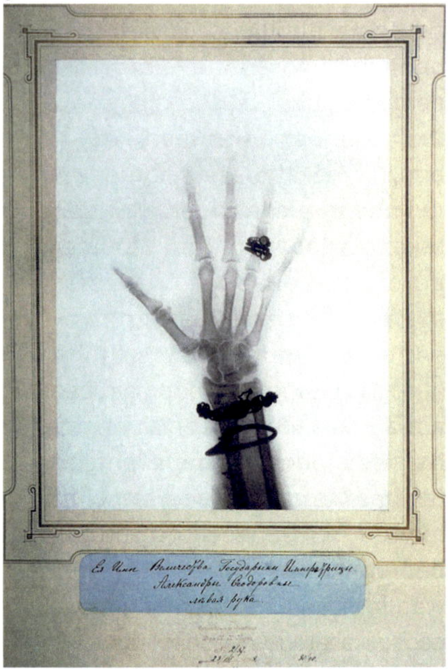

4 Wilhelm Röntgen, X-ray photograph of the left hand of his wife Anna Bertha Ludwig with wedding ring, 22 December 1895
5 Wilhelm Röntgen, X-ray photograph of the hand of Professor Albert von Kölliker, January 1896
6 X-ray of the hand and wrist of Alexandra, Empress of Russia, ca. 1898
7 X-rays of the hands of King Georges and Queen Mary, plate from the *Illustrated London News*, April 30, 1896

7

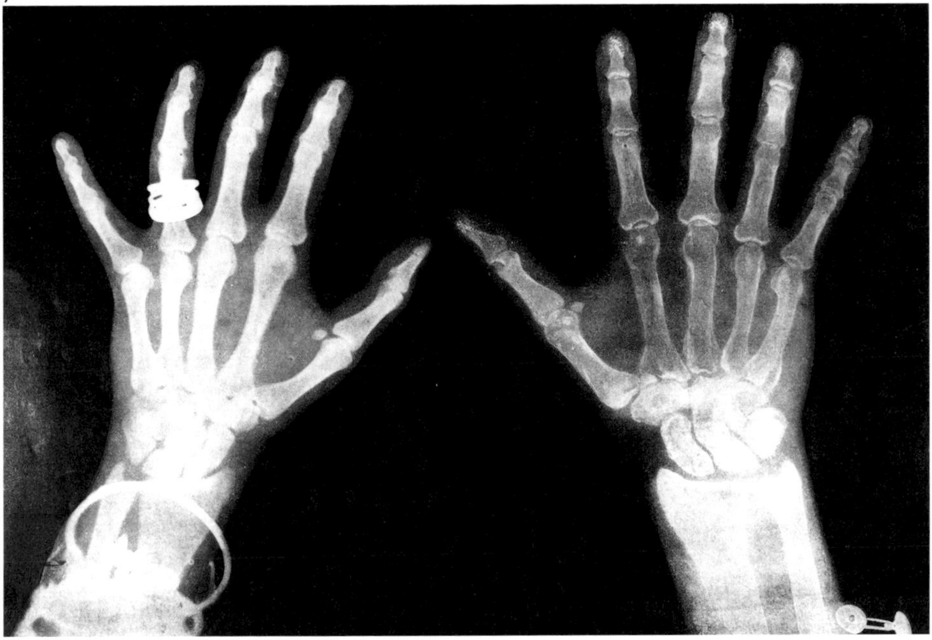

A poem in *Life* magazine on March 12, 1896, captures this new intimacy as the body becomes a halo, "misty in line":

Lines on an X-ray Portrait of a Lady

She is so tall, so slender; and her bones—
Those frail phosphates, those carbonates of lime—
Are well produced by cathode rays sublime,
By oscillations, amperes, and by ohms.
Her dorsal vertebrae are not concealed
By epidermis, but are well revealed.
Around her ribs, those beauteous twenty-four,
Her flesh a halo makes, misty in line,
Her noseless, eyeless face looks into mine,
And I but whisper, "Sweetheart, je t'adore."
Her white and gleaming teeth at me do laugh.
Ah! Lovely, cruel, sweet cathode-a-graph!

Röntgen had named the mysterious phenomenon "X-rays" because he didn't know what they were. Kölliker had proposed, after Röntgen's Würzburg lecture, that the new rays be called "Röntgen rays," but self-effacing Röntgen preferred to continue to call them X-rays. The justification of the term "rays," he claimed in that first article, lay in the "shadow pictures" produced by interposing a body between the source of the X rays and a photographic plate or a screen. He wrote that in the two months before he X-rayed his wife's hand, he had "observed and photographed many such shadow pictures," including a set of weights inside a wooden box and a compass card and needle completely enclosed in a metal case.[9]

Röntgen considered this ability to make photographs of the "shadow pictures" on the screen of "special interest," because it made it possible to "exhibit the phenomena so as to exclude the danger of error."[10] The main advantage for him, therefore, was to provide proof, to confirm the observations already made multiple times with the fluorescent screen. Soon after its initial publication, he sent reprints of the article together with prints of the X-ray images he had taken to many scientists, including Emil Warburg in Berlin and Henri Poincaré in Paris.[11] Warburg immediately added the X-ray images to an exhibition that was mounted on the occasion of the anniversary of the Berlin Physical Society at Berlin University. This was the first public exhibition of X-ray images.

Without these images, the discovery of the X-rays would have had less of an impact in both scientific and lay circles. It was front-page news in many newspapers world-wide. FIG. 7 On January 5, 1886, *Die Presse* in Vienna was the first to report on the discovery, with an article entitled "Eine Sensationelle Entdeckung" (A sensational discovery).[12] In their haste, they misspelled Röntgen's name as "Routgen." The next day, *The Standard* newspaper in London cabled the following news release to the world, repeating the misspelled name and misidentifying Bertha's hand as that of a man:

> The noise of war's alarm should not distract attention from the marvellous triumph of Science which is reported from Vienna. It is announced that Professor Routgen of Würzburg has discovered a light which, for the purpose of photography, will penetrate wood, flesh and most other organic substances. The Professor has succeeded in photographing metal weights which were in a closed wooden case, also a man's hand, which shows only the bones, the flesh being invisible.[13]

When *The Standard* reported on the story in the newspaper of January 7, 1896, they felt obliged to add: "The *Presse* assures its readers that there is no joke or humbug in the matter. It is a serious discovery by a serious German Professor."[14] The *Frankfurter Zeitung* published the news, also on January 7, and was the first to print the images. Newspapers around the world, from *Le Matin and L'Illustration* in Paris, to the Krakow-based *Czas,* to the *New York Times, St. Louis Dispatch,* and *Sydney Telegraph,* among many others, continued to sensationalize the discovery and anticipate its

8, 9 Josef Maria Eder and Eduard Valenta, *Photographie mittelst der Röntgen-Strahlen*, 1896, cover and Chamäleon cristatus
10 Spread from L. Moholy-Nagy, *Malerei, Fotografie, Film*, Bauhausbücher 8, 1925

medical uses, something about which Röntgen was skeptical. Since only text could be sent by cable telegraphy, most of these early overseas reports where not illustrated, also prompting skepticism among readers and journalists. *Czas*, for example, wrote: "the problem, although it seems an All Fools' Day joke, is seriously considered in serious circles."[15]

A MAGIC SCREEN

Following Röntgen's invention, many people developed techniques for photographing the X-ray effect. Röntgen had refused several offers to patent his discovery, declaring that it belonged to humanity. Sadly, he died in near poverty. From the beginning, he provided detailed accounts of his method, allowing others to experiment. Within a month of Röntgen's publication, Josef Maria Eder (director of an Austrian institute for graphic processes and author of an early history of photography)[16] and the photo chemist Eduard Valenta published *Versuche über Photographie mittelst der Röntgen'schen Strahlen* (Research on photography with Röntgen rays), **FIG. 8** an album of fifteen photogravures made from X-rays, in which they described in great detail the procedure used and the improvements they had made to Röntgen's apparatus.[17] Human hands and feet, fish, frogs, a snake, a chameleon, **FIG. 9** a lizard, a rat, and a newborn rabbit were among the images in this album, a kind of zoo echoing nineteenth-century naturalist albums of animals, insects, and plants, but also anticipating the "new vision" of photography of Moholy-Nagy and others in the 1920s. **FIG. 10** This new vision of photography would also become encyclopedic.

8

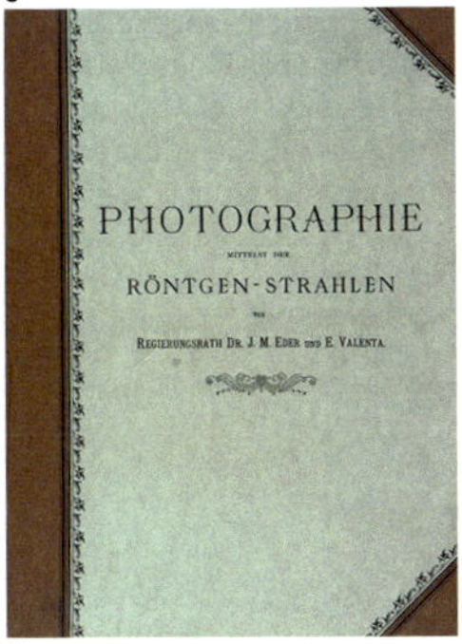
PHOTOGRAPHIE
RÖNTGEN-STRAHLEN
REGIERUNGSRATH DR. J. M. EDER UND E. VALENTA.

9

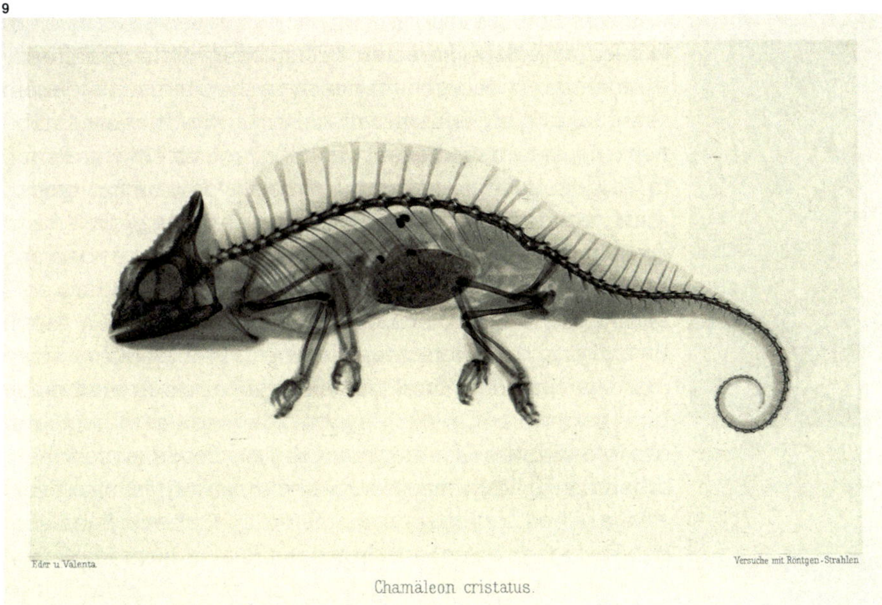
Eder u. Valenta.
Versuche mit Röntgen-Strahlen
Chamäleon cristatus.

10

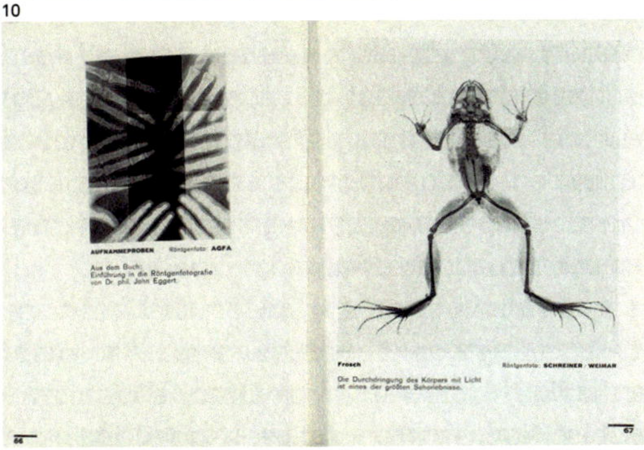
AUFNAHMEPROBEN
Röntgenfoto: AGFA
Aus dem Buch:
Einführung in die Röntgenfotografie
von Dr. phil. John Eggert.
66
Frosch
Röntgenfoto: SCHREINER / WEIMAR
Die Durchdringung des Körpers mit Licht
ist eines der größten Seherlebnisse.
67

11 Annie Besant, theosophist and women's rights activist, 1885
12 Annie Besant and C. W. Leadbeater, "Forms Produced by Pendulums," illustration in *Thought-Forms,* 1901
13 L. Aubert, "Radioscopic Shadow of a Thorax in Expiration," in *La Photographie de l'Invisible: Les rayons X suivi d'un glossaire, les livres d'or de la science,* 1898
14 L. Aubert, "Shadow on a fluorescent screen of a frog fixed with pins on a sheet of cork"
15 L. Aubert, *La Photographie de l'Invisible: Les rayons X suivi d'un glossaire, les livres d'or de la science,* 1898, cover
16 August Dittmar, *Prof. Röntgen's "X" RAYS and their applications in the New Photography,* 1896

11

12

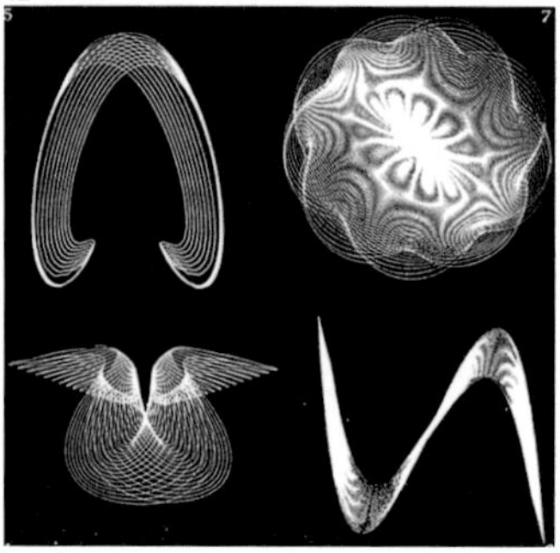

It was as if the whole world had to be seen again, or more precisely, as if it were a whole new world. Moholy-Nagy would later write:

> The passion for transparencies is one of the most spectacular features of our time. In x-ray photos, structure becomes transparency and transparency manifests structure. The x-ray pictures, to which the futurist has consistently referred, are among the outstanding space-time renderings on the static plane. They give simultaneously the inside and outside, the view of an opaque solid, its outline, but also its inner structure.[18]

What interests me here is how X-ray images had transformed the visual field long before the so-called avant-garde. The X-ray was a new kind of realism, a realism that was in no way in opposition to a new kind of mysticism or spiritualism. William Crookes, the scientist who developed the cathode-ray tube used by Röntgen, was the president of the Society for Psychical Research and within a year of the discovery of X-rays announced that they produced a new sense of reality based not on outer surfaces, but inner vibrations, closer to consciousness itself, as Linda Henderson has pointed out.[19] The Theosophist and women's rights activist Annie Besant was likewise trying to give visible form to the invisible. Not by chance, many of the images of what she called "thought-forms" have the appearance of X-rays.[20] **FIGS. 11, 12** The X-ray was an optical and philosophical revolution that swept the world at astonishing speed. The first

13

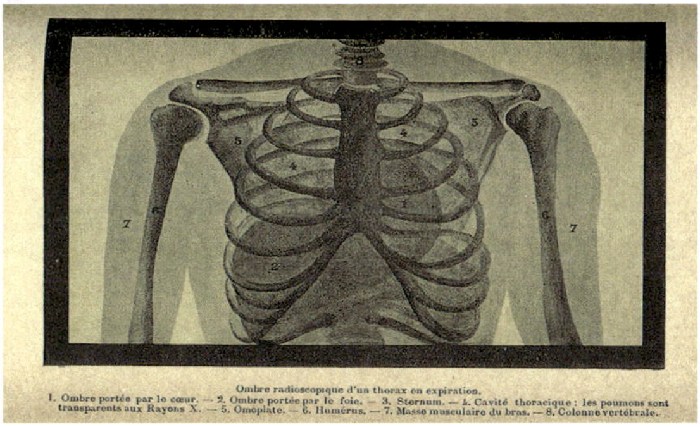

14

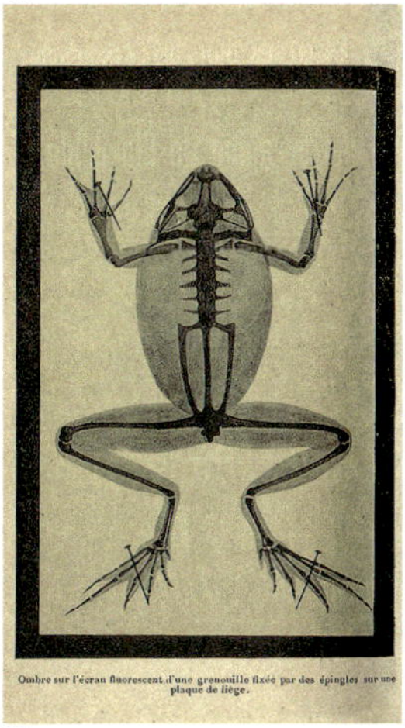

15

16

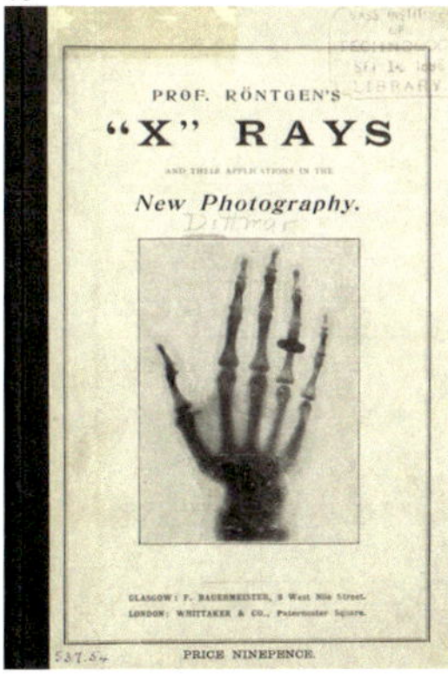

surgery with X-rays was carried out in the United States within two months of the discovery, and the first fully fledged department of radiology was established at the Glasgow Royal Infirmary within a year. **FIG. 17**

It is important to note that in the albums of X-rays that proliferated everywhere at the turn of the century, X-rays were still presented as images of screens. Even books aimed at popularizing science, such as the 1898 French book *La photographie de l'invisible,* **FIG. 15** carefully note below each image that it is a "shadow on a screen." For example, under the X-ray of a frog we read: "shadow on a fluorescent screen of a frog fixed with pins on a sheet of cork" **FIG. 14** or "shadow of a hand on a screen of platinum cyanide of barium."[21] The caption is needed because the screen itself disappears, since the paper support of the screen has the same color as the page in the publication. The caption reminds the reader that there is a screen there, a screen that was originally chemicals on paper. The "shadow image" takes the place and the modality of a drawing, a ghostly trace hanging before the viewer and offering a deep gaze into the secrets of a body or even of the cosmos itself. **FIG. 13** The floating, disappearing screen becomes the most powerful of instruments.

Röntgen was fascinated that he could also produce the effect directly on a photographic plate. **FIG. 16** Within a year of the discovery of X-rays, Eastman developed a special plate for X-rays and a thin transparent surface would eventually take over the responsibility of the screen when Eastman introduced film, replacing the glass photographic plate. But the doubling, the eerie status of the shadow image,

17

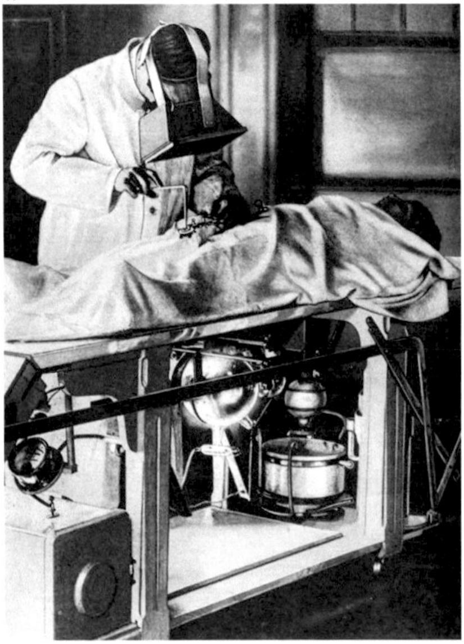

18

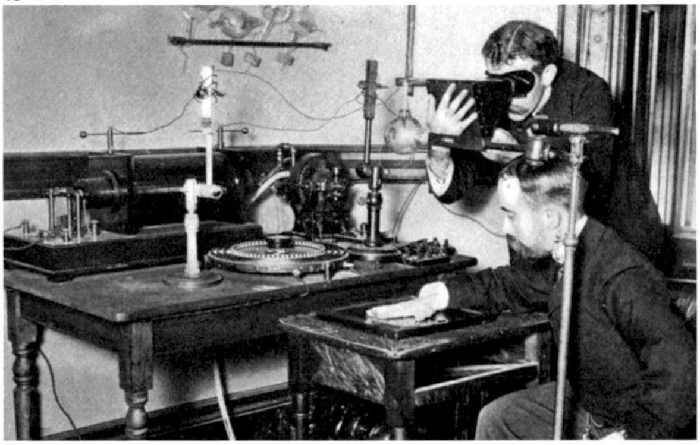

19

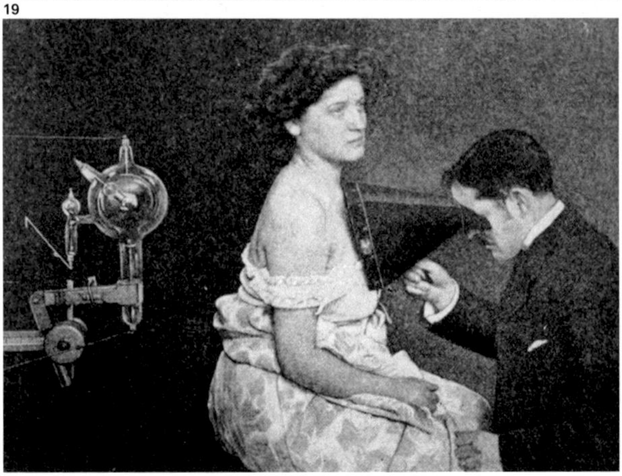

17 Surgical operation during World War I using a fluoroscope to find embedded bullets, 1917
18 Experimenter (top right) examining his hand with fluoroscope, 1890s
19 Fluoroscopy of the chest, *New York Medical Journal*, February 23, 1907

remained. The photograph of Bertha's hand was the image of an image, the proof of what Röntgen had seen countless times on the screen. It is still the image of the screen. This magical and threatening screen effect rippled through society, becoming a new form of spectacle. It was as if nothing could be seen the same way. Everything needed to be rethought. Every field seemed to be affected by the magic screen—science and medicine, of course, but also policing and entertainment, religion and spiritualism, where many seized upon the X-ray as proof of what they believed all along.

The screen was a site of intense speculation. From the very beginning, this visual revolution was understood as an assault on privacy and even a form of indecency. **FIG. 19** The London newspaper *Pall Mall Gazette* wrote in 1896: "We are sick of the Röntgen rays.... It is now said that you can see other people's bones with the naked eye.... On the revolting indecency of this there is no need to dwell."[22] Cartoons and comical poems explored the new space of exposure. The fear that X-rays would allow people to see through clothing was there from the beginning. Another poem of 1896, this time in *Electrical Review* goes:

X-ACTLY SO!

The Roentgen Rays, the Roentgen Rays,
What is this craze?
The town's ablaze
With the new phase
Of X-ray's ways.

20

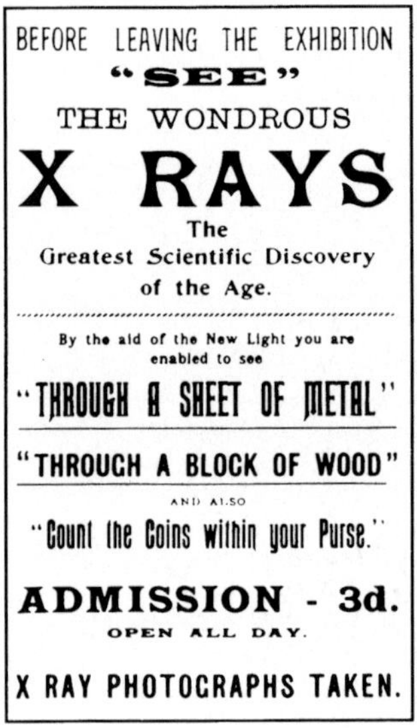

I'm full of daze,
Shock and amaze;
For nowadays
I hear they'll gaze
Thro' cloak and gown—and even stays,
These naughty, naughty Roentgen Rays.[23]

Shortly after the invention, merchants offered X-ray–proof underwear (as happened again in more recent years when customs and security introduced full-body scanners in airports). And a New Jersey assemblyman is supposed to have introduced a bill to ban X-ray opera glasses, should they ever be invented. Thomas Edison, who exhibited X-rays to the public in the New York Electrical Exhibition of 1896, even imagined that the X-ray would eventually read people's thoughts.

The X-ray was also an immense form of entertainment. There were X-ray machines in every scientific and popular fair. A leaflet distributed at an 1896 exhibition at the Crystal Palace, London, reads: "BEFORE LEAVING THE EXHIBITION, 'SEE', THE WONDROUS X RAYS. The Greatest Scientific Discovery of the Age.... X RAY PHOTOGRAPHS TAKEN." **FIG. 20** In Paris, the *Grands Magasins Dufayel* alternated demonstrations of an X-ray machine with demonstrations of the Lumière brothers' moving pictures. **FIG. 21** Customers could have an X-ray taken of their hand or their feet as a souvenir.

In fact, cinematography and X-rays were discovered within a few months of each other, in late 1895. X-ray equipment was bought not just by scientists, but by entrepre-

20 Leaflet announcing X-ray demonstrations, distributed at a 1896 exhibition at the Crystal Palace, London
21 Advertisement of the Grands Magasins Dufayel, announcing daily cinematographic and X-ray performances, ca. 1880

21

22 Customs officers using X-rays to inspect luggage in Paris, 1897
23 A technician takes an X-ray of a patient in 1940. This image was used to argue that radiation exposure during X-raying was negligible
24 X-ray device is used to expose a woman hiding a bottle of liquor under her dress, 1897

neurs, some of whom believed that X-rays would offer more entertainment value than the cinema. Business trade journals carried ads from impresarios trying to exchange their movie projectors for X-ray equipment.[24] In 1896, Bloomingdales hired Columbia University physics senior Herbert Hawks to conduct public demonstrations of the X-rays. There were X-ray studios in all major cities. Coin-operated X-ray machines were installed in Chicago, where you could have an X-ray for one dollar.

It was a nervous kind of entertainment. The X-ray had undone the logic of what is private and what is public. It represented a complete transformation not just of privacy, but also of public life. Changing what is seen is equally a changing of what is shared—willingly or not. In that sense, it was a shock to social life and unleashed fears of intrusion and control.

BUILDING THE NEW VISUAL FIELD

X-rays were almost immediately used for policing in customs checkpoints, where suitcases and people were subjected to exposure. In Paris railways stations, the police subjected passengers and their luggage to X-rays as early as 1898. FIG. 22 An illustration in a Parisian newspaper shows how a woman hiding a bottle of liquor under her dress is exposed by the machine as the glass with lead becomes visible next to her femur in the X-ray. FIG. 24 What is crucial here is the architecture of the scene. She is suspended behind a floating screen held in place by the assistant. She is occupying a new space of radical exposure.

22

23

24

The X-ray thus was architectural from the beginning and remains so, as can be seen in image after image, like the photograph of an attractive blond woman behind a screen made in 1940 as a publicity image to reassure the public that radiation from X-rays was negligible. **FIG. 23**

She is occupying a new technological space defined by a screen, rather than by walls, a glowing screen with its shadow image. We are still in the territory of Bertha Röntgen and the ur-image of her hand. The mysteries of the interior are brought to the surface by a screen, and the flesh becomes just a faint outline. The body is literally turned inside out.

Western architecture, at least since the Italian Renaissance, has modeled itself on the human body, but the body is inverted with the arrival of X-ray—with the inside becoming the outside. Modern architecture absorbed the logic of the screen and even of the shadow image. Glass architecture echoes the logic of the X-ray. There is an outer screen that disappears in order to register a ghostly image of the inside. It is X-ray architecture. As with Röntgen's transformative images, X-ray architecture is an image of an image—the effect of an X-ray, rather than an actual X-ray. It's not so much that the inside of the building is exposed, but that the building represents exposure, and this exposure occurs on a screen. Glass is called on to simulate transparency.

This X-ray effect was integral to a new discourse about transparency. Arthur Korn's extraordinary 1929 book *Glas im Bau und als Gebrauchsgegenstand* (Glass in construction and as a commodity), **FIG. 26** translated into English as *Glass*

25 Walter Gropius, Bauhaus Dessau, 1920s, illustration in Arthur Korn, *Glas im Bau und als Gebrauchsgegenstand*, 1929
26 Arthur Korn, *Glas im Bau und als Gebrauchsgegenstand*, 1929, cover

25

26

in Modern Architecture, catalogues the new use of glass in architecture in 181 remarkable images, including not just architecture, but some furniture, light bulbs, and laboratory equipment. Korn notes, as if surprised:

> The outside wall is no longer the first impression one gets of a building. It is the interior, the spaces in depth and the structural frame which delineates them, that one begins to notice through the glass wall. This wall is barely visible, and can only be seen when there are reflected lights, distortions or mirror effects.... Glass is noticeable yet not quite visible. It is the great membrane, full of mystery, delicate yet tough.[25]

This sense of mystery, which X-rays share, infuses Korn's book, as in a photograph of the Bauhaus building in Dessau where the glass wall is a kind of ripple. FIG. 25 The volume of the building within looms without definition, an effect found throughout the book.

Korn's discussion of transparency is an uncanny echo of Röntgen's discussion of new forms of transparency in the first publication of his discovery of X-rays. Just as the body of the Bauhaus building appears, in this photograph, strangely blurry through the not-quite-visible glass, Röntgen writes about the flesh becoming a kind of mysterious shadow while the bones are perfectly visible.

Modern buildings even started to look like medical images. The impact of the technology of the X-ray is evident in the work of many avant-garde architects of the early decades of the twentieth century. Mies van der Rohe wrote about his work as "skin and bones" architecture and rendered his projects for the Friedrichstrasse Skyscraper of 1919 and his Glass Skyscraper of 1922 as if seen through an X-ray machine. **FIG. 28** Mies was deeply interested in X-ray images and used them as illustrations in his articles, as in the April 1926 issue of *G*, where the silhouette of the head of a woman appears next to the X-ray of the same head.[26] **FIG. 27** He even put an image of a bone alongside his glass skyscraper in an issue of the magazine *Merz* to drive the point home.[27] **FIG. 29**

Mies was not alone. Books on modern architecture are filled with images of glowing glass skins revealing inner bones and organs; they look like albums of X-rays, reminiscent of the X-ray atlases that proliferated in the early decades of the twentieth century.[28] Think, for example, about Le Corbusier's project for the Glass Skyscraper (1925) **FIG. 31**, Walter Gropius and Adolf Meyer's Bauhaus (1925–1926), Brinkman and van der Vlugt's Van Nelle Factory (1925–1927) in Rotterdam **FIG. 33**, Erich Mendelsohn's Schocken Department Store (1926–1928) in Stuttgart **FIG. 32**, Buckminster Fuller's 4D Tower (1928) **FIG. 36**, George Keck's Crystal House (1933–1934) at the World's Columbian Exhibition in Chicago **FIG. 35**, Paul Nelson's Suspended House (1935), Frits Peutz's Schunck Glass Palace (1935) in Heerlen **FIG. 37**, Jaromír Krejcar's Czech pavilion at the International Exhibition in Paris (1937) **FIG. 30**, and countless other examples. This is more than a dominant aesthetic. It is a symptom of a deep-seated philosophy of design deriving from medical discourse.

27

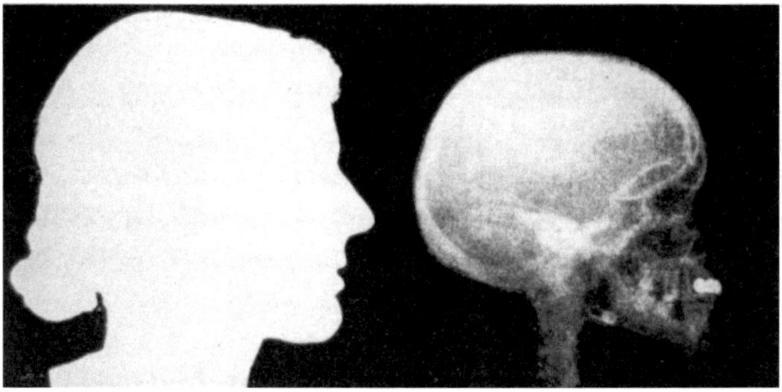

28

27 Silhouette and X-ray of the same head, used as illustration in Mies van der Rohe's article in *G: Zeitschrift für elementare Gestaltung*, no. 5–6, April 1926
28 Mies van der Rohe, Glass Skyscraper, Berlin, 1922, photomontage
29 Double spread of *Merz*, no. 8–9, April–July 1924, pp. 81–82

29

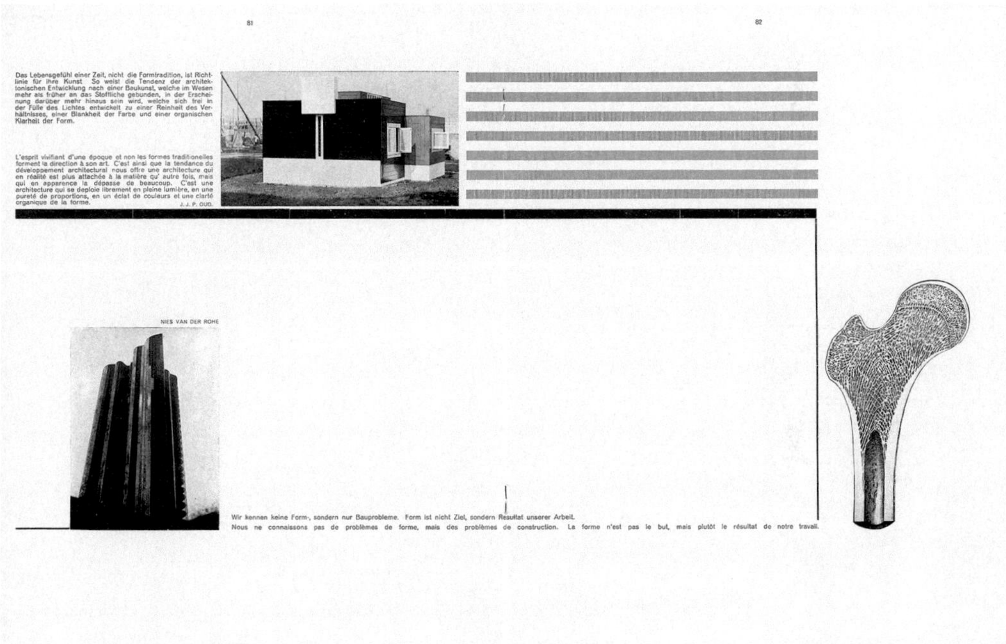

81

82

Das Lebensgefühl einer Zeit, nicht die Formtradition, ist Richtlinie für ihre Kunst. So weist die Tendenz der architektonischen Entwicklung nach einer Baukunst, welche im Wesen mehr als früher an das Stoffliche gebunden, in der Erscheinung darüber mehr hinaus sein wird, welche sich frei in der Fülle des Lichtes entwickelt zu einer Reinheit des Verhältnisses, einer Blankheit der Farbe und einer organischen Klarheit der Form.

L'esprit vivifiant d'une époque et non les formes traditionelles forment la direction à son art. C'est ainsi que la tendance du développement architectural nous offre une architecture qui en réalité est plus attachée à la matière qu' autre fois, mais qui en apparence la dépasse de beaucoup. C'est une architecture qui se deploie librement en pleine lumière, en une pureté de proportions, en un éclat de couleurs et une clarté organique de la forme.

J. J. P. OUD.

MIES VAN DER ROHE

Wir kennen keine Form-, sondern nur Bauprobleme. Form ist nicht Ziel, sondern Resultat unserer Arbeit.
Nous ne connaissons pas de problèmes de forme, mais des problèmes de construction. La forme n'est pas le but, mais plutôt le résultat de notre travail.

30

31

32

33

34

30 Jaromir Krejcar, Czech pavilion at the Paris World Exhibition of 1937
31 Le Corbusier's project for the Glass Skyscraper, 1925
32 Erich Mendelsohn, Schocken store, Stuttgart, Germany, 1926–1928
33 Brinkman and van der Vlugt's Van Nelle Factory in Rotterdam, 1925–1927
34 Bernard Bijvoet and Pierre Chareau, Maison de Verre, Paris, 1932
35 George Keck, Crystal House, 1933–1934, exhibited at the World's Columbian Exhibition in Chicago, 1934. A Dymaxion car by R. Buckminster Fuller is parked in the garage.
36 R. Buckminster Fuller, Streamlined Dymaxion Shelter prototype, 1932
37 Frits Peutz, Schunck Glass Palace, Heerlen, the Netherlands, 1935

35

36

37

38

39

Maison de Verre, the house and clinic in a Paris courtyard for the prominent gynecologist Dr. Jean Dalsace, designed by Bernard Bijvoet and Pierre Chareau from 1928 to 1932, is especially emblematic of this resonance between architecture and medicine, with the internal elements of the building revealed like organs through the translucent glass-block facade in a ghostly X-ray effect. FIG. 34 Not by chance, Dalsace was very engaged with radiography and published articles on it in medical journals during the house's construction.[29]

The development of the X-ray and that of modern architecture coincide; they evolved in parallel. Although experiments with glass were numerous in the early years of the twentieth century, they still tended to be isolated esoteric projects by avant-garde architects—many developed as temporary buildings for fairs. Only by the mid–twentieth century did the see-through house become realized in Mies's Farnsworth House (1945–1951) in Plano, Illinois, FIG. 38 and Philip Johnson's Glass House (1949) in New Canaan, Connecticut, FIG. 39 for example. Just as the X-ray exposes the inside of the body to the public eye, the glass house exposes its interior. This exposure became a mass phenomenon with the ubiquitous picture window of the suburban American house at midcentury, perhaps not by chance at exactly the same time that the X-ray itself became a mass phenomenon.

By midcentury, the mass X-raying of US citizens on a regular basis was established. With this development, the now-visible interior of the body became not just a tool for diagnosis, but also the site of a new form of public surveillance. The postwar mobilization against TB included pro-

38 Mies van der Rohe, Farnsworth House, Piano, Illinois, 1949
39 Philip Johnson, Glass House, New Canaan, CT, 1949
40 "Helping those who help the sick," advertisement for mobile X-ray unit published in *Life* magazine, December 1945
41 Dr. Scholl's Fluoroscopic Shoe X-Ray, 1940s
42 "Cooking Taught with Loving Care," advertisement for Pyrex, 1940
43 Ad for transparent plastic wrap Pliofilm, developed by Goodyear in 1934

40

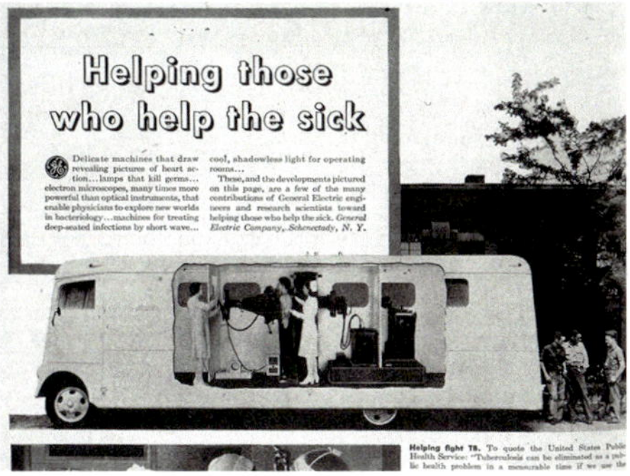

41

grams for the mass X-ray surveying of the entire population using mobile X-ray machines in places such as department stores, industries, schools, suburban streets, and public markets. **FIG. 40** Over a period of a half century, an experimental medical tool had been transformed into a mechanism of surveillance for the whole population.

42

This was more than a medical paradigm. Shoe stores, for example, used X-ray machines for shoe fittings without any kind of protection from radioactivity. **FIG. 41** The machines were not banned in the United States until the 1970s. X-rays had evolved from being radical images representing the hidden truth of things to become almost routine elements of everyday life.

43

At exactly the same time, everything, not just the house, all of a sudden needed to be see-through: from Pyrex cookware and Saran Wrap to windows in ovens and washing machines that expose their contents. **FIGS. 42, 43** Likewise, everything had to be subjected to X-rays—even cars, as in a 1946 image of a Jeep featured in *Life* magazine as the "World's Biggest X-Ray"[30] **FIG. 45** and appropriated by the Independent Group to be used in the exhibition "Parallel of Life and Art" at the Institute of Contemporary Arts in London in 1953. The front cover of the catalogue of this exhibition was a 1941 X-ray image of a man using an electric shaver, taken from László Moholy-Nagy's 1947 book *Vision in Motion*, where it is described as the work of two doctors in a New Jersey laboratory. **FIG. 44** The image had been published in *Mechanix Illustrated*, which is where Moholy-Nagy found it. But he also took images of X-rays from a 1923 issue of

44

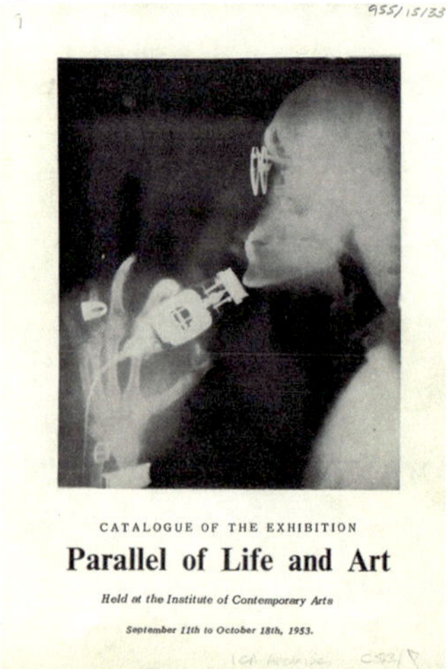
CATALOGUE OF THE EXHIBITION
Parallel of Life and Art
Held at the Institute of Contemporary Arts
September 11th to October 18th, 1953.

45

WORLD'S BIGGEST X-RAY
Huge machine records life-size image of jeep

44 Catalogue of the exhibition *Parallel of Life and Art* held at the Institute of Contemporary Arts, September 11 to October 18, 1953
45 "World's biggest X-Ray," life size X-ray image of a jeep, *Life* magazine, March 25, 1946
46 Stills from *Highlights and Shadows* by James Sibley Watson, Jr., Kodak, 1937

46

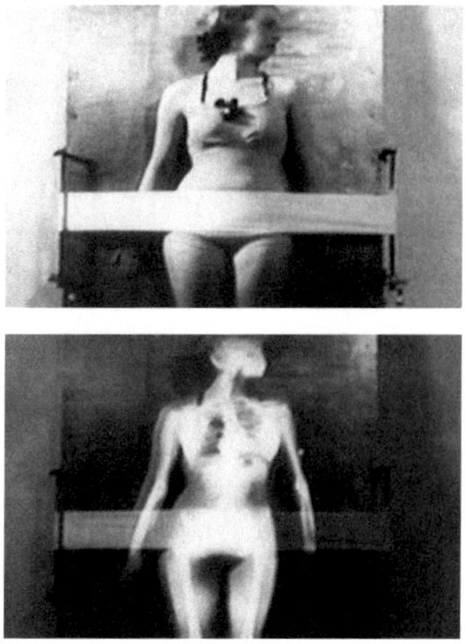

Wendingen magazine. In fact, architectural magazines had an eye on X-ray images from early on. It is as if X-rays had steadily infiltrated and transformed diverse popular, professional, scientific, and artistic discourses—virally expanding from a new way of seeing the world to a new world, from diagnosis to symptom, or even as generator of symptoms.

GLASS TERROR

The association between X-rays and glass houses became commonplace in midcentury popular culture. For example, in *Highlights and Shadows*, a 1937 Kodak Research Laboratories film on the virtues of X-rays for disease prevention by the filmmaker-radiographer James Sibley Watson, Jr., a woman wearing a swimsuit is shown strapped to a laboratory table while her body is subjected to X-rays. As her photographic image gives way to the image of her X-rayed body, the narrator declares: "This young lady, to whom henceforth a glass house should hold no terrors, will after an examination of her radiographs, be reassured that she is indeed physically fit."[31] **FIG. 46** The glass house acted as a symbol of both the new form of surveillance and health.

A similar set of associations can be found in the discourse surrounding canonical works of modern architecture. In an interview in *House Beautiful,* Edith Farnsworth, a successful doctor in Chicago, compared her famous weekend house, designed by Mies in 1949, to an X-ray:

> I don't keep a garbage can under my sink. Do you know why? Because you can see the whole "kitchen" from the

47

48

> road on the way in here and the can would spoil the appearance of the whole house. So I hide it in the closet further down from the sink. Mies talks about "free space": but his space is very fixed. I can't even put a clothes hanger in my house without considering how it affects everything from the outside. Any arrangement of furniture becomes a major problem, because the house is transparent, like an X-ray.[32] **FIGS. 47, 48**

Modern architecture was again understood as a piece of medical equipment. While the house was for Farnsworth like an X-ray, the nearby village thought of the white building full of glass as a sanatorium. Farnsworth goes on to claim: "There is already the local rumor that it's a tuberculosis sanatorium."[33]

The association was not accidental. Modern architecture not only thought of itself as providing sanatorium conditions for everyday life, but even thought of buildings as diagnostic instruments with the power of an X-ray. As Le Corbusier already had put it in *L'Art décoratif d'aujourd'hui* in 1925: "If the house is all white ... everything stands out from it and is recorded absolutely, black on white; it is honest and dependable.... It is rather like an X-ray of beauty."[34]

The metaphor of the X-ray was not accidental, either. Diagnosis of tuberculosis continued to be difficult in the 1920s. Physicians often confused it with other illnesses, including bronchitis, chronic indigestion, malaria, neurasthenia, and typhoid fever. To evaluate the condition, they needed to see inside the body. X-ray technology, which had

47 Mies van der Rohe, Farnsworth House, 1949, exterior view of kitchen
48 Mies van der Rohe, Farnsworth House, 1949, interior view of kitchen
49 Stills from *Mass Radiography*, 1944
50 Advertisement for Victor Roentgen Stand, Model 3, 1920

49

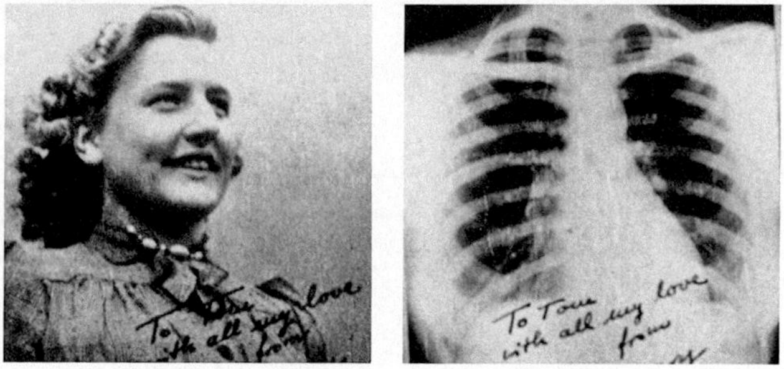

50

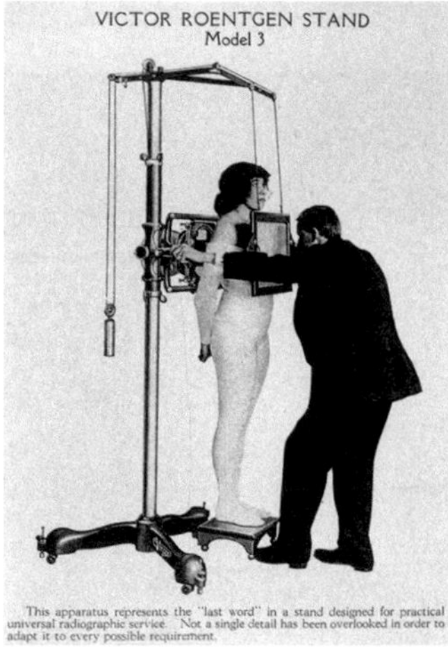

been available in sanatoriums since the beginning of the century, became by the 1920s a routine part of the examination of those with visible symptoms. Screening the body for tuberculosis meant optically penetrating areas of the body previously invisible. X-rays created a new kind of vision, a new paradigm of the inside/outside relationship. Nothing could have been more architectural.

The discourse about transparency in modern architecture is an echo of the discourse about transparency that was part of Röntgen's first scientific paper announcing the discovery of X-rays in 1895 and immediately captivating the popular imagination. The ability to see through material challenged all assumptions and social protocols about privacy and psychological well-being and therefore all architectural concepts of shelter and comfort. Everyone became a permanent patient in need of a new kind of medical domesticity. The intrusive logic of medical and police surveillance, with the body unable to resist a newly penetrating gaze, gave way to a tender intimacy. The attempt to discipline the body—with a new regime of synchronized medical, technological, and architectural protocols—also produced new psychological, social, philosophical, and emotional interactions to which architects responded. **FIGS. 49–51**

Just as the X-ray exposes the inside of the body to the public eye, the modern building exposed its interior. What was previously private is now subjected to public scrutiny. But the X-ray is not simply an image of the body. It is an image of the body being imaged. The X-ray is not simply about showing an inside. The exterior envelope is still a kind

51 Winning models Marianne Baba (*left*), Lois Conway (*center*) and Ruth Swensen (*right*) standing next to plates of their X-rays during a chiropractor beauty contest, *Life* magazine, May 1956

51

of shadow or a blur, and you feel yourself looking through it. To look at an X-ray is to feel your eye penetrating the surface of the body. The very act of looking is exposed. You feel the eye moving through space. It is inevitably voyeuristic. Perhaps that's what attracted architects to the X-rays from the beginning. In glass architecture, the glass is never completely transparent. Even at night, you feel the outer limit of the building and your eye passing through that limit. You feel the exposure. Modern architecture exposes itself, but not by revealing everything. Rather, it stages the act of exposure, calling the eye in.

The seemingly fragile cloudy space of the X-ray becomes an architecture in its own right that can be inhabited and is inhabited. All the ostensible sharpness and clarity of modern architecture gives way to soft layers of reflections and translucencies. X-ray architecture is an occupiable blur.

1 Susan Sontag Archives, UCLA, Box 43. In *Illness as Metaphor* (New York: Farrar, Straus and Giroux, 1977), p. 33, she wrote: "The TB sufferer was a dropout, a wanderer."
2 Sontag, *Illness as Metaphor,* p. 12.
3 Thomas Mann, *The Magic Mountain* (New York: Alfred Knopf, 1945), pp. 348–49.
4 Wilhelm Röntgen, "On a New Kind of Rays," *Nature,* January 23, 1896, p. 275; English translation of the 1895 original text "Über eine neue Art von Strahlen" published in *Sitzungsberichte der Physikalisch-Medizinischen Gesellschaft in Würzburg* 137, December 28, 1895, pp. 132–41.
5 Röntgen, "On a New Kind of Rays," p. 274.
6 Ibid. p. 274
7 The original article did not include illustrations, but the English version published in *Nature* a few weeks later did.
8 Multiple sources repeat this story, including Gottfried Landwehr and A. Hasse, eds., *Röntgen Centennial: X-rays in Natural and Life Sciences* (Singapore: World Scientific, 1997), pp. 7–8.
9 Röntgen, "On a New Kind of Rays," p. 276
10 Ibid., p. 274
11 Röntgen also sent the reprint and images to the Arthur Schuster in Manchester, Friedrich Kohlrauch in Göttingen, Lord Kelvin in Glasgow, and Franz Exner in Vienna.
12 It was Franz Exner who alerted the Vienna newspaper to Röntgen's discovery.
13 *Electrical Engineer,* New York, January 8, 1896, quoted in Otto Glaser, *Wilhelm Conrad Röntgen and the Early History of the Roentgen Rays* (San Francisco: Norman, 1993), p. 199.
14 *The Standard* (London), January 7, 1896, quoted in Glaser, *Wilhelm Conrad Röntgen and the Early History of the Roentgen Rays,* p. 200.
15 Quoted in A. Urbanik, "History of Polish Gastrointestinal Radiology," *Journal of Physiology and Pharmacology.* 54, no. 3 (2003), p. 211, and in "The Beginnings of Radiology in Poland—19th Century," Polish Medical Society of Radiology, polradiology.org., https://archive.li/z7zl.
16 Josef Maria Eder, *Ausführliches Handbuch der Photographie* (Halle: W. Knapp, 1884).
17 Josef Maria Eder and Eduard Valenta, *Versuche über Photographie mittelst der Röntgen'schen Strahlen* (Vienna: R. Lechner; Halle, Wilhelm Knapp, 1896).
18 László Moholy-Nagy, "Space-Time Problems," first published in *American Abstract Artists Yearbook* (New York, 1946). Reprinted in Moholy-Nagy, *Vision in Motion* (Chicago: P. Theobald, 1947), p. 252.
19 Linda Dalrymple Henderson, *Duchamp in Context: Science and Technology in the Large Glass and Related Works* (Princeton: Princeton University Press, 1998). See also Tom Gunning, "Invisible Worlds, Visible Media," in *Brought to Light: Photography and the Invisible 1840–1900,* ed. Corey Keller (New Haven: Yale University, 2008).
20 Annie Besant and C. W. Leadbeater, *Thought-Forms* (London: The Theosophical Publishing House, 1901).
21 L. Aubert, *La photographie de l'invisible: Les rayons X suivi d'un glossaire* (Paris: Les livres d'or de la science, 1898), frontispiece and p. 65.
22 *Pall Mall Gazette,* March 1896, quoted in Jon Queijo, *Breakthrough!: How the 10 Greatest Discoveries in Medicine Saved Millions and Changed Our View of the World* (London: FT Press, 2010), p. 99.
23 Wilhelma, *Electrical Review,* April 17, 1896, quoted in Akash Ganguly and Rezaul Karim, *Essential Physics For Radiology and Imaging* (Kolkata: Academic Publishers, 2009), p. iv.
24 Gunning, "Invisible Worlds," p. 52.
25 Arthur Korn, *Glass in Modern Architecture* (London: Barrie & Rockliff, 1967), p. 6.
26 Mies van der Rohe, "The Pure Form is the Natural," *G,* no. 5–6, April 1926.
27 *Merz,* no. 8–9, April–July 1924, pp. 81–82.
28 Rudolf Grashey's *Typische Röntgenbilder von normalen Menschen,* for example, went through six printings between 1905 and 1939. See Lorraine Daston and Peter Galison, "The Image of Objectivity," in "Seeing Science," special issue, *Representations* 40 (Autumn 1992), pp. 81–128.
29 Emma Cheatle, *Part-Architecture: The Maison de Verre, Duchamp, Domesticity and Desire in 1930s Paris* (London: Routledge, 2017), p. 112 n. 83.
30 "World's Biggest X-Ray: Huge Machine Records Life-Size Image of Jeep," *Life,* March 25, 1946, pp. 84–85. The X-ray taken at the University of Rochester laboratory was twelve feet, one inch long and four feet high.
31 James Sibley Watson, Jr., *Highlights and Shadows,* Kodak, 44 mins., black and white, 35 mm, 1937, quoted in Lisa Cartwright, *Screening the Body: Tracing Medicine's Visual Culture* (Minneapolis: University of Minnesota Press, 1995), p. 155.
32 Edith Farnsworth, quoted in Joseph A. Barry, "Report on the American Battle between Good and Bad Modern," *House Beautiful,* May 1953, p. 270.
33 Edith Farnsworth, "Memoirs" (unpublished manuscript), quoted in Alice T. Friedman, *Women and the Making of the Modern House: A Social and Architectural History* (New York: Abrams, 1998), p. 143.
34 Le Corbusier, *L'Art décoratif d'aujourd'hui* (Paris: G. Crès et Cie, 1925), p. 190, my translation.

CHAPTER 4

Blurred Visions

Transparency is not what it seems. The very act of looking through glass destabilizes the eye. Space now "fluctuates," as György Kepes put it in his *Language of Vision* (1944): "Transparency means a simultaneous perception of different spatial locations. Space not only recedes but fluctuates in a continuous activity."[1] Forms "interpenetrate" ambiguously without dissolving each other. They vibrate, forcing the brain of the viewer to speculate on what is there without ever being able to pin things down. In reverse, overlapping forms produce an effect of transparency. In Colin Rowe and Robert Slutzky's canonic reading of Kepes: "By definition, the transparent ceases to be that which is perfectly clear and instead becomes that which is clearly ambiguous."[2]

For example, at first sight, the work of SANAA, the office of Kazuyo Sejima and Ryue Nishizawa, appears as the perfect case of transparency in architecture and has been celebrated as such. In this sense, SANAA has inherited the Miesian tradition of radical transparency, absorbing and refining the X-ray effect. Take their Glass Pavilion (2006) in the Toledo Museum of Art, **FIG. 1** an all-glass pavilion for all-glass objects in the "Glass City," Toledo, Ohio. In the standard publicity image of the project, the white-trimmed pavilion sits in the park, uncannily echoing some of Mies's canonical projects, particularly the Farnsworth House and the Fifty-by-Fifty House. **FIG. 2** Mies famously deployed sheer glass walls to expose the interior. But what really fascinated architects such as Mies and those inspired by him, such as Philip Johnson, was not the way the gaze passes through the glass, but the way it seems to get caught in the layers of reflection.

1

2

3

1 SANAA, rendering of the Glass Pavilion at the Toledo Museum of Art, Ohio, 2006
2 Mies van der Rohe, model of Fifty-by-Fifty House, 1951–1952
3 Reflections in the Glass House, Philip Johnson, New Canaan, Connecticut, 1949
4, 5 Mies van der Rohe, model of the Glass Skyscraper, Berlin, 1922

In canonical photographs, Johnson's Glass House (1949) becomes opaque, clad in what he described as "wallpaper." **FIG. 3** In a 1961 television interview, Johnson said that the Glass House "works very well for the simple reason that the wallpaper is so handsome. It is perhaps a very expensive wallpaper, but you have wallpaper that changes every five minutes throughout the day and surrounds you with the beautiful nature that sometimes, not this year, Connecticut gives us."[3]

For Mies and Johnson, reflections consolidate the wall's plane. Complex lines of reflected trees become like the veins of marble in Mies's buildings. When explaining his Glass House, Johnson cited Mies' words from twenty-five years earlier, when Mies said: "I discovered by working with actual glass models that the important thing is the play of reflections and not the effect of light and shadow, as in ordinary buildings."[4] Mies must have been referring to the glass model of his Glass Skyscraper that he had repeatedly photographed in a garden in Berlin **FIGS. 4, 5** before arriving at the few canonical images released in 1922 that quickly went viral internationally in architectural magazines and books. It is hard to find an avant-garde magazine that didn't include at least one of the images. Most professional magazines feature them, as does every book on modern architecture. Not by chance, they are the opening images of Arthur Korn's 1929 book *Glas im Bau*. The images rapidly became an icon of modernity itself. The eye is pulled into the center of the image, through the glass to the skeleton, but the skeleton is not crystal clear. It is a kind of amorphous, murky presence.

4

5

6 Mies van der Rohe, Friedrichstrasse skyscraper project, 1921–1922
7 Mies van der Rohe, Friedrichstrasse skyscraper project, 1921
8 Mies van der Rohe, Sketch for a glass house on a hillside, 1934
9 Charles and Ray Eames, model of first version of Case Study House 8, which they called "Bridge House," 1948
10, 11 Reflections of trees on the glass facade of the Eames House, Pacific Palisades, California, 1949

6

7

The center of the image is totally obscure. The image stages exposure, but finally what is exposed is unclear. It is precisely this quality that makes it an X-ray.

The X-ray effect is not a sharply defined structure seen through an almost invisible surface, but rather a mysterious inner reality suspended in the ghostly medium of a translucent mass—an effect perfectly captured in the photomontages and even the huge charcoal renderings of the Friedrichstrasse Skyscraper of 1921 and the Glass Skyscraper of 1922. **FIGS. 6, 7**

Charles and Ray Eames also went to considerable trouble to study the reflections of the trees by placing a glass model of the initial project of the Eames House, the all-glass Bridge House of 1948 **FIG. 9** (which had been directly inspired by the unbuilt 1934 Glass House on a Hillside project by Mies), **FIG. 8** on the site of their future house in Santa Monica and photographing it from all angles.[5] The interior of the house becomes mysterious and blurred with the reflected exterior of trees and sky. The whole point is again not transparency, but blur. With the built version of the Eames house, the Eameses took Mies's experiment one step further. The glass plane is now broken, and the reflections of the eucalyptus tree endlessly multiply and relocate. The house dissolves in the play of reflections. As Ray said after thirteen years of living in the house, "The structure long ago ceased to exist. I am not aware of it."[6] They lived in reflections and the reflections of reflections.[7] **FIGS. 10, 11**

SANAA goes even further in producing a layering of reflection on the inside as well as the outside. The blurring

8

9

10

11

12

13

14

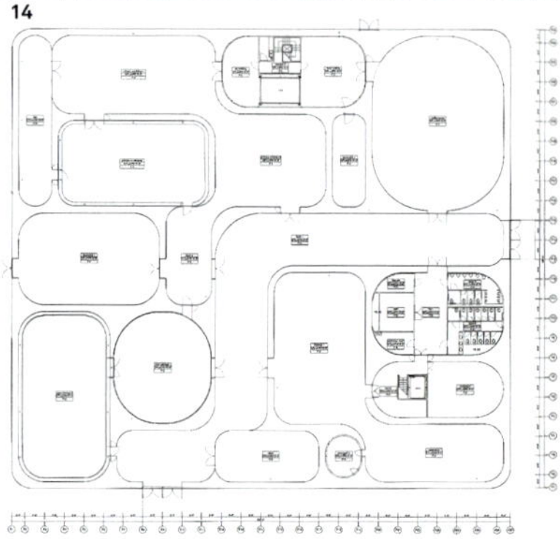

SANAA
12 Rendering of the Glass Pavilion at the Toledo Museum of Art, Ohio, 2006
13 Novartis Pharma Headquarters, Basel, 2002
14 Plan of the Glass Pavilion at the Toledo Museum of Art, Ohio, 2006
15 Rendering of the Glass Pavilion at the Toledo Museum of Art, Ohio, 2006
16 Model study of Christian Dior Building, Tokyo, 2001–2003
17 Christian Dior Building, Tokyo, 2001–2003

15

no longer stops at the space's outside limit. The whole space is the limit. **FIG. 13** There is no clear-cut boundary between inside and outside. The space is neither in nor out, but seems to extend infinitely. In such a space, walls are not optical barriers, but optical intensifiers. They are exposed, along with the people and the objects. **FIG. 12** In the Glass Pavilion, the inner and outer edges of the wall are revealed, and the inaccessible gap between them takes over to become the real space of the project. **FIG. 15** The double line of the wall establishes and then undoes any sense of solidity. **FIG. 14**

16

SANAA's vision is far from crystal clear. In fact, their work appears to be more interested in further blurring the view, softening the focus, **FIG. 16** than in sustaining the supposed transparency of early avant-garde architecture. Within SANAA's architecture, structure is never revealed. Their buildings are optical devices without any visible mechanisms. The real view is not just from the outside looking in or the inside looking out, it is from the inside looking even further inward, not to discover the inner secret of the building, but to be suspended in the view itself. The visitors are often literally between walls of glass or acrylic. What they see, through the shiny layer in front of them, is another layer and then another and then another, with the juxtaposed reflections off each surface dissolving any line between inside and outside. Peering through all the layers, vision softens and distorts, with the curves and ripples of the glass accentuating the distortion. **FIG. 17**

17

If SANAA is the inheritor of Miesian transparency, the latest in a long line of experiments, they are the ultimate

18

19

SANAA
18 Rendering of the Glass Pavilion at the Toledo Museum of Art, Ohio, 2006
19 Rendering of Lumiere Park Café, Almere, the Netherlands, 1999
20 "Transparència nipona," clipping from Newspaper *Avui*, Barcelona, June 14, 2010

20

L'estudi d'arquitectura Sanaa dialoga amb Mies van der Rohe amb un mur de plàstic instal·lat al bell mig del pavelló barceloní

Transparència nipona

Miesians, leaping beyond his investigation of transparency into a whole new kind of mirage effect. After centuries of architecture organized by the straight lines of the viewing eye, we now have an architecture formed by the soft distortions of the gaze—a more tactile experience of vision. To enter a SANAA project is to be caressed by a subtle softening of the territory. Even the reflections of trees in the outer layer of glass have a delicacy that one does not find in Mies's work, whether in the renderings or the one-to-one scale models. **FIG. 18**

With such a tactile sense of vision, models are crucial. In the working of the studio, countless models are made of every possible solution in order that the effects can be felt before being fixed in a drawing. Indeed, SANAA seeks variations whose effects are unclear. As they put it in an interview: "We try not to select options for which we can already imagine the outcome."[8] Theirs is an architecture of deliberately unclear vision. **FIG. 19** Mies's experiments in the garden to see the shift in what is seen get multiplied. The lack of transparency of glass is used to expose glass that exposes glass in a kind of vertigo of vision. SANAA's architecture is not so much layerings of glass and acrylic as layerings of opacity—blurs, rather than lines.

CHOREOGRAPHED OPACITY

SANAA's installation in the Barcelona Pavilion in 2008 was the ultimate encounter, since SANAA is widely considered the inheritor of Miesian transparency **FIG. 20**—"a challenge," as Sejima admitted in an interview—a return to the scene of

21 View of SANAA's installation in the Mies van der Rohe Pavilion, Barcelona, 2008
22 Poster for SANAA's installation in the Mies van der Rohe Pavilion, 2008

the crime, one could argue. The installation carefully marks off a part of the pavilion with an acrylic curtain acting as a kind of crime-scene tape, leaving, as SANAA put it "the existing space of the Barcelona Pavilion undisturbed." And yet a completely new atmosphere was created.

> We decided to use acrylic to make transparent curtains. We imagined an installation design that leaves the existing space of the Barcelona Pavilion undisturbed.
>
> The acrylic curtain stands freely on the floor and is shaped in a calm spiral. The curtain softly encompasses the spaces within the pavilion and creates a new atmosphere. The view through the acrylic will be something different from the original with soft reflections slightly distorting the pavilion.[9] **FIG. 22**

But what crime has been committed here? What has been cordoned off? Is it the freestanding golden onyx wall at the center of the pavilion? Or the two Barcelona chairs for King Alfonso XIII and Queen Victoria Eugenia of Spain, where they were to sign the golden book during the building's opening ceremony? **FIG. 21** Or is it the space outside the spiral that has been marked off, preserved, "undisturbed"?

In any case, the cordon is loose, the spiral is open. **FIG. 24** We can walk in, but not so easily. First we have to find the entrance, slide around the outside of the curtain. Only when we are on the other side, having squeezed between the acrylic curtain and the front glass wall of the pavilion,

21

22

The Fundació Mies van der Rohe presents the installation by the architects Kazuyo Sejima and Ryue Nishizawa until the 18th January 2009 at the Mies van der Rohe Pavilion.
Avinguda Marquès de Comillas s/n, Parc de Montjuïc

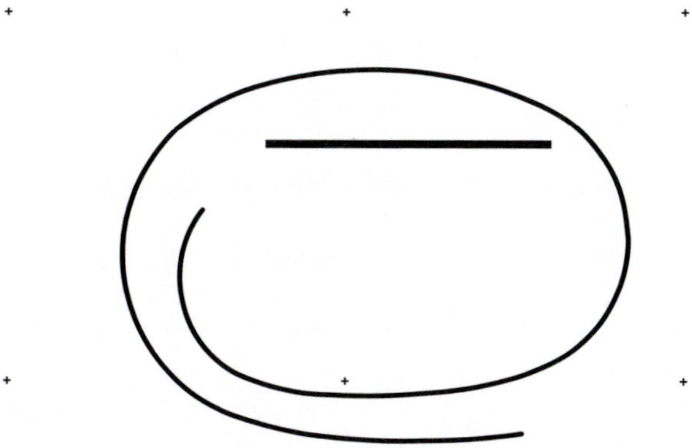

"We decided to use acrylic to make transparent curtains.

We imagined an installation design that leaves the existing space of the Barcelona Pavilion undisturbed.

The acrylic curtain stands freely on the floor and is shaped in a calm spiral.

The curtain softly encompasses the space within the pavilion and creates a new atmosphere.

The view through the acrylic will be something different from the original with soft reflections slightly distorting the pavilion".

SANAA

26.11.2008 - 18.01.2009

mies barcelona

can we suddenly fold back into the spiral by making a 180-degree turn, which echoes the two 180-degree turns already required to enter the Barcelona Pavilion. Just as Mies narrowed the entrance down, subtly constraining the visitor with a folded path, SANAA spins and squeezes the visitor between the narrow planes of acrylic that curve around until suddenly one is inside, facing the two Barcelona chairs—or rather, the chairs are facing us, as if the king and queen were still there, sitting down, presiding over everything.

There is a new chair, as if for us. It is the SANAA plywood chair with two asymmetrical bunny ears: **FIG. 23** whimsical, childlike, fragile, uncomfortable, funny—a kind of inexpensive school or cafeteria chair facing the wide, ceremonial, orthogonal, plush, leather-and-chrome chairs of Mies as in some kind of playful challenge. Another bunny chair is placed outside the acrylic curtain, behind the Barcelona chairs, as if guarding the crime scene. The new chair represents SANAA just as much as the old one represents Mies. The bunny belongs to the acrylic curve, while the Barcelona belongs to the onyx plane. As with Mies, is the new chair for sitting in and looking from? Or is it what is looked at: a solitary object suspended in the play of reflections, as unattainable as a royal appointment? Or is it the inexpensive, antiaristocratic chair, a subversive object that has infiltrated the luxury space? Or is it some kind of prisoner of the spiral? Or a kind of calling card left by SANAA? In any case, the role of Mies's heavy furniture in light of his blurring of the visual field is called into question. Each chair is like a kind of ship floating in the liquid reflections of the shiny floor, walls, and glass. X-ray vision surely means a shift in the status of objects. SANAA turns the pavilion itself into a ready-made object, even a piece of furniture, that can now be seen differently.

But what does SANAA mean when they say that the space of the pavilion is left "undisturbed"? Something has changed. In fact, everything seems to have changed. The simple spiral makes a new pavilion out of the old one—a pavilion inside a pavilion, each transforming the other to produce a whole new architecture. The most famous pavilion of the twentieth century becomes something far from itself, but contained within itself. All the classic images imbedded in the brain of every architect now have additional layers of reflections. **FIG. 26**

SANAA returns the curtain to the pavilion—or is it the pavilion to the curtain? The acrylic freestanding curtain recalls the Velvet and Silk Café, **FIG. 25** the brilliant collaborative work of Lilly Reich and Mies for the Exposition de la Mode in Berlin, two years before Barcelona, where draperies in black, orange, and red velvet and black and yellow-lemon silk hung from metal rods to form the space. In its radical approach to defining the space by suspending sensuous surfaces, the café was a kind of prototype of the pavilion. In the pavilion, the richly veined onyx surfaces took over the role of the curtains—the hard surfaces absorbing softness. In fact, Mies pretended that they were curtains, denying their structural role, even if we now know better. The forensic work for the reconstruction revealed many veiled secrets of

23, 26, 27 View of SANAA's installation in the Mies van der Rohe Pavilion, Barcelona, 2008
24 Plan of SANAA's installation in the Mies van der Rohe Pavilion, 2008
25 Mies van der Rohe and Lilly Reich, Café Samt und Seide, *Mode der Dame* exhibition, Berlin, 1927

23

24

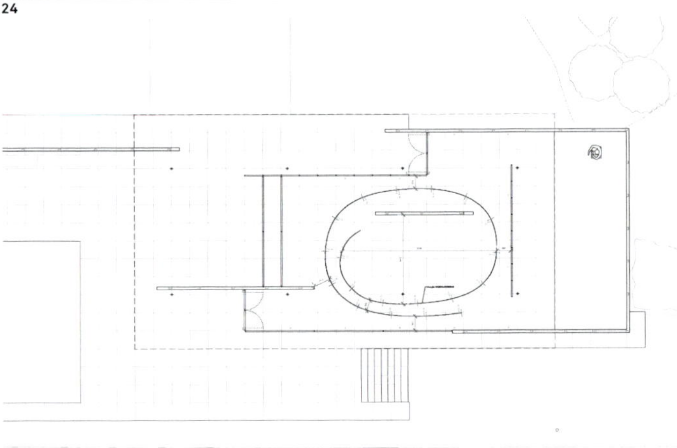

25

26

27

28 Mies van der Rohe with King Alfonso XIII, Barcelona Pavilion opening, May 27, 1929
29 Lilly Reich in the Barcelona Pavilion, 1929
30 Francisco de Goya, *El Rey Fernando VII con Manto Real*, 1814

the building—the theatrical quality of its main polemical effects, the illusion of modernity. That the walls are curtains may also explain why we don't enter the Barcelona Pavilion frontally, but at an angle, as if entering from backstage.

SANAA's project reminds us that the Barcelona Pavilion comes from curtains, from a soft material. The beginnings of architecture were textile. It is a Semperian idea of architecture, beautifully adopted by Adolf Loos, who wrote:

> The architect's general task is to provide a warm and livable space. Carpets are warm and livable. He decides for this reason to spread one carpet on the floor and to hang up four to form the four walls. But you cannot build a house out of carpets. Both the carpet on the floor and the tapestry on the wall require a structural frame to hold them in the correct place. To invent this frame is the architect's second task.[10]

The space that SANAA has wrapped with the new transparent curtain is precisely the center of the pavilion, the throne room with its poignantly empty chairs for the king and queen of Spain. In old photographs, the space is marked by a black carpet on the floor, which nobody dares to step on—as in the image of the mysterious woman (is it Lilly Reich?) **FIG. 29** standing outside its border, her back to the camera, looking in. SANAA's curtain is the invisible cloak that further protects that space—a kind of royal transparent cloak. **FIG. 30** The garment moves. It billows outward, allowing us to enter between its folds. Space is defined in a kind of invisible movement,

28

29

30

neither limited nor unlimited, a paradox that the spiral has always communicated.

> "My house," writes Georges Spyridaki, "is diaphanous, but it is not of glass. It is more of the nature of vapor. Its walls contract and expand as I desire. At times, I draw them close about me like protective armor.... But at others, I let the walls of my house blossom out in their own space, which is infinitely extensible." Spyridaki's house breathes. First it is a coat of armor, then it extends ad infinitum, which amounts to saying that we live in it in alternate security and adventure. It is both cell and world. Here geometry is transcended.[11]

SANAA's diaphanous curtain preserves the pavilion by allowing it to breathe. It is a kind a life support in a moment in which the subtlety of Mies's pavilion might so easily be forgotten precisely because the building is so insistently celebrated. The single curtain slows us down, allowing us to enter the pavilion again, as if on the day of its opening. **FIG. 28** Once again, the fact that Mies and Reich did so little, when asked so much (represent Germany in Barcelona), can be appreciated. Yet what allows SANAA to take us back, or to bring the pavilion again forward toward us, is that the curtain is precisely not transparent. What is added is not a clear window or a magnifying glass, but a delicate veil. SANAA's acrylic, like their glass, is never neutral.

The modern discourse of X-rays—cutting through the outer layers to reveal secrets—gives way to inner translu-

31 Philip Johnson's Glass House in the snow, New Canaan, Connecticut, 1949
32 Mies van der Rohe, Farnsworth House flooded, 1950–1951

cent layers, endlessly folded and overlapping, intensifying the mystery, rather than removing it. The X-ray logic absorbed by modern architecture culminates in a dense cloud of ghostly shapes. The clearest of glass is now used to undermine clarity. With the acrylic curtain in Barcelona, the ghost is unambiguously modern architecture, preserved, rather than transformed, by subtle deflections. It is the disturbance that allows things to return to us undisturbed.

The effect of this architecture is not unmediated transparency, but rather a vision that is more blurry, veiled, nebulous, vaporous, as if in a snowstorm or a dense fog, seemingly infinite. This architecture is much lighter than that of Mies, Johnson, or even the Eameses. It is as if the architecture wants to disappear, to evaporate.

In one of the most evocative accounts of the Glass House, Johnson describes it as a "celestial elevator in which when it snows, you seem to be going up because everything is coming down."[12] **FIG. 31** The house levitates in the snow, but remains a box. SANAA's glass pavilions are permanently in a storm, as if producing their own weather. Theirs is a more oceanic view, a liquid architecture. It is not by chance that lately, their own language also expresses this feeling. In the La Samaritaine project, they describe the "soft waves of the glass"; in Nishizawa's Office Building in Hatsudai, the "undulating mesh"; in Louvre-Lens, the play of reflections that "allows the building to dissolve in its surroundings" and the glass foyer that allows the park "to flow through the structure." In reverse, the interior is "spilling outside, blurring the boundaries of the museum itself."[13] Everything becomes liquid.

31

32

Liquidity was already part of the modern project. In his book on Mies accompanying the 1947 exhibition at MoMA, Johnson described the Farnsworth House type as a "floating self-contained cage."[14] **FIG. 32** He later used the same metaphor for his own house, describing it as floating on the sea, even if he apparently hated the sea: "That's why I don't like the seaside. There's nothing there, unless it's a boat. If there's a boat, it's O.K. In the East River [of New York] wonderful barges go by. But God keep me from the Atlantic Ocean. There are a lot of glass houses that face the ocean, and people like them. But I say there's nothing there."[15]

The glass houses of Mies and Johnson are sealed floating boxes. A SANAA building is "porous." It is no longer a sealed box on the move. It breathes. Breathing—this is what was missing in Mies's and Johnson's glass houses, which in the summer had to leave the doors open to let fresh air in, even if the mosquitoes also came in, because screens would spoil the effect. SANAA loves screens, filters, slits, membranes, curtains, mesh. The flows are not just optical. One breathes the landscape. The building "dissolves in its surrounding," absorbing "the colors of the sky and vegetation, its appearance changing with the season and the time of the day."[16]

BUT WHY IS ARCHITECTURE DISAPPEARING?

The light footprints of Le Corbusier's pilotis, of Mies's glass walls, of thin walls, big windows, roof gardens, and so on have given way to ever more ethereal structures. Junya Ishigami, for example, not by chance coming out of the SANAA studio, takes this dissolution to the extreme by imagining a barely visible architecture of the most delicate threads. Has this dematerialization of architecture to do with a world increasingly mediatized? Old media made modern architecture modern.[17] New media makes it disappear.

With the X-ray and glass architecture, the most inner secrets of our bodies and private life were exposed in public. Kodak understood this new paradigm. Their 1937 film *Highlights and Shadows* implied that there was nothing to fear in glass houses. The X-ray had acclimatized us to living in a new, mediated condition. The threshold of the private was no longer the outside limit of a building. It had relocated. Privacy was now, paradoxically, established in public, something that is all too obvious today with the use of a cell phone, for example, to create an intimate space in the heart of a public space, or in the opposite direction, projecting from the supposed privacy of the interior, or even the bed, the most intimate details of one's life to a wider and wider audience through social media.[18] The most inner secrets of our bodies, movements, sexuality, medical histories, domestic life, and finances are now public. The X-ray effect has migrated to all dimensions of contemporary life. The role of architecture is once again challenged. In a world of extreme exposure in which walls no longer offer privacy, new strategies emerge by entering the mechanisms of exposure to find the blind spots.

1 György Kepes, *Language of Vision* (Chicago: Paul Theobald, 1944), p. 77.
2 Colin Rowe and Robert Slutzky, "Transparency Literal and Phenomenal," *Perspecta* 8 (1963), p. 45.
3 Philip Johnson, in "The Architect (Philip Johnson and Louis Kahn)," *Accent*, CBS, May 14, 1961.
4 Mies van der Rohe, *Frühlicht* 1, no. 4, 1922, quoted in Philip Johnson, *Mies van der Rohe* (New York: MoMA, 1947), p. 187.
5 Charles and Ray Eames, photograph of the model of first version of Case Study House 8, which they called Bridge House, *Arts & Architecture,* March 1948, cover. For more on this project and its relationship to Mies van der Rohe's Glass House on a Hillside (1934), see my *Domesticity at War* (Cambridge, MA: MIT Press, 2006), pp. 100–101.
6 Ray Eames quoted in Esther McCoy, *Modern California Houses,* 1962, reprinted as *Case Study Houses 1945–1962* (Los Angeles: Hennessey & Ingalls, 1977), p. 54.
7 See my *Domesticity at War,* chapter 3.
8 Kazuyo Sejima, interview about the Rolex Center.
9 Kazuyo Sejima and Ryue Nishizawa, *Intervention in the Mies van der Rohe Pavilion* (Barcelona; ACTAR, 2010), p. 8.
10 Adolf Loos, "The Principle of Cladding" (1898), in *Spoken into the Void: Collected Essays 1897–1900,* trans. Jane O. Newman and John H. Smith (Cambridge, MA: MIT Press, 1982), p. 66. Compare with Gottfried Semper statement: "Hanging carpets remained the true walls, the visible boundaries of space. The often solid walls behind them were necessary for reasons that had nothing to do with the creation of space; they were needed for security, for supporting a load, for their permanence, and so on. Wherever the need for these secondary functions did not arise, the carpets remained the original means of separating space. Even where building solid walls became necessary, the latter were only the inner, invisible structure hidden behind the true and legitimate representatives of the wall, the colorful woven carpets." Gottfried Semper, "The Four Elements of Architecture: A Contribution to the Comparative Study of Architecture" (1851), in Gottfried Semper, *The Four Elements of Architecture and Other Writings,* trans. Harry Francis Mallgrave and Wolfgang Herrmann (Cambridge: Cambridge University Press, 1989), p. 104.
11 Gaston Bachelard, *The Poetics of Space,* trans. Maria Jolas (Boston: Beacon Press, 1969), p. 51. Bachelard is quoting Georges Spyridaki, *Mort lucide* (Paris: P. Seghers, 1953), p. 35.
12 Quoted in Kenneth Frampton, "The Glass House Revisited," *Catalogue* 9, September–October 1978, reprinted in David Whitney and Jeffrey Kipnis, eds., *Philip Johnson: The Glass House* (New York, Pantheon Books, 1993), p. 99.
13 Kazuyo Sejima, Ryue Nishizawa, in *SANAA 2011–2015, El Croquis 179–180* (2015), pp. 68, 369, 55.
14 Philip Johnson, *Mies van der Rohe* (New York: Museum of Modern Art, 1947), p. 154.
15 Quoted in Rosamond Bernier, "Improving His View," in *House & Garden,* June 1986; reprinted in Whitney and Kipnis, eds., *Philip Johnson,* p. 149.
16 SANAA, "Louvre Lens," *SANAA 2011–2015, El Croquis 179–180,* p. 47.
17 Beatriz Colomina, *Privacy and Publicity: Modern Architecture as Mass Media* (Cambridge, MA: MIT Press, 1994).
18 Beatriz Colomina, "Privacy and Publicity in the Age of Social Media," in *2000+: The Urgencies of Architectural Theory,* ed. James Graham (New York: GSSAP Books, 2015).

CHAPTER 5

Hyperpublic: An Afterword

At the turn of the twenty-first century, the CAT scan (Computerized Axial Tomography), also known as CT (Computed Tomography) may have been for architects what the basic X-ray was early in the twentieth century. Like the X-ray, the CAT scan is not an image of the body, but of the body being imaged. In fact, the CAT scan (invented in 1972 and widely available in hospitals since 1980)[1] is simply multiple X-ray images compiled by a computer to generate cross-sectional views and three-dimensional images of the body's internal organs. The word "tomography" comes from the Greek *tomos,* meaning "slice" or "section" and *graphia,* meaning "writing" and "drawing," as in the word "photography," meaning "drawing with light." Unlike X-rays, the CT makes visible hard and soft tissues inside the body. A large donut-shaped machine takes X-rays at many different angles around the body as the body, lying horizontal, is moved slowly through the apparatus. FIG. 1 The camera effectively spirals around the whole body. A typical medical brochure describes the procedure thus: "Imagine the body as a loaf of bread and you are looking at one end of the loaf. As you remove each slice of bread, you can see the entire surface of that slice from the crust to the center." The crust, skin, or envelope has become an almost invisible line. What matters is the dense interior, which is rendered like a new, more complex kind of facade.

As with the X-ray, architects were quick to respond to the new technology. While architectural publications from the beginning to the middle of the twentieth century were full of X-rays—from Mies and Le Corbusier to Alison and Peter Smithson—and their architecture reflects this

1

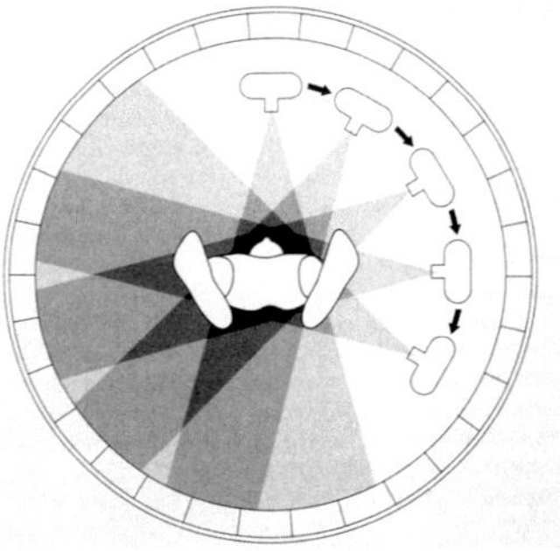

1 CAT scan section, from patient's brochure, ca. 1999

2

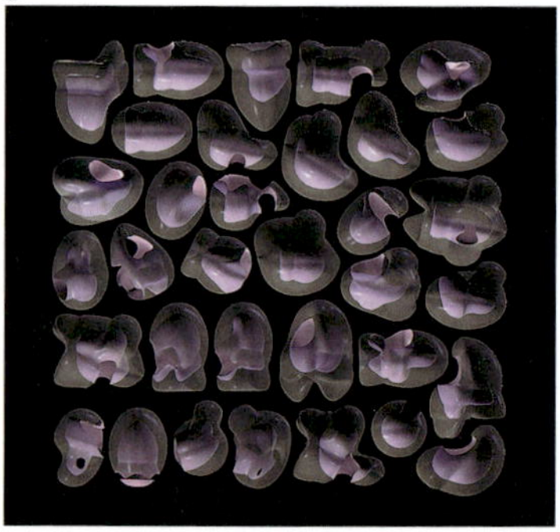

3

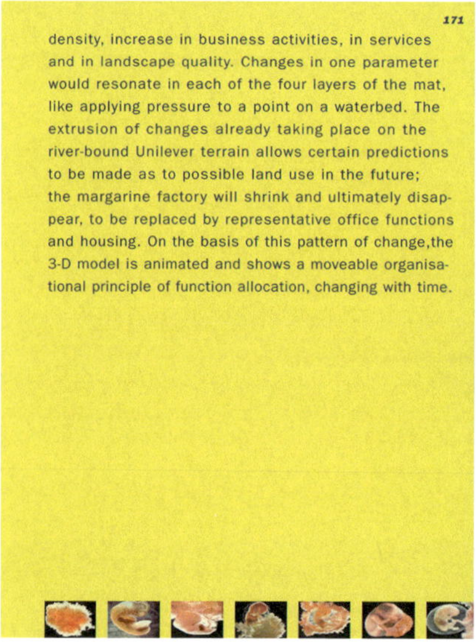

171

density, increase in business activities, in services and in landscape quality. Changes in one parameter would resonate in each of the four layers of the mat, like applying pressure to a point on a waterbed. The extrusion of changes already taking place on the river-bound Unilever terrain allows certain predictions to be made as to possible land use in the future; the margarine factory will shrink and ultimately disappear, to be replaced by representative office functions and housing. On the basis of this pattern of change,the 3-D model is animated and shows a moveable organisational principle of function allocation, changing with time.

4

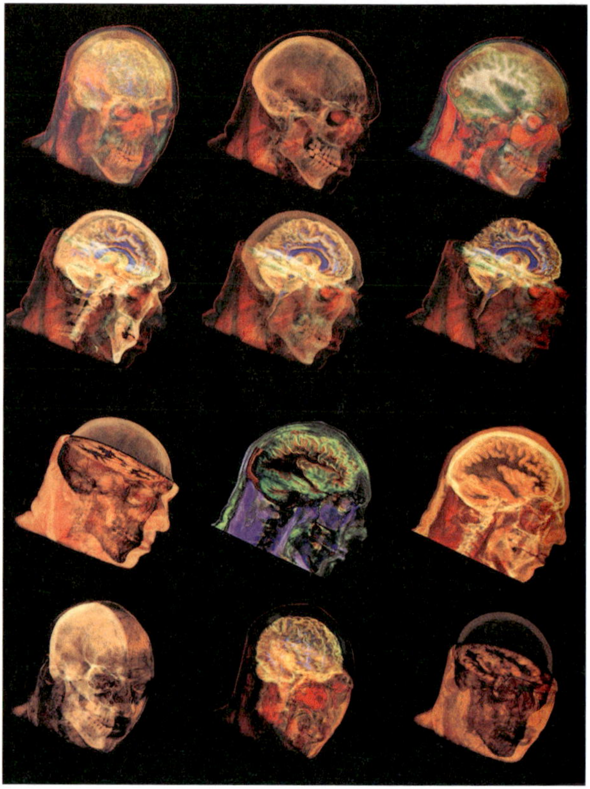

2 Greg Lynn, Embryonic Space, ca. 1998
3 Page from UN Studio, *MOVE* Vol. 2, 1999, showing photographs of fetuses in different states of development
4 Page from UN Studio, *MOVE* Vol. 2, 1999, showing CAT scans of the brain
5 Cover of catalogue *Jose Luis Mateo, MAP architects* with CAT scan of the brain
6 Cryosectional images from the Visible Male, US National Library of Medicine

5

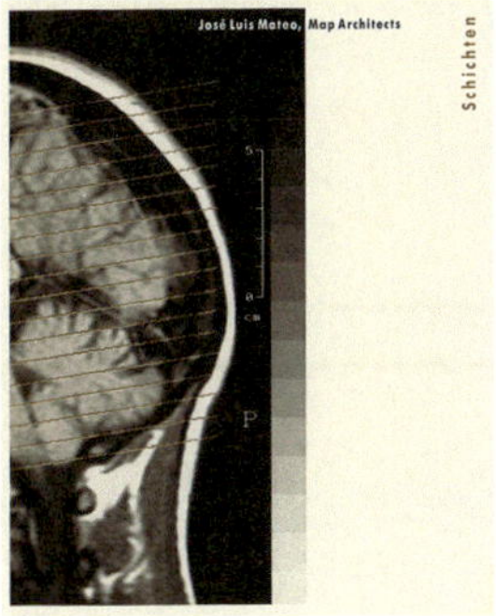

6

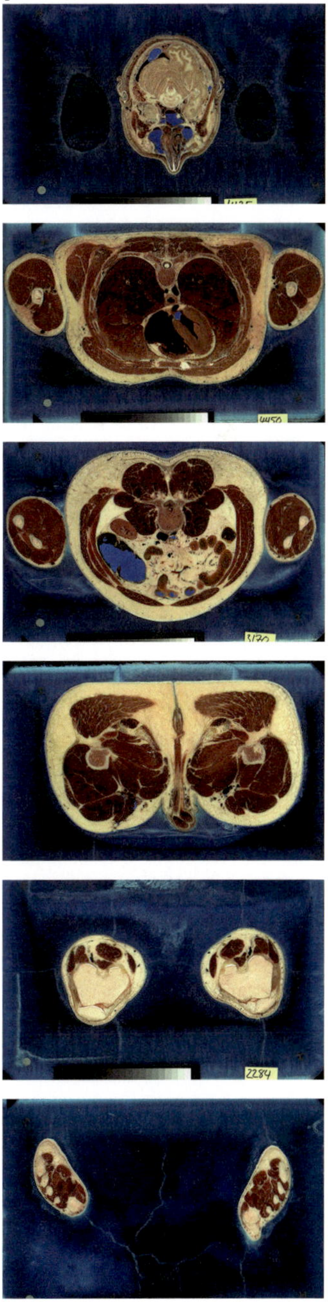

interest, architectural publications at the turn of the twenty-first century were full of CAT-scan images. A 1992 catalogue of an exhibition of Josep Lluís Mateo's work, for example, shows a CAT scan of a brain on the cover FIG. 5 and insists inside that "the architect has to act with the callousness of the medic: he cuts, analyses, researches. But he must never mummify an organism that lived once."[2] Likewise, UN Studio showed CAT scans of the brain alongside their projects in their 1999 book *Move.*[3] FIG. 4 The Renaissance obsession with the brain continued into the twenty-first century, as did interest in the fetus, as evidenced by the "embryological" work done by so-called "digital architects."[4] FIGS. 2, 3 This new generation of architects, emerging in the late 1990s, started to produce experimental work under the influence of computer-assisted technologies that allowed complete three-dimensional modeling of the inside of the body.

Not by chance, these architects were also fascinated by another medical procedure that parallels the CAT scan, the Visible Human Project, FIG. 6 completed in 1995, which acts out physically the operation of the CAT scan, cutting a body in one-millimeter sections, which are then used to generate an animation moving steadily through the whole body. Just as with the Renaissance dissections, the invaded male body is that of a criminal, who in this case donated his body to science. The female donor remains anonymous. Architecture has always referenced the medical body, but the human body now is a digital artifact in its own right, experienced from the inside and generating new kinds of thinking about the interior.

7

8

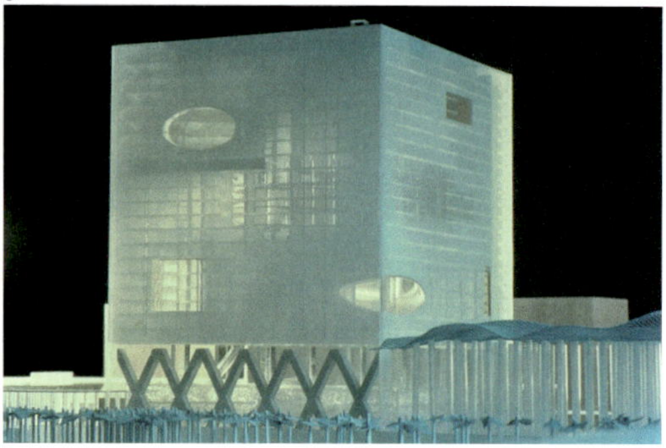

9

The influence of the CAT scan and of the MRI scan, invented a few years later to provide more detail of soft tissue, is reflected in architectural envelopes. In the Bibliothèque Nationale competition entry of 1989 by OMA (Office for Metropolitan Architecture), **FIGS. 7–9** the Miesian exposure of a skeleton behind a glass skin gives way to translucent bodies, revealing organs as in an MRI, without any visible envelope. The winning entry by FOA (Foreign Office Architecture) in the Yokohama Port Terminal's competition of 1995, on the other hand, seems to follow the logic of the CAT scan: **FIG. 10** an endless series of section cuts was used to assemble a three-dimensional body that can be thought of as either all envelope or no envelope. **FIG. 11** There is no simple opposition between the outside and the inside. Its dream is to be a continuously folded surface where structure and skin are one and where there are no bones or discrete organs. **FIG. 12**

When Alejandro Zaera Polo interviewed Frank Gehry's team in 1995, he asked where they had obtained the 3-D digitizers that were in use in the office, and they answered that they were originally used for guiding lasers in brain surgery.[5] The state-of-the-art medical technology was being used in an architectural studio to generate 3-D models on the computer. A series of 3-D points is taken from the physical model, and the computer interpolates the surfaces between them to build the precise geometry of the building. The model is treated like a body about to be operated on, rebuilt through a kind of plastic surgery.

Today, there are new instruments of medical diagnosis, new systems of representation. The latest techniques

7–9 OMA, Très Grande Bibliothèque, Paris, France, competition 1989
10–12 Foreign Office Architects, Yokohama Port and Ferry Terminal, Yokohama, Japan, 1995

10

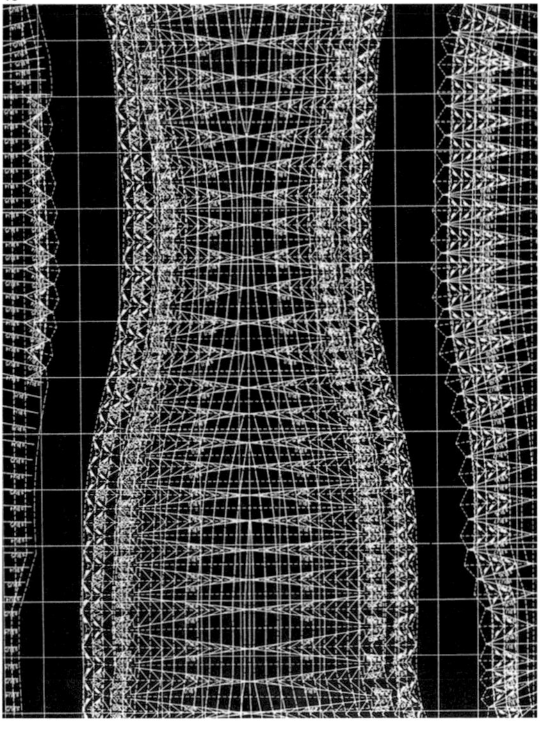

11

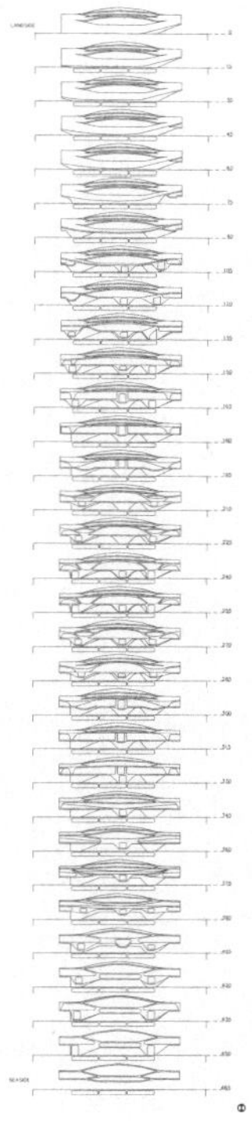

12

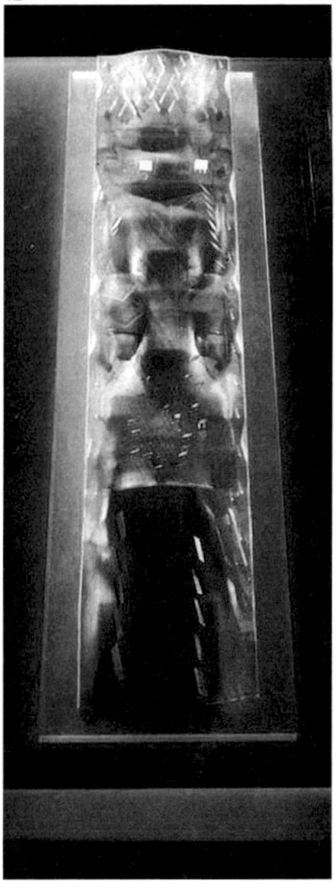

13

14

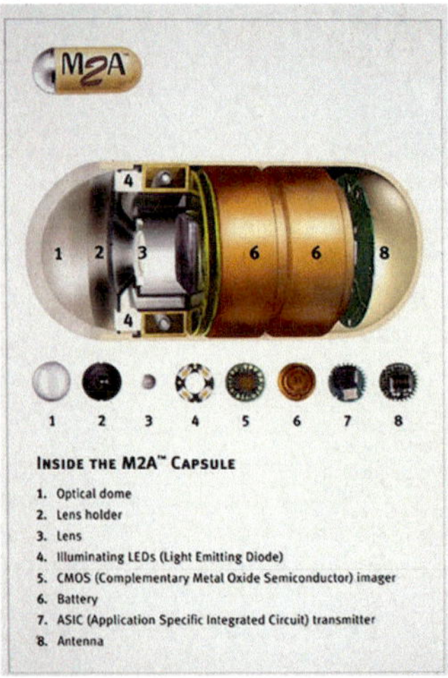

15

represent yet another radical transformation of our thinking between inside and outside. For example, the M2A camera **FIG. 13** that was approved by the FDA in 2001 is a one-inch-long disposable camera that is swallowed as a pill and snaps two color pictures a minute for eight hours as it passes through the twenty-two-foot-long digestive tract. "M2A" is short for "mouth to anus." A recorder, advertised at the time as being "the size of a Walkman," collects 57,000 color images while a person goes about his or her normal day. The images are then downloaded to a computer to produce a video of the camera's trip through the digestive tract.

Much of this technology began with the military, entertainment, communications, and consumer electronics industries. The M2A was the brainchild of an Israeli missile researcher who applied his knowledge of video systems used as smart bombs and took advantage of the miniaturization developed by NASA. So the M2A is a merging of space and military technology, and in fact, it looks like a little spaceship. **FIG. 14** Scientists in laboratories have been developing microscopic nanomachines that supposedly one day will prowl through the human body like "miniature repairmen," fixing what ails us.

Like the 1966 movie *Fantastic Voyage,* **FIG. 15** starring Raquel Welch, in which a team of scientists is shrunk and injected into the body to repair a brain injury, the M2A transforms the body into an occupiable interior. The body is turned inside out, making the skin irrelevant. All that remains is an endless interior, bathed in the light from the little capsule's video camera. The capsule itself looks like

13, 14 M2A capsule endoscope
15 Still from Richard Fleischer (director), *Fantastic Voyage*, 1966

a hybrid of the buildings inspired by X-rays and CAT scans. A translucent envelope exposes the outlines of the inner mechanisms, while a transparent head acts as the viewing apparatus. This hybrid displaces both the transparent and translucent systems in favor of the skinless body, one no longer even experienced as a body.

All this is somehow reminiscent of Frederick Kiesler, and it is not by chance that so many "digital architects" have echoed his fluid geometries, and in particular, his Endless House, which he explicitly understood as a digestive system, giving architectural form to the first mouth-to-anus system. But with Kiesler and with much of the computer-generated architecture of the turn of the twenty-first century, the skin is turned into the structure, the whole building becoming a kind of flowing, self-supporting skin, a hyperenvelope. What the M2A camera creates, on the other hand, is the possibility of the radically skinless body, the skinless building, the building turned completely inside out to such an extent that it may not be clear that it is a building.

What exactly this complete loss of the envelope means for architecture is unclear, but in an age in which the public/private distinction has been so radically dissolved, an architecture without envelope may very well be upon us.

Privacy is increasingly defined by a kind of blur within a hyperpublic space. The intentional blurring of the airport scan that strips the outer layer of clothing away to look for hidden weapons or contraband is supposed to protect those worried about the loss of privacy. Privacy is no longer established by a line but by a blurring within the most public space, and one can hide for a while within that blur. This blur might be treated as a kind of space, a new kind of interior that can be designed.

The space of the airport is no longer defined by the building, but by the layers of surveillance machines that carve out a new kind of space, a seemingly public space that can be occupied only by surrendering private information about the body, bank account, history, movements, employment, family, and friends. The scanner that literally acts as the doorway is reinforced by explosives sniffers, retina scans, heat sensors looking at the face for evidence of contagion, facial-recognition software, fingerprinting, and so on. The body does not simply pass through an airport, but through multiple devices and through the space of data.

Architecture is increasingly defined by these new instruments for looking, being looked at, and looked into. Multiple descendants of the X-ray machine are dispersed through the contemporary city, patrolling and defining the limits of existing architecture, but also defining new architectures.

Today, new forms of advanced surveillance technologies operate in the city, and these models of vision act as the new paradigms for transparency. Hand-held scanning devices capable of seeing through clothing, walls, and buildings are in use by the military and, increasingly, also by the police. These devices effectively make solid walls behave like glass, and they open up the possibility, even the inevitability, of new kinds of architectural experiments.

Forward-looking infrared radar (FLIR), for example, detects the electromagnetic frequencies at which heat

16

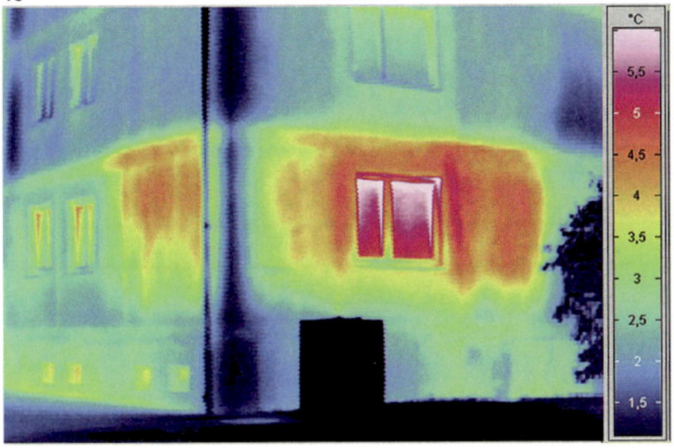

radiates from organisms and structures, exposing heat-emitting bodies. **FIG. 16** Seemingly solid walls no longer offer privacy. Indeed, FLIR scans reveal activities that have already finished. One can be exposed even after one has left, because heat signatures remain for a while. This time delay is incorporated into a new kind of vision. Bodies are treated the same as buildings. Just as the airport scanners strip the body, the KAYA lens filter that can be attached to a regular camera or even a cell-phone camera can see through clothing by concentrating on the infrared spectrum. These technologies are controversial. The backscatter X-ray machines installed in all US airports were removed a few years later because of the failure to blur the images of naked citizens, and the use of passive millimeter imaging (PMI) machines instead has been restricted to the production of a cartoon image of the body due to the privacy concerns. **FIG. 17**

The midcentury fear of loss of privacy in the glass house and with the X-ray has reappeared. It seems as if each new technology that exposes something private is perceived as threatening, then quickly absorbed into everyday life. The fear of the glass box or X-ray seems quaint today. Even the grainy images of video surveillance cameras seem less invasive now, almost reassuring. Perhaps today's scanning technologies will also seem quaint in the future as each new technology delves deeper and deeper into the private. With each new invasion, our definition of "private" changes.

All of these shifts in the technologies of viewing take their meaning relative to the massive levels of personal exposure through data mining today. Not only is the most private information transiting through vast networks and being mined by companies and governments, but the private itself is now staged in a hyperpublic. The line between private and public is no longer drawn around a body, a relationship, a social group, or a building. Rather, it is drawn in the space of data, with multiple forms of privacy continuously established and violated. The body itself is now suspended in data. The medical body around which architecture has always organized itself is at once flesh and information.

The point of this small book is simply to show that in changing our definitions of public and private, the new medical technologies that emerged in the early years of the last century changed our understanding of architecture. The question now is not how transparency is dislocated into other fields, or how architecture affects other fields, but how architecture absorbs transformations of public and private and reflects on those transformations.

"Every age has its signature afflictions," Byung-Chul Han writes in *The Burnout Society.*[6] We can now add that each affliction has its architecture. The age of bacterial diseases—particularly tuberculosis—gave birth to modern architecture, to white buildings detached from the "humid ground where disease breeds," as Le Corbusier had put it,[7] smooth surfaces, big windows, and terraces to facilitate taking the sun and fresh-air cure. When the discovery of antibiotics put an end to that age, in the postwar years, attention shifted to psychological problems. The same architects once concerned with the prevention of tuberculosis became obsessed with the psyche, with the house seen as not just a medical device for the prevention of disease, but as a way to provide psychological comfort, what Neutra called "nervous health,"[8] with the architect as a psychologist.

The twenty-first century, according to Han, is the age of neurological disorders: depression, ADHD, borderline personality disorders, and burnout syndrome. What is the architecture of these afflictions? Not by chance the turn of the twenty-first century is also the age of the sick building syndrome, in which modern buildings turn on their occupants, literally rendering them unhealthy. It is the age of allergies, the age of the "environmentally hypersensitive" unable to live in the modern world and its buildings. Never at any one time in history have there been so many people allergic to chemicals, buildings, electromagnetic fields (EMF), fragrances.... Since the environment is now almost completely man-made, we have become allergic to ourselves, to our own hyperextended body in a kind of autoimmune disorder.

What do these developments mean for design? Architecture finds itself increasingly unable to present itself as a cure. Escaping architecture becomes the only architectural strategy. There are communities of the afflicted living in a kind of replay of the 1960s in bubbles, tents, and old cars that have been "cleaned" of all toxic materials, usually in the desert or far away from civilization–nomads moving at the very sniff of a chemical coming from a shifting wind that brings "whiffs of industry, detergent, fabric softener, fertilizers, pesticides, herbicides ... exhaust from cars," as Dodie Bellamy puts it in "When the Sick Rule the World."[9]

Implied in all of this is a different city—and new questions for design, or very ancient questions about the limits of the body and mind, and how to take shelter in a threatening world. The correlation of architecture with the medical body has finally come full circle with the rise of the "sick building syndrome." The type of architecture that was meant to inoculate its occupants against disease has become a source of disease. We are becoming physically allergic to buildings. New bodies will probably have to be designed. A new theory of architecture is likely to follow.

1 Computer Tomography (CT) was invented in 1972 by two people working independently: British engineer Godfrey Hounsfield of EMI Laboratories, England, and South Africa–born physicist Allan Cormack of Tufts University, Massachusetts. Hounsfield and Cormack were later awarded the Nobel Peace Prize for their contributions to medicine and science.
2 *Josep Lluís Mateo—MAP Architects* (Barcelona: Dragados y Construcciones, 1991), exh. cat. Architekturgalerie e.V., Munich, 1991.
3 Ben van Berkel, Caroline Bos, UN Studio, *MOVE* (Amsterdam, The Netherlands: Goose Press, 1999).
4 See for example Greg Lynn's Embryological House (1997–2001).
5 Alejandro Zaera-Polo, "Information Technology at Frank O. Gehry & Associates," *Frank O. Gehry: 1991–1995, El Croquis 74–75* (1995), p. 153.
6 Byung-Chul Han. *The Burnout Society* (Stanford: Stanford University Press, 2015), p. 1.
7 Le Corbusier, *The Radiant City* (1935; Orion Press 1967), pp. 55–56.
8 Richard Neutra, *Survival through Design* (New York: Oxford University Press, 1953), p. 194.
9 Dodie Bellamy, *When the Sick Rule the World* (South Pasadena: Semiotext(e), 2015), p. 35. On the other side of the spectrum, there is the "burnout society" that Han writes about—those who, in working for themselves, push themselves harder than anybody else could have pushed them. This is what Han calls "the achievement-subject," who turns out to be much more disciplined than "the obedience-subject," despite the fact that he obeys only himself—master and slave conflated. No one can be as brutal with anyone as with oneself. Pushing the limits of the imaginable, this creature does not experience the brutality as pain or as obligation, but as self-realization. The horror of fascist control of body and brain from the outside has given way to a kind of dictatorship of the self.

17 Passive millimeter imaging (PMI)

17

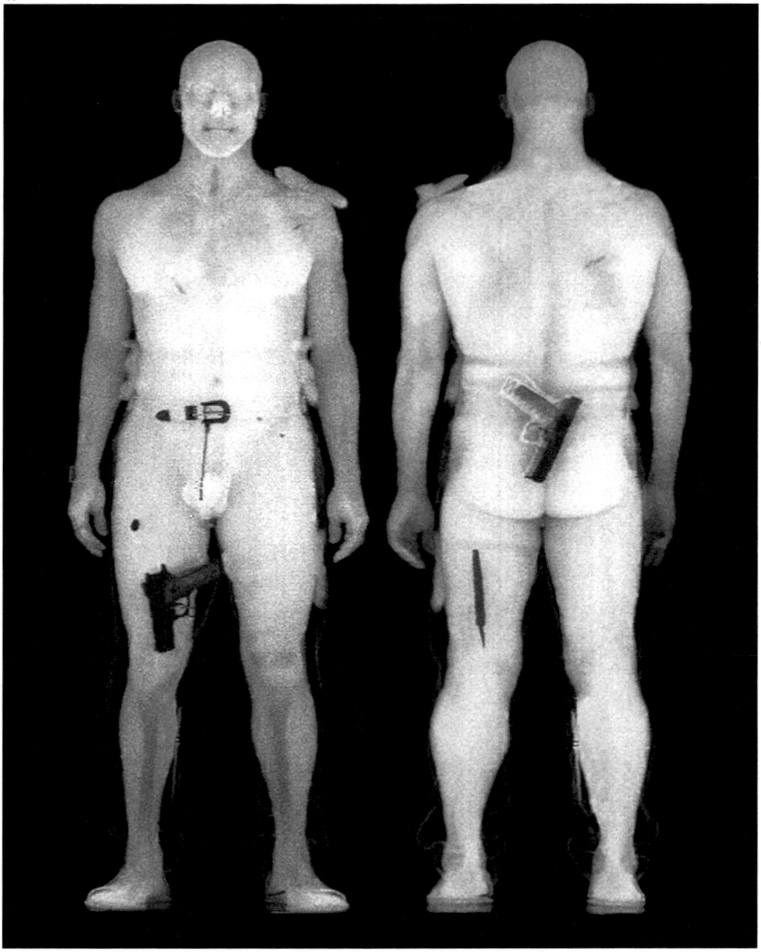

Beatriz Colomina is the Howard Crosby Butler Professor of the History of Architecture in Princeton University School of Architecture and a 2018–2019 fellow at the Wissenschaftskolleg zu Berlin. She has written extensively on questions of architecture, art, sexuality and media. Her books include *Sexuality and Space* (Princeton Architectural Press, 1992), *Privacy and Publicity: Modern Architecture as Mass Media* (MIT Press, 1994), *Domesticity at War* (MIT Press, 2007), *The Century of the Bed* (Verlag für Moderne Kunst, 2015), *Manifesto Architecture: The Ghost of Mies* (Sternberg, 2014), *Clip/Stamp/Fold: The Radical Architecture of Little Magazines 196X–197X*, with Craig Buckley (Actar, 2010), and *Are We Human? Notes on an Archaeology of Design*, with Mark Wigley (Lars Müller Publishers, 2016). She has curated a number of exhibitions including *Clip/Stamp/Fold* (2006), *Playboy Architecture* (2012) and *Radical Pedagogies* (2014). In 2016 she was co-curator of the third Istanbul Design Biennial. Colomina was born in Madrid and lives in New York. She has a professional degree in architecture and a Ph.D. in the History and Theory of Architecture from the Polytechnic University of Barcelona. In 2018 she was appointed doctor honoris causa by the KTH, Royal Institute of Technology, Stockholm.

Index

Image Credits

INTRODUCTION

1 © 1975, Susan Sontag. Photo: Beatriz Colomina.
2 Photo: Jean-Regis Rouston/Roger Viollet/Getty Images
3 CC BY-SA 3.0
4 Photo: Stefan Müller and Simon Menges

CHAPTER 1

1 Cesare Cesariano, *Di Lucio Vitruvio [...],* (Como: Gotardus de Ponte, 1521), fol. 49r.
2 Wellcome Collection
3 Dennis Hallinan/Alamy Stock Photo
6 Photo: Boyer/Roger Viollet/Getty Images
7 Eugène Viollet-le-Duc, *Dictionnaire raisonné de l'architecture francaise du XIe au XVIe siècle,* tome 4ième, (Paris: B. Bance, 1870), p. 93
8 Illustration by Jean-Baptiste Marc Bourgery in *Traité complet de l'anatomie de l'homme comprenant la médecine opératoire,* Vol. 1, (Paris: Atlas, 1831)
9 From: *Wasmuths Monatshefte für Baukunst,* Jan. 1929, vol. 1, p. 83.
10 Photo: Jacques Boyer/Roger Viollet/Getty Images
12 © 2018 Artists Rights Society (ARS), New York / VG Bild-Kunst, Bonn
13 Photo: Marcel Breuer. From: Richard Döcker, *Terrassentyp,* (Stuttgart: Akademischer Verlag Wedekind, 1929), p. 99
14 From: *Le Corbusier: The Art of Architecture,* (Weil am Rhein: Vitra Design Museum, 2007)
15–17, 33 © F.L.C. / ADAGP, Paris / Artists Rights Society (ARS), New York 2018
18, 20, 21, 34 Le Corbusier, *The Radiant City,* (New York: Orion Press, 1967)
19 From: Le Corbusier, *La Ville Radieuse,* (Paris: Editions Vincent, 1933), p. 100
22 From: *L'Esprit nouveau,* vol. 2, (Paris: Editions de l'esprit nouveau, 1920), p. 185
24 Bibliothèque nationale de France, département Réserve des livres rares, RES P-V-790
25 *L'Esprit nouveau,* vol. 15, (Paris: Editions de l'esprit nouveau, 1922), p. 1755
26 Photo: Lotte Jacobi. From: Sigfried Giedion, *Befreites Wohnen,* (Zurich: Orell Füssli, 1929; Reprint: Lars Müller Publishers, 2019), plate 26
27 Photo: Wanda von Debschitz-Kunowski
28 Harvard Art Museums/Busch-Reisinger Museum, Gift of Ise Gropius, BRGA.45.66. Imaging Department © President and Fellows of Harvard College
29 © 2019 Artists Rights Society (ARS), New York / VG Bild-Kunst, Bonn
30 © Collection Het Nieuwe Instituut/LEPP, d28-1
31 © The Museum of Architecture in Wroclaw
32 From: Pierre Winter, "Le point du vue du biologiste," *Architecture et Urbanisme,* (Paris: Les Publications techniques/Galerie Charpentier, 1933)
36 Otto Wilhelm Thomé, *Flora von Deutschland, Österreich und der Schweiz,* (Gera: Eugen Köhler, 1885)
37 From: *L'Esprit nouveau,* vol. 21, (Paris: Editions de l'esprit nouveau, 1924)
38 From: Burkhardt Rukschcio and Roland Schachel, *Adolf Loos: Leben und Werk,* (Vienna: Residenz, 1982), p. 221, image 215
39 From: Burkhardt Rukschcio and Roland Schachel, *Adolf Loos: Leben und Werk,* (Vienna: Residenz, 1982)
40 Universität Zürich, Archiv für Medizingeschichte (AfM) IN 47.08.10:03
41, 44–46, 49, 50, 52 © 2018 Austrian Frederick and Lillian Kiesler Private Foundation
42, 43 © 2018 Austrian Frederick and Lillian Kiesler Private Foundation. Photo: J. Alex Langley
47 © 2018 Austrian Frederick and Lillian Kiesler Private Foundation. Photo: Irving Penn
48 © 2018 Austrian Frederick and Lillian Kiesler Private Foundation. Photo: Hans Namuth
51 Photo: Renate Ponsold
53 R.M. Schindler papers, Architecture and Design Collection. Art, Design & Architecture Museum, UC, Santa Barbara
54 R.M. Schindler papers, Architecture and Design Collection. Art, Design & Architecture Museum, UC, Santa Barbara. Photo: JT Beals. From: David Gebhard, *Schindler,* (Santa Barbara: Peregrine Press, 1980), pp. 84–85
56 © Gerhard Riebicke / Bodo Niemann Berlin
57–59 Courtesy of Thomas Hines
60 Richard Neutra Archives, UCLA
61 Richard J. Neutra, *Survival of Design,* (New York: Oxford University Press, 1954)
63 Anonymous, Security Pacific National Bank / Los Angeles Public Library
64 © J. Paul Getty Trust. Getty Research Institute, Los Angeles (2004.R.10, Job 2920). Photo: Julius Shulman
65 U.S. Department of Health and Human Services
66, 67, 71 © 2018 Eames Office, LLC (eamesoffice.com)
69 Photo: Dmitri Kessel/The LIFE Picture Collection/Getty Images
70 © J. Paul Getty Trust. Getty Research Institute, Los Angeles (2004.R.10, Job 2717). Photo: Julius Shulman

CHAPTER 2

1 Alvar Aalto Museum, no. 50-759
2 Alvar Aalto Museum, no. 50-003-091. Photo: Alvar Aalto
3 Alvar Aalto Museum, no. 50-003-361. Photo: Gustaf Welin
4 Alvar Aalto Museum, no. 50-003-360. Photo: Gustaf Welin
5 Alvar Aalto Museum, no. 50-395. Drawing: Alvar Aalto
6 Alvar Aalto Museum, no. 50-950. Drawing: Alvar Aalto
7 Alvar Aalto Museum, no. 50-23b. Drawing: Alvar Aalto
8 Alvar Aalto Museum, no. 50-003-266. Photo: Gustaf Welin
10 Alvar Aalto Museum, no. 50-209
11 From: Alvar Aalto, "The Humanizing of Architecture," Technology Review, vol. 43, no. 1, (November 1940), p. 16
12 Alvar Aalto Museum, no. av 2118. Photo: Maija Holma
13 Alvar Aalto Museum, no. digi 2078. Photo: Maija Holma
14 Alvar Aalto Museum, no. 50-410. Drawing: Alvar Aalto
15 Alvar Aalto Museum, no. 50-405. Drawing: Alvar Aalto
16 Alvar Aalto Museum, no. 50-003-419. Photo: Gustaf Welin
17 Alvar Aalto Museum, no. AFmn 8-3. Photo: unknown
18, 19 Granger Historical Picture Archive / Alamy Stock Photo
20 From: *Josef Hoffmann. Sanatorium Purkersdorf,* ed. Breckner, Meyer, et al., (Vienna: Galerie Metropol, 1970). Courtesy Georg Kargl
21 From: Richard Döcker, *Terrassentyp,* (Stuttgart: Akademischer Verlag Wedekind, 1929), p. 70
22 From: Geretsegger, Peintner, Pichler, *Otto Wagner 1841–1918. The Expanding City,* (New York: Rizzoli, 1979)
24 From: Sigfried Giedion, *Befreites Wohnen,* (Zurich:

Orell Füssli, 1929; Reprint: Lars Müller Publishers, 2019), plate 5
26 HB-05962-P2, Chicago History Museum, Hedrich-Blessing-Collection
27 C. Eberth
28 Revista Nacional de Arquitectura, vol. 126, June 1952. Official body of the Higher Council of the Spanish Architects' Associations. Published by the Colegio Oficial de Arquitectos de Madrid
29 From: Karel Teige and Jaromir Krejcar, *Práce Jaromira Krejcara* [The work of Jaromir Krejcar], (Prague: V. Petr, 1932)
30 Brochure Gallois, ca. 1930, collection C. Raynal, T. Lefebvre. Thierry Lefebvre, Cécile Raynal, *Les Solariums tournants du Dr Jean Saidman,* Paris, Editions Glyphe, 2010.
31 From: Larissa Anisimova, Pavel Khoroshilov, *Nudo per Stalin: Il Corpo nella fotografia sovietica negli anni venti,* (Rome: Gangemi editore, 2009), p. 203
32, 35 Collection Archives d'Aix-les-Bains
34 Ullstein bild. Photo: André Kertesz
36 From: *L'architecture d'aujourd'hui,* ed. André Bloc, September 1934, p. 78
37 From: *L'architecture vivante,* ed. Jean Badovici, 1931, p. 48
39 Richard von Krafft-Ebing, *Über gesunde und kranke Nerven,* 3rd edition, (Tübingen: H. Laupp'schen, 1885)
41 © ÖNB Wien 461.759B
42, 44, 46 © MAK – Österreichisches Museum für angewandte Kunst/Gegenwartskunst
43 From: *Josef Hoffmann. Sanatorium Purkersdorf,* ed. Breckner, Meyer, et al., (Vienna: Galerie Metropol, 1970)
45 Photo: Imagno/Getty Images
47 From: C. Sitte, *L'arte di costruire le città. L'urbanistica secondo i suoi fondamenti artistici,* (Milano: Jaca Book, 1980), p. 223
48 Camillo Sitte, Der Städtebau nach seinen künstlerischen Grundsätzen [City planning according to artistic principles], (Vienna: Graeser, 1889)
50 Collection Beatriz Colomina
55 Collection Jewish Historical Museum, Amsterdam. Collection J. van Velzen.
57 Photo: Arnold Itten. From: E. J. Jelles, C. A. Alberts, *Duiker. 1890–1935,* (Amsterdam: Architectura et amicitia, 1972)
58 Jan Verboom. Oudhilversum.nl. Photo: Jan van Zutphen, International Institute of Social History (Amsterdam).
60, 63 From: Geretsegger, Peintner, Pichler, *Otto Wagner 1841–1918. The Expanding City,* (New York: Rizzoli, 1979), p. 40
61 © Rowohlt Verlag
64 Arkivi-Bildagentur
65 From: E. J. Jelles, C. A. Alberts, Duiker. 1890–1935, (Amsterdam: Architectura et amicitia, 1972)
66 From: *Le Visage de l'enfance,* (Paris: Horizon, 1937), p. 201
68–71 MUS – Musée d'Histoire Urbaine et Sociale de Suresnes
72 From: Richard Döcker, *Terrassentyp,* (Stuttgart: Akademischer Verlag Wedekind, 1929), p. 57
74 Photo: Richard Poehlmann. From: Richard Döcker, *Terrassentyp,* (Stuttgart: Akademischer Verlag Wedekind, 1929), p. 24
75 From: Richard Döcker, *Terrassentyp,* (Stuttgart: Akademischer Verlag Wedekind, 1929), p. 62
77 © Richard-Döcker-Archiv, Deutsches Architekturmuseum, Frankfurt am Main. From: Sigfried Giedion, *Befreites Wohnen,* (Zurich: Orell Füssli, 1929; Reprint: Lars Müller Publishers, 2019), plate 58
78 Photo: *Illustriertes Blatt* no. 5, (Frankfurt a.M., 1929). From: Sigfried Giedion, *Befreites Wohnen,* (Zurich: Orell Füssli, 1929; Reprint: Lars Müller Publishers, 2019), plate 83
79 From: Richard Döcker, *Terrassentyp,* (Stuttgart: Akademischer Verlag Wedekind, 1929), p. 70
80 © 2018 Artists Rights Society (ARS), New York / ADAGP, Paris. From: Sigfried Giedion, *Befreites Wohnen,* (Zurich: Orell Füssli, 1929; Reprint: Lars Müller Publishers, 2019), plate 82
81 © gta Archives/ETH Zurich (Sigfried Giedion Archive). From: Sigfried Giedion, *Befreites Wohnen,* (Zurich: Orell Füssli, 1929; Reprint: Lars Müller Publishers, 2019), plate 76
82 © Man Ray 2015 Trust / Artists Rights Society (ARS), NY / ADAGP, Paris 2018
83, 85 From: Richard Döcker, *Terrassentyp,* (Stuttgart: Akademischer Verlag Wedekind, 1929), pp. 116–117.
84 From: André Lurçat, portfolio sheets "Terrasses et jardins," *L'Art international d'aujourd'hui* (Paris: Charles Moreau, 1930).
86 Privat Collection. © villaNoailles
87 © Man Ray 2015 Trust / Artists Rights Society (ARS), NY / ADAGP, Paris 2018. Photo: Telimage, Paris
88 © Man Ray 2015 Trust / Artists Rights Society (ARS), NY / ADAGP, Paris 2018
91 Alvar Aalto Museum, no. 50-003-257. Photo: Alvar Aalto
93 © Peter Blake. All rights reserved, DACS / Artists Rights Society (ARS), New York 2018. From: Franz Schulze, *Mies van der Rohe. Interior Spaces,* (Chicago: Arts Club, 1982), p. 21
94 From: Christian Norbert-Schulz, *Casa Tugendhat. Tugendhat House. Brno,* (Rome: Officina Edizioni, 1984), p. 44
95 Photo: Fritz Tugendhat. Courtesy of Daniela Hammer-Tugendhat. From: Daniela Hammer-Tugendhat, Ivo Hammer, Wolf Tegethoff, *Tugendhat House. Ludwig Mies van der Rohe,* (Basel: Birkhäuser, 2015), p. 101, fig. 132
96 Courtesy of Daniela Hammer-Tugendhat. From: Daniela Hammer-Tugendhat, Ivo Hammer, Wolf Tegethoff, *Tugendhat House. Ludwig Mies van der Rohe,* (Basel: Birkhäuser, 2015)
97 Tony Garnier, *Une cité industrielle,* (Paris: Vincent, 1917), plate 58
98 Private archive Arthur Rüegg

CHAPTER 3

1 Wilhelm Röntgen, *Über eine neue Art von Strahlen* [On a New Kind of Rays, a Preliminary Communication], Sitzungsberichte der Physikalisch-Medizinischen Gesellschaft in Würzburg 137, December 28, 1895. CC BY-NC 3.0 DE15:34 Deutsches Textarchiv
2 Otto Glasser, *W.C. Röntgen,* (Springfield, Illinois: Charles Thomas Publisher, 1945), p. 51
3 Photo: © CORBIS/Corbis via Getty Image
5 Reproduction by permission of the Buffalo & Erie County Public Library, Buffalo, New York
6 From: Tom Gunning, Corey Keller, Jennifer Tucker, *Brought to Light: Photography and the Invisible, 1840–1900,* (San Francisco: San Francisco Museum of Modern Art, 2008)
7 Photo: Science and Society Picture Library/Getty Images
9 Purchase, Alfred Stieglitz Society Gifts, Joyce F. Menschel Photography Library Fund, and Maureen and Noel Testa Gift, 2011. The Metropolitan Museum, 2011.66.1–.15. http://www.metmuseum.org/art/collection/search/296322

10 L. Moholy-Nagy, *Malerei, Fotografie, Film,* Bauhausbücher 8, (Munich: Albert Langen Verlag, 1925), pp. 60–61
11 Photo: Hayman Selig Mendelssohn (1848–1908)
12 From: Annie Besant and C.W. Leadbeater, *Thought-Forms,* (London: The Theosophical Publishing House, 1901, fig. 10
13–15 L. Aubert, *La Photographie de l'invisible: Les rayons X suivi d'un glossaire, les livres d'or de la science,* (Paris: Librairie C. Reinwald, Schleicher Frères, Éditeurs, 1898)
16 August Dittmar, *Prof. Röntgen's "X" RAYS and their applications in the New Photography,* (Glasgow: F. Bauermeister, 1896)
18 William J. Morton and Edwin W. Hammer, *The X-ray, or Photography of the Invisible and its value in Surgery,* (New York: American Technical Book Co., 1896), fig. 54
22 Published in *La Ilustración Española y Americana,* July 16, 1897, p. 20; and in *Scientific American,* August 7, 1897
23 National Cancer Institute, AV-4000-3979
24 Private collection. From: L'Illustration, July 3, 1897
25 Photo: Lucia Moholy. © 2018 Artists Rights Society (ARS), New York / VG Bild-Kunst, Bonn. From: Arthur Korn, *Glas im Bau und als Gebrauchsgegenstand,* (Berlin: Ernst Pollak, 1929)
26 Arthur Korn, *Glas im Bau und als Gebrauchsgegenstand,* (Berlin: Ernst Pollak, 1929)
27 From: Mies van der Rohe, "The Pure Form is the Natural," *G. Zeitschrift für elementare Gestaltung,* no. 5–6, April 1926
28 © 2018 Artists Rights Society (ARS), New York / VG Bild-Kunst, Bonn
29 Kurt Schwitters, "Nascy," *Merz,* no. 8/9, Hannover, April-July 1924, pp. 81–82
30 From: Werner Oechslin, *Gregor Harbusch, Sigfried Giedion und die Fotografie,* (Zurich: gta Verlag, 2010), p. 279. Photo: Hugo P. Herdeg
31 © F.L.C. / ADAGP, Paris / Artists Rights Society (ARS), New York 2018
32 From: Bruno Zevi, *Erich Mendelsohn,* (New York: Rizzoli, 1985), pp. 86–87
33 NAI Collection Database – Het Nieuwe Instituut
34 Architectural Press Archive from the RIBA collection
35 HB-09789-A, Chicago History Museum, Hedrich-Blessing Collection
36 Courtesy The Estate of Buckminster Fuller. From: *Shelter,* no. 5, November 1932
37 Photo: J. Cohnen. Collection Rijckheyt
38 Courtesy of Edward Duckett
39 New York, Museum of Modern Art (MoMA). Gelatin silver print, 7 1/2 × 9 3/4" (19.1 × 24.8 cm). Architecture & Design Study Center. Inv. no.: AD1375. Digital image © 2019, The Museum of Modern Art, New York/Scala, Florence
40 From: *LIFE* magazine, December 31, 1945
42 Reproduced with kind permission from the Corning Museum of Glass/Rakow Research Library
45 From: *LIFE* magazine, March 25, 1946, p. 84–85
46 © J.S. Watson. Used With Permission from the Eastman Kodak Company.
48 From: *Architectural Forum,* October 1951, p. 158
49 Lisa Cartwright, *Screening the Body: Tracing Medicine's Visual Culture,* (Minneapolis: University of Minnesota Press, 1995), p. 158
50 From: Victor X-Ray Company, *X-Ray Supplies,* (Chicago, 1920), p. 25
51 Photo: Wallace Kirkland for LIFE Magazine/Getty Images

CHAPTER 4

1, 12–19 SANAA
2 CCA, Fonds Myron Goldsmiths, Canadian Center for Architecture, 032 ARC 135. © 2018 Artists Rights Society (ARS), New York / VG Bild-Kunst, Bonn
3 Photo: Arnold Newman/ Getty Images
4 © 2018 Artists Rights Society (ARS), New York / VG Bild-Kunst, Bonn. Photo: Oswald Herzog
5–7 © 2018 Artists Rights Society (ARS), New York / VG Bild-Kunst, Bonn
8 © 2018 Artists Rights Society (ARS), New York / VG Bild-Kunst, Bonn. From: Philip Johnson, *Mies van der Rohe,* (New York: MoMA, 1947, 1978), p. 109 (bottom)
9 From: *Arts & Architecture,* March 1948.
10 © 2018 Eames Office, LLC (eamesoffice.com). Photo: Julius Shulman
11 © 2018 Eames Office, LLC (eamesoffice.com). Photo: Charles Eames
20 Photo: Miquel Anglarill
21, 23 © Fundació Mies van der Rohe, Barcelona. Photo: Ivan Blasi
22, 24, 27 © Fundació Mies van der Rohe, Barcelona
25 Courtesy of Hendrich Blessing
26 Photo: © Ramon Prat Homs
28 Photo: José Maria Sagarra. Courtesy of Familia Sagarra. From: *On Diseño,* no. 73, 1986, p. 12
29 From: *Diario Oficial de la Exposición Internacional Barcelona,* 1929
30 © Photographic Archive Museo Nacional del Prado
31 © Michael Moran
32 HB-30037, Chicago History Museum, Hedrich-Blessing Collection

CHAPTER 5

2 From: Greg Lynn, *Folds, Bodies,and Blob,* (Brussels: La Lettre volée, 1998)
3 UN Studio, *MOVE* Vol. 2, (Netherlands: Goose Press, 1999), p. 171
4 UN Studio, *MOVE* Vol. 1, (Netherlands: Goose Press, 1999), p. 154
6 US National Library of Medicine, Visible Human Project, http://erie.nlm.nih.gov/~dave/vh
7–9 © 2018 Artists Rights Society (ARS), New York / c/o Pictoright Amsterdam
10–12 From: FOA, *Phylogenesis,* (Barcelona: Actar, 2004)
13, 14 Given Imaging
15 Photo: John Springer Collection/Getty Images
16 Courtesy of the United States Customs and Border Protection
17 American Science & Engineering / Science Photo Library

The editors have endeavored to identify all copyright holders and photographers. Should despite our intensive research any person entitled to rights have been overlooked, legitimate claims shall be compensated within the usual provision.

Acknowledgments

With a project of such long duration, I feel indebted intellectually and emotionally to many people and institutions. I am grateful to the New York Institute for the Humanities, my first host in New York and where this project was incubated—even if then abandoned for a long time. I am grateful to Richard Sennett for his generosity as director, inviting me to the Institute as a research scholar, and to the fellows of 1980–81, particularly Susan Sontag, Wolfgang Schivelbusch, and Carl Schorske for their profound inspiration. I could never see architecture the same way again.

In the long hiatus where I tried to suppress this project, several people and institutions invited me to speak and write about the question, unwittingly keeping the flame alive. They include Werner Oechslin, Cynthia Davidson, Bernard Tschumi, Stephan Trüby, Andrea Phillips, Detlef Mertins, Sylvia Lavin, Antoine Picon, Jennifer Sigler, Brett Steele, Andrea Simitch, Carolyn Christov-Bakargiev, and Nikolaus Hirsch.

The American Academy in Berlin, where I was a fellow in the fall of 2014, provided the ideal setting to revive this project, which continued at the Getty Center in Los Angeles in the spring of 2015. I am immensely grateful to the feedback of the fellows and their partners at both institutions, particularly Anthony McCall, Annabelle McCall, Myles Jackson, Daniel Eisenberg, Ellen Rothenberg, Monica Black, Adam Ross, Tacita Dean, Mathew Hale, Thordis Arrhenius, Thomas Hines, Katja Müller-Helle, and Carolyn Christov-Bakargiev. Back in the forests of Berlin and again at the edge the water, as a 2018–19 fellow at the Wissenschaftskolleg zu Berlin, has been the perfect place to complete this book.

Generous support for the research and publication was provided by the Graham Foundation for Advanced Studies in the Fine Arts and the Barr Ferree Foundation Publication Fund, Department of Art and Archeology, Princeton University.

I am grateful to Bud Bynack for his subtle editing and to Bart-Jan Polman and Esther Choi for their help with the index and the image sourcing respectively. It has been a pleasure to work again with Lars Müller, "the last bookmaker," and his team. I am particularly thankful to Maya Rüegg for the careful coordination and to Martina Mullis and Lars for the design.

Special thanks to my colleagues and friends for their support, particularly Giuliana Bruno, Jean-Louis Cohen, Elizabeth Diller, Hal Foster, Alice Friedman, Sarah Herda, Francesca Hughes, Sylvia Lavin, Dietrich Neumann, Felicity Scott, and Tony Vidler. I am especially grateful to Monica Ponce de Leon, my colleagues, and the students at the School of Architecture at Princeton, who continuously create such an energizing academic environment. In the end, this book comes out of my teaching and the pleasure of testing ideas.

Above all, I am super grateful to the non-boring endless conversation with Mark Wigley about these ideas.

Beatriz Colomina

Beatriz Colomina
X-RAY ARCHITECTURE

Copyediting: Bud Bynack
Proofreading: David Koralek
Coordination: Maya Rüegg
Image rights: Chris Reding, Maya Rüegg
Design: Integral Lars Müller/Lars Müller and Martina Mullis
Production: Martina Mullis
Lithography: prints professional, Berlin, Germany
Printing and binding: DZA Druckerei zu Altenburg, Germany
Paper: Profibulk 1.3, 135 gsm

Lars Müller Publishers is supported by the Swiss Federal Office of Culture with a structural contribution for the years 2016–2020.

Lars Müller Publishers
Zürich, Switzerland
www.lars-mueller-publishers.com

ISBN 978-3-03778-443-3

Distributed in North America by ARTBOOK | D.A.P.
www.artbook.com

Printed in Germany

Publication is made possible in part by grants from the Barr Ferree Foundation Publication Fund, Department of Art and Archaeology, Princeton University, and from the Graham Foundation for Advanced Studies in the Fine Arts.